Ultimate Elastic Stack for Observability and Real-Time Analytics

Design, Build, Secure and Optimize Elastic Stack Environments for Data Analytics, Monitoring and Real-Time Search Across Modern Infrastructures

Agus Kurniawan

www.orangeava.com

First Published: October 2025

Published By: Orange Education Pvt Ltd, AVA®

Address: 9, Daryaganj, Delhi, 110002, India

275 New North Road Islington Suite 1314 London,
N1 7AA, United Kingdom

ISBN (PBK): 978-81-97396-65-6
ISBN (E-BOOK): 978-81-97396-62-5

Scan the QR code to explore our entire catalogue

www.orangeava.com

Dedicated To

My Wife, Ela Juitasari

And

My Children, Thariq and Zahra.

About the Author

Agus Kurniawan stands out as an emblem of dedication and innovation in the world of Information Technology (IT). Boasting an illustrious career as an IT consultant, advisor, trainer, and author, he has carved a niche for himself as a beacon of knowledge and expertise.

Recognized for his exceptional contributions, he was honored with the prestigious Microsoft MVP Award continuously from 2004 to 2022. Such an accolade speaks volumes about his commitment to excellence, and his prowess in the realm of technology.

Specializing in Software Engineering, Agus's interests are diverse and encompassing. He has ventured deep into the avenues of Machine Learning (ML), exploring its endless possibilities, and bringing innovations to life. His intrigue does not stop there, as the domains of Internet of Things (IoT) and Cloud Computing have also seen his pioneering touch. As the digital era evolves, Agus has continually emphasized the importance of DevOps, ensuring streamlined operations in IT projects.

Beyond his technical pursuits, he is an advocate for continuous learning. His belief that adaptability and knowledge are the pillars of success in the tech landscape shines through in his role as a trainer. Through his courses, he empowers individuals, from novices to seasoned professionals, ensuring that they are well-equipped with the latest skills and knowledge.

In personal spheres, he enjoys exploring the technological advancements of the modern age, while valuing the lessons of the past. His approach to technology is holistic, viewing it as a tool to bridge gaps, connect cultures, and pave the way for a brighter, more integrated future.

About the Technical Reviewers

Saravanan Shanmugam is a product-driven technology leader with 13+ years of experience delivering scalable infrastructure, observability, and DevOps solutions aligned with business goals. With expertise spanning product management and deep technical execution, he builds platforms that enhance operational efficiency, developer productivity, and customer outcomes.

Saravanan's product leadership is rooted in collaboration with engineering, operations, and business teams. He excels at defining strategic roadmaps, prioritizing features, and delivering infrastructure and observability products that drive measurable value.

He brings strong expertise in Linux systems, automation, and scripting with Shell and Python, and has designed highly available; cloud-native environments. With eight years in observability and data platforms, he's built end-to-end pipelines for ingestion, processing, and analytics, specializing in Elasticsearch for scalable search and real-time insights. An advocate of CNCF and open source, he has implemented Kubernetes, Prometheus, and Fluentd to build resilient, automated systems that reduce downtime, accelerate releases, and improve services.

Rahul Shriram Funde is a seasoned software engineer and technical consultant with 9+ years of experience designing and delivering scalable software systems across industries including hospitality, GPS tracking, CRM, legal tech, and telecommunications. He specializes in building tailored solutions that solve complex business challenges.

Rahul is a full-stack developer skilled in Angular, Node.js, TypeScript, and Couchbase, with expertise in backend API design, Linux (CentOS), and Hyper-V virtualization. His DevOps experience with Chef, Docker, Grafana, Prometheus, and the ELK Stack enables him to build reliable, observable systems. As a Technical Reviewer for *Ultimate Elastic Stack for Observability and Real-Time Analytics* published by Orange Education Pvt Ltd, he contributes expert insights on log analytics and enterprise observability. Having worked on fleet tracking, CRM, and telecom backends, Rahul combines versatility with a passion for clean code, mentoring, and continuous learning.

Acknowledgments

I would like to express my sincere gratitude to the vibrant Elastic community whose contributions, discussions, and shared experiences have been invaluable in shaping this handbook. Special thanks to the Elastic team for creating such powerful and innovative tools that continue to transform how we handle data at scale.

My appreciation extends to the system administrators, developers, and data analysts who shared their real-world challenges and solutions, providing the practical insights that make this book truly useful. Their feedback during the writing process helped ensure that the content addresses the genuine needs in the field.

I am grateful to the technical reviewers who meticulously examined each chapter, offering constructive feedback that significantly improved the accuracy and clarity of the content. Their expertise in various aspects of the Elastic Stack was instrumental in creating a comprehensive and reliable resource.

Finally, I want to thank my family and colleagues for their patience and support throughout this writing journey. Their encouragement made it possible to dedicate the time and energy necessary to create a handbook that truly serves the Elastic Stack community.

Preface

The Elastic Stack has revolutionized the way organizations collect, store, search, and analyze their data. What began as a simple search engine has evolved into a comprehensive platform capable of handling everything from application logs and system metrics to complex business analytics and security monitoring. This handbook represents a culmination of years of hands-on experience, community insights, and practical implementations across diverse industries and use cases.

In today's data-driven world, the ability to quickly ingest, process, and gain insights from vast amounts of information is not just an advantage—it is a necessity. The Elastic Stack, comprising Elasticsearch, Logstash, and Kibana, along with the broader ecosystem of Beats, APM, and other Elastic products, provides the tools to meet these challenges. However, mastering these tools requires more than just understanding their individual capabilities; it demands knowledge of how they work together, how to deploy them effectively, and how to optimize them for real-world scenarios.

Ultimate Elastic Stack for Observability and Real-Time Analytics bridges the gap between basic tutorials and enterprise-level implementations. Hence, whether you are just starting your journey with the Elastic Stack or looking to enhance your existing knowledge with advanced techniques, this book provides practical guidance based on real-world experience.

Rather than focusing solely on theoretical concepts, this handbook emphasizes practical application. Each chapter builds upon the previous one, creating a comprehensive learning path that takes you from initial setup to advanced deployment strategies. The inclusion of real-world case studies demonstrates how organizations across various industries have successfully leveraged the Elastic Stack to solve complex challenges.

The book covers not just the traditional ELK stack, but also explores the broader Elastic ecosystem, including Beats for data shipping, Elastic APM for application performance monitoring, and advanced features like machine learning and security. This comprehensive approach ensures that readers gain a complete understanding of what is possible with modern Elastic deployments.

This handbook is designed to be both a learning guide and a reference resource. If you are new to the Elastic Stack, start with Chapter 1, and work through sequentially. Each chapter builds upon concepts from previous sections, creating a solid foundation of knowledge.

For experienced users, individual chapters can serve as focused deep-dives into specific topics. The extensive table of contents and cross-references make it easy to find information about particular features or implementation strategies.

The case studies in Chapter 9 are particularly valuable for understanding how theoretical concepts translate into practical solutions. These real-world examples demonstrate the decision-making process behind successful Elastic Stack implementations, and can serve as templates for your own projects.

The Elastic Stack continues to evolve rapidly, with new features and capabilities being added regularly. While this book focuses on stable, production-ready features, the principles and best practices covered will remain relevant as the platform continues to grow. The foundation you build with this handbook will serve you well as you explore new developments in the Elastic ecosystem.

So, welcome to your journey into the world of the Elastic Stack! Whether you are building your first search application, implementing enterprise-wide logging, or creating sophisticated analytics platforms, this handbook will be your trusted companion in unlocking the full potential of these powerful tools.

Get a Free eBook

We hope you are enjoying your recently purchased book! Your feedback is incredibly valuable to us, and to all other readers looking for great books.

If you found this book helpful or enjoyable, we would truly appreciate it, if you could take a moment to leave a short review with a 5 star rating on Amazon. It helps us grow, and lets other readers discover our books.

As a thank you, we would love to send you a free digital copy of this book, and a **30%** discount code on your next cart value on our official websites:

www.orangeava.com

www.orangeava.in (For Indian Subcontinent)

☑ **Here's how:**

Leave a review for the book on Amazon.

Take a screenshot of your review, and send an email to **info@orangeava.com** (it can be just the confirmation screen).

Once, we receive your screenshot, we will send you the digital file, within 24 hours.

Thank you so much for your support – it means a lot to us!

Downloading the code bundles and colored images

Please follow the links or scan the QR codes to download the
Code Bundles and Images of the book:

https://github.com/ava-orange-education/Ultimate-Elastic-Stack-for-Observability-and-Real-Time-Analytics

The code bundles and images of the book are also hosted on
https://rebrand.ly/bfb068

In case there's an update to the code, it will be updated on the existing GitHub repository.

Errata

We take immense pride in our work at **Orange Education Pvt Ltd,** and follow best practices to ensure the accuracy of our content to provide an indulging reading experience to our subscribers. Our readers are our mirrors, and we use their inputs to reflect and improve upon human errors, if any, that may have occurred during the publishing processes involved. To let us maintain the quality and help us reach out to any readers who might be having difficulties due to any unforeseen errors, please write to us at :

errata@orangeava.com

Your support, suggestions, and feedback are highly appreciated.

DID YOU KNOW

Did you know that Orange Education Pvt Ltd offers eBook versions of every book published, with PDF and ePub files available? You can upgrade to the eBook version at **www.orangeava.com** and as a print book customer, you are entitled to a discount on the eBook copy. Get in touch with us at: **info@orangeava.com** for more details.

At **www.orangeava.com**, you can also read a collection of free technical articles, sign up for a range of free newsletters, and receive exclusive discounts and offers on Print Books and eBooks.

PIRACY

If you come across any illegal copies of our works in any form on the internet, we would be grateful if you would provide us with the location address or website name. Please contact us at **info@orangeava.com** with a link to the material.

ARE YOU INTERESTED IN AUTHORING WITH US?

If there is a topic that you have expertise in, and you are interested in either writing or contributing to a book, please write to us at **business@orangeava.com**. We are on a journey to help developers and tech professionals to gain insights on the present technological advancements and innovations happening across the globe and build a community that believes Knowledge is best acquired by sharing and learning with others. Please reach out to us to learn what our audience demands and how you can be part of this educational reform. We also welcome ideas from tech experts and help them build learning and development content for their domains.

REVIEWS

Please leave a review. Once you have read and used this book, why not leave a review on the site that you purchased it from? Potential readers can then see and use your unbiased opinion to make purchase decisions. We at Orange Education would love to know what you think about our products, and our authors can learn from your feedback. Thank you!

For more information about Orange Education, please visit **www.orangeava.com**.

Table of Contents

CHAPTER 1
Introduction and Initial Setup

Introduction

Welcome to the "*Ultimate Elastic Stack Handbook*," your comprehensive guide to mastering Elastic Stack, a powerful trio of tools for searching, analyzing, and visualizing data in real-time. Whether you are a system administrator, a developer, a data analyst, or just an enthusiast looking to extract valuable insights from your data, this handbook is designed to take you from the basics to advanced implementations of the Elastic Stack.

In this first chapter, we will start by laying the groundwork for your Elastic Stack journey. We will cover the overview and evolution of the Elastic Stack, discuss its benefits and various use cases, detail the system requirements you will need to get started, walk through the installation and configuration of Elasticsearch, Logstash, and Kibana, and finally, show you how to verify your installation to ensure that you are ready to proceed.

By the end of this chapter, you will have a strong foundational understanding of what the Elastic Stack is, and how it can be a game-changer for your data needs. You will also have a fully functioning Elastic Stack environment set up, and ready for action. So, let us dive in!

Structure

In this chapter, we will discuss the following topics:

- Overview and Evolution of the Elastic Stack
- Benefits and Use Cases
- System Requirements: Hardware, Software, and Cluster Considerations
- Installing and Configuring: Elasticsearch, Logstash, and Kibana

- Setting up Lab Environment
- Verifying Your Installation

Overview and Evolution of the Elastic Stack

The Elastic Stack – formerly known as the ELK Stack – comprises three open-source projects: Elasticsearch, Logstash, and Kibana, often complemented by Beats, a collection of lightweight, single-purpose data shippers. It is a robust suite of tools that allows for the ingestion, storage, analysis, and visualization of data.

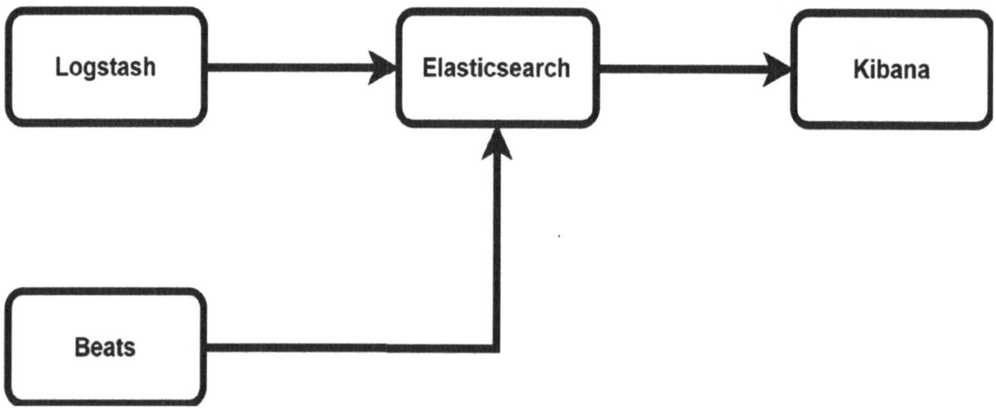

***Figure 1.1**: Relationship between the Elastic Stack Components*

Figure 1.1 provides a simplistic representation of the core components of the Elastic Stack, often referred to as the ELK stack. At the center, we have **Elasticsearch**, the heart of the system, responsible for indexing and querying data. **Logstash** is positioned on the left, emphasizing its role as a data processing and ingestion pipeline that feeds data into Elasticsearch. On the right, **Kibana** stands as the visualization and user interface tool, enabling users to create dashboards, and visualize the data stored in Elasticsearch. Lastly, at the bottom, **Beats** acts as lightweight data shippers that collect and send data directly to either Elasticsearch or Logstash, showcasing its role as the foundation for data collection in the stack. Together, these components form a cohesive and powerful ecosystem for data analysis and visualization.

Elasticsearch: The Heart of Elastic Stack

Elasticsearch is much more than just a search engine; it is a versatile, distributed data store that allows for the storage, retrieval, and analysis of large volumes of data in near real-time. At its core, Elasticsearch is built on the Apache Lucene library, which provides robust, reliable full-text search capabilities. However, Elasticsearch enhances

Lucene with distribution features, RESTful API, and a JSON-based query DSL (Domain-Specific Language), making it both powerful and user-friendly.

The distributed nature of Elasticsearch means it is inherently scalable. You can start with a single node on your laptop, and scale out to hundreds of nodes, handling petabytes of data seamlessly. This scalability is managed by dividing each index into shards which can be distributed across the cluster of nodes. Each shard can have zero or more replicas, providing high availability and redundancy. This design allows Elasticsearch to handle large-scale operations, without compromising performance.

Elasticsearch is schema-less, which means that documents can be indexed without predefining the structure of the data. When a document is indexed, Elasticsearch automatically infers the data structure, creates an index if necessary, and adds the document to the index. This dynamic mapping makes it easy to get started with Elasticsearch, but it also offers the power and flexibility of defining custom mappings to optimize your data storage and search capabilities.

The search capabilities of Elasticsearch are one of its most powerful features. It is not limited to simple full-text searches, but also supports structured searches, filters, geospatial searches, and many more. It offers complex query combinations and aggregations, providing the ability to perform advanced analytics and summaries of your data directly within the search engine.

To demonstrate making a request to an Elasticsearch server, let us imagine you have an Elasticsearch cluster running, and want to index a new document into the **products** index. You would issue an HTTP POST request with a JSON body representing the document:

```
POST /products/_doc/
{
  "name": "Ultimate Elastic Stack Handbook",
  "description": "A comprehensive guide to mastering the Elastic
Stack.",
  "price": 42.00,
  "in_stock": true
}
```

This request can be made using tools like **curl**, Postman, or any HTTP client in a programming language of your choice. Elasticsearch will then respond with a JSON object indicating the successful creation of the document, including a generated ID, if one was not specified.

For a search example, if you want to find products with the word **Elastic** in their name, your HTTP request would look like this:

```
GET /products/_search
{
  "query": {
```

```
        "match": {
          "name": "Elastic"
        }
      }
    }
```

This search request tells Elasticsearch to look into the **`products`** index for any documents where the **`name`** field contains the word, **`Elastic`**. The response will be a JSON object containing the search results, including the document itself, and metadata such as the document's **`_id`**.

Elasticsearch's real-time analytics and full-text search capabilities are revolutionizing the way companies approach their data. From log and event data analysis to full-blown search engines, the application possibilities are nearly limitless which has solidified Elasticsearch's role as the heart of the Elastic Stack.

Logstash: The Data Processing Pipeline

Logstash is a powerful open-source data processing pipeline that ingests data from a multitude of sources simultaneously, transforms it, and then sends it to a "*stash*" like Elasticsearch. It is an integral part of the Elastic Stack, providing the muscle to handle data intake and filtration, before it is indexed into **`Elasticsearch`**.

Designed with an emphasis on versatility and performance, Logstash has a pluggable framework featuring over 200 plugins to connect with various types of inputs, filters, and outputs. This flexibility allows Logstash to unify data processing across different databases, applications, and log files. For instance, it can ingest data from sources such as log files, metrics, web applications, data stores, and various AWS services, apply sophisticated transformations, and then send it to Elasticsearch for indexing.

The configuration files for Logstash are separated into three parts: Input, filter, and output. The **input** plugins consume data from various sources, the **filter** plugins modify the data as you specify, and the **output** plugins write the data to a destination, often Elasticsearch. Logstash filters can perform numerous transformations and enhancements to the data, such as geo-enrichment, anonymization, splitting, and grokking to structure the unstructured log data.

Logstash's pipeline is capable of buffering the incoming data, and applying back-pressure when the system is processing at peak volumes, which is critical for maintaining the integrity of a system under load. It is also fault-tolerant, with a number of features designed to ensure that data processing can continue without loss, even when there are network or hardware failures.

The power of Logstash lies not just in its ability to process large volumes of data, but also in its rich ecosystem of input and output plugins that can be easily mixed and matched to create a customized data processing pipeline that suits any requirement.

Here is an example of how you could send data to Elasticsearch using Logstash. Assume that you have a simple log file, **`weblogs.log`**, which you want to parse and send to Elasticsearch. You would create a Logstash configuration file, **`logstash.conf`**, with the following content:

```
input {
  file {
    path => "/path/to/your/weblogs.log"
    start_position => "beginning"
  }
}

filter {
  grok {
    match => { "message" => "%{COMBINEDAPACHELOG}" }
  }

  date {
    match => [ "timestamp", "dd/MMM/yyyy:HH:mm:ss Z" ]
  }

  geoip {
    source => "clientip"
  }
}

output {
  elasticsearch {
    hosts => ["http://localhost:9200"]
    index => "weblogs-%{+YYYY.MM.dd}"
  }
}
```

In this configuration:

- The **`input`** section defines the path to the log file.
- The **`filter`** section uses the **`grok`** plugin to parse and structure the log data, the `` `date` `` plugin to parse the timestamp, and the **`geoip`** plugin to add geographical information about the IP addresses found in the logs.
- The **`output`** section specifies that the processed data should be sent to an Elasticsearch server running on **`localhost,`** and indexing the data into daily indices named **`weblogs-YYYY.MM.dd`**.

To run Logstash with this configuration, and start processing the data, you would use the following command:

```
bin/logstash -f path/to/your/logstash.conf
```

Upon execution, Logstash reads the log file, processes each line using the specified filters, and sends the transformed data to the Elasticsearch server, where it is indexed and stored. This setup allows for real-time monitoring and analysis of log data through Elasticsearch and Kibana, demonstrating just one of the many powerful capabilities of Logstash within the Elastic Stack.

Kibana: The Window to Your Elastic Data

Kibana is the visualization layer of the Elastic Stack that allows users to create powerful visualizations and dashboards from their Elasticsearch data. It provides a user-friendly web interface that enables users to explore, analyze, and visualize the data stored in Elasticsearch indices. By translating the complexities of raw data into graphical representations, Kibana facilitates a better understanding of the data patterns, trends, and anomalies.

The strength of Kibana lies in its ability to provide real-time summary and analysis of large datasets in a coherent and user-friendly manner. It supports a variety of charts, tables, and maps which can be combined to create comprehensive dashboards that provide actionable insights. These dashboards are dynamic, easily shareable among team members, and can be customized to the unique requirements of each user.

One of Kibana's key features is its deep integration with Elasticsearch. All the visualizations and searches in Kibana are made possible through Elasticsearch's aggregation capabilities which can handle complex queries and aggregations at scale. This tight integration ensures that Kibana can provide a fast and responsive experience, even when working with large data sets and complex queries.

Kibana also offers features like machine learning, graph exploration, and log and infrastructure monitoring out of the box. These advanced features empower users to detect anomalies, build relevant relationships in data, and monitor their infrastructure and applications, all within the same tool. Moreover, with the addition of Canvas, users can create pixel-perfect infographics and presentations that pull the live data directly from Elasticsearch.

The continuous development and integration of new features keep Kibana at the forefront of data visualization tools. Elastic's commitment to enhancing user experience is evident in features like Lens, which simplifies the process of creating complex visualizations through a more intuitive interface, and the introduction of "*Spaces*", which allows for better organization and management of dashboards and visualizations across different teams within an organization.

Kibana has evolved from a simple visualization tool to a powerful application capable of handling a variety of use cases, from simple log data visualizations to complex business analytics. It stands out not only for its ability to visualize data, but also for its role in the operational management of the Elastic Stack, including features for managing indices, users, and advanced settings. Kibana's versatility, ease of use, and extensive customization options make it an indispensable tool for anyone working with the Elastic Stack.

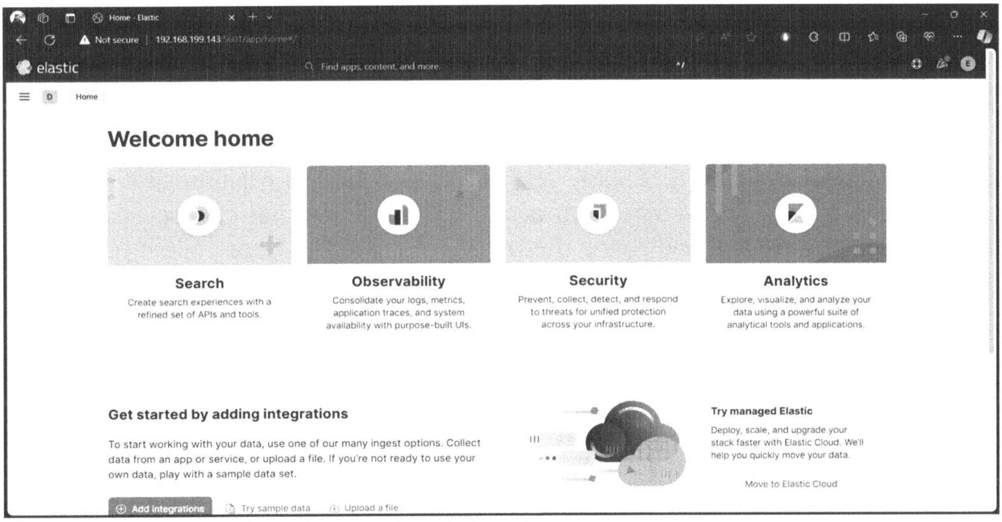

***Figure 1.2**: Kibana Portal*

Figure 1.2 showcases the initial landing page of the Kibana web portal which is a part of the Elastic Stack offering a visual interface for users to manage their Elasticsearch data. Upon successful setup and access configuration, users are greeted with this home screen that provides a user-friendly dashboard for navigating the platform's features. The portal is divided into sections such as Search, Observability, Security, and Analytics, each representing a core capability of the Elastic Stack. Search offers tools to create search experiences, Observability consolidates various data points for system monitoring, Security aids in threat detection and infrastructure protection, and Analytics provides tools for data visualization and analysis. The homepage also prompts users to get started by adding data integrations, uploading files, or experimenting with sample datasets, making it straightforward for newcomers to begin exploring the full potential of Elastic services. The interface's clean and structured layout, with clear call-to-action buttons such as '**`Add Integrations`**' and **`'Try sample data'`**, illustrate Kibana's focus on the ease of use, and swift user onboarding.

Beats: The Data Shippers of the Elastic Stack

Beats form the collection layer of the Elastic Stack, a suite of lightweight, single-purpose data shippers that can be installed on servers to capture all sorts of operational data from logs, metrics, network packet data, to runtime metrics, and ship them directly into Elasticsearch or Logstash for further processing. As the agents on the ground, Beats are responsible for the initial collection of data points that form the foundation of the stack's powerful analytics capabilities.

Each Beat is designed to be lean and performant, with a small footprint which ensures that they can efficiently collect the data, without impacting the system performance. This design philosophy makes Beats an ideal solution for a decentralized data collection strategy where data is generated across multiple servers, containers, and even cloud environments. With various types of Beats available, such as Filebeat for log files, Metricbeat for metrics, Packetbeat for network data, and many more, users can choose the specific Beat that fits their data collection needs.

Beats are incredibly easy to deploy and manage which is a significant advantage for operation teams. They come with a range of modules that can be enabled with minimal configuration, allowing for the automatic setup of data collection, parsing, and visualization for common log formats and systems. This modularity and ease of configuration mean that Beats can start sending the relevant data to Elasticsearch or Logstash within minutes of installation, greatly simplifying the operational overhead, typically associated with data shippers.

The versatility of Beats is further enhanced by their extensibility. If the existing Beats do not cover a specific use case, developers can create custom Beats, using the libbeat framework. This developer-friendly aspect allows for the creation of custom data shippers tailored to unique requirements, ensuring that the Elastic Stack can be extended to cover practically any data collection scenario that might arise.

Beats play a crucial role in securing and monitoring data flows as well. With the addition of features like SSL encryption for data in transit, and integration with Elasticsearch security features, they ensure that the sensitive data is protected from the endpoint to Elasticsearch. Moreover, Beats come with built-in monitoring and diagnostic features that provide insights into their operational health, ensuring that any issues can be identified and rectified quickly.

In the context of the Elastic Stack, Beats are not just the first step in the data pipeline, but are also key to providing the granularity and specificity required for advanced data analysis and insight. They are often the unsung heroes of the stack, quietly and efficiently collecting and delivering the data that drives analysis, visualization, and decision-making in Kibana. The evolution of Beats continues to reflect the broader trends in data collection and monitoring, focusing on the ease of use, automation, and integration with the ever-growing ecosystem of technologies in the IT landscape.

The evolution of the Elastic Stack has been marked by its transformation from a set of independent products into a tightly integrated platform. The continuous addition of new features and tools, such as Elastic APM for application performance monitoring, Elastic SIEM for security information and event management, and various other solutions, are a testament to its expanding capabilities and adaptability to modern data needs.

Benefits and Use Cases

The Elastic Stack has a myriad of benefits, making it an invaluable tool across various industries. Its real-time data processing capabilities, powerful search functions, and flexible data ingestion options make it suitable for numerous applications. It shines in situations such as log and event data management, security analytics, performance monitoring, and many more.

Some of the key use cases include:

- **Log Analysis**: Centralizing logs from various systems and applications to detect anomalies, track events, and troubleshoot issues.
- **Security Information and Event Management (SIEM)**: Providing insights into security-related data for real-time analysis of security events.
- **Application Performance Monitoring (APM)**: Capturing data about application performance and errors, helping developers and operation teams understand the performance of their software.
- **Full-Text Search**: Enabling sophisticated search functionalities across diverse sets of documents.
- **Data Visualization**: Allowing businesses to visualize their data in various formats to extract business intelligence.

System Requirements: Hardware, Software, and Cluster Considerations

Before diving into the setup of the Elastic Stack, it is crucial to understand the system requirements needed to run the software efficiently. These requirements vary, based on the scale at which you plan to operate.

- **Hardware**: Depending on your data volume, you will need to consider the CPU, memory, and disk space. Elastic provides guidelines for hardware sizing to help make the right choices.
- **Software**: Elasticsearch and Kibana are Java applications, so you will need a supported Java Runtime Environment (JRE). Logstash and Beats have specific requirements, depending on the operating system.
- **Cluster Considerations**: For production environments, you will need to consider the setup of an Elasticsearch cluster to ensure high availability and failover capabilities.

The Elastic Cloud Enterprise, commonly known as the ELK Stack, is a robust and scalable platform designed for comprehensive data search, analysis, and visualization. To ensure optimal performance and reliability, specific hardware prerequisites must be met. The following is a concise list of these requirements:

- **Physical Memory (RAM)**: At least 64GB, with half or more dedicated to the Elastic Stack.
- **CPU Cores**: A minimum of 16 cores.
- **Disk Space**: Fast storage with at least 1TB SSDs. It is advised to use RAID 0 and NVMe storage.
- **Network**: 10GbE network recommended. High bandwidth and low latency internal networks are crucial for efficient node-to-node communication.
- **Operating System**: Elastic Cloud Enterprise supports various Linux distributions.
- **Other Considerations**: Hardware isolation is vital. It is advisable to run Elastic Cloud Enterprise on dedicated hosts, and not share with other services. This ensures optimal performance.

For further details and considerations, refer to the official website for Elastic Cloud Enterprise Hardware Requirements, **https://www.elastic.co/guide/en/cloud-enterprise/current/ece-hardware-prereq.html**.

Installing and Configuring: Elasticsearch, Logstash, and Kibana

When diving into the installation and configuration of the Elastic Stack, it is paramount to consider the variety of hosting and deployment options available. Your choice will significantly influence performance, scalability, and management complexity. Hence, whether you are looking to leverage the raw power of dedicated hardware, the flexibility of cloud services, or the reproducibility of containerized environments, each option has its distinct advantages and trade-offs. Let us now delve into the most popular installation avenues for the Elastic Stack (Elasticsearch, Logstash, and Kibana) and explore the pros and cons of each.

Bare Metal

Installing the Elastic Stack directly onto physical hardware means that there is no virtualization layer in between the software and the machine's resources. This method harks back to traditional computing setups where software applications had direct access to server hardware. Opting for a bare-metal installation is often a choice for those who prioritize performance, and seek the fullest control over their environment, ensuring that there is no additional layer potentially inhibiting the software's operations. While it offers raw power and extensive customization options, it requires a careful selection of hardware components, and a more hands-on approach to management.

- **Method**: Installing the Elastic Stack directly on physical hardware, without any virtualization layers.
- **Pros**:
    - Maximum performance due to no virtualization overhead.
    - Full control over hardware specifications and configurations.
    - Better resource utilization as there is no intermediary layer.
    - Extended customization possibilities tailored to specific needs.
    - Often results in predictable performance metrics.
- **Cons**:
    - Scaling requires significant manual intervention.
    - Higher upfront costs due to hardware investments.
    - Physical failures can lead to longer downtimes.
    - More complex disaster recovery scenarios.
    - Potentially underutilized resources, if not managed efficiently.

Virtual Machines (VMs)

Virtual Machines have revolutionized IT infrastructures by allowing multiple operating systems to run on a single physical server. By using hypervisors, VMs abstract the Elastic Stack from the underlying hardware, offering flexibility and efficiency. This method is like having several computers operating within one physical machine. Each VM has its own dedicated resources, and runs independently, ensuring isolation from others. It is a preferred choice for organizations that seek a balance between performance, scalability, and resource management, allowing for more dynamic IT operations.

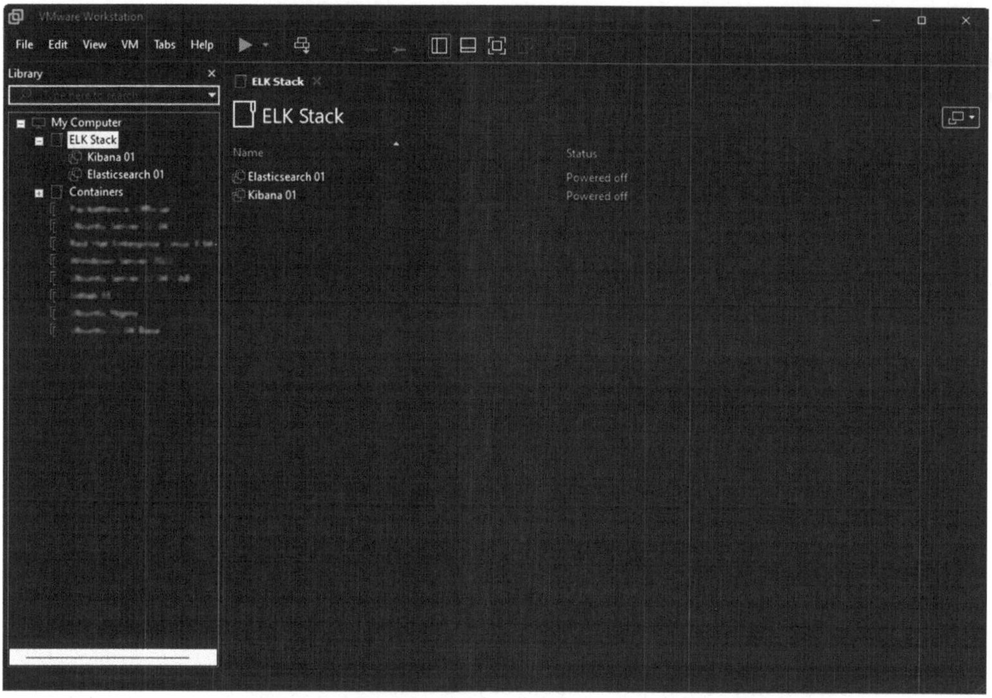

Figure 1.3: *Deploying ELK Stack on VMWare*

Figure 1.3 showcases a virtual machine environment for deploying the Elastic Stack. The author has opted for VMWare for running instances of Elasticsearch and Kibana. While VMWare is a robust solution for virtualization, allowing fine control over resource allocation and offering strong isolation, it is important to note that there are other viable options for setting up your Elastic Stack. You can use VirtualBox, Hyper-V, or any other virtualization software of your choice. These alternatives include running on bare metal for performance-critical applications, leveraging containerization with Docker for portability, or utilizing cloud services for their elasticity and managed services.

- **Method**: Installing on virtual machines that run on hypervisors.
- **Pros**:
  - Enhanced scalability by easily creating or cloning VMs.
  - Effective resource isolation, ensuring smooth operations.
  - Snapshots make backup and recovery simpler.
  - Migration between hardware becomes feasible.
  - Hardware maintenance, without affecting the virtual environment.
- **Cons**:
  - Performance overhead because of virtualization.

- Additional licensing costs for hypervisor software.
- Requires robust hardware for optimal performance.
- VM sprawl can lead to management challenges.
- Dependencies on the underlying host system.

Cloud Services

The evolution of cloud computing has brought about a paradigm shift in how software is hosted and accessed. Leveraging cloud services for the Elastic Stack means utilizing the infrastructure of providers such as AWS, Azure, or GCP. Instead of investing in and maintaining physical hardware, organizations can rent resources on-demand, making it easier to scale as needs change. Cloud-based installations offer a blend of convenience, scalability, and managed services, ideal for businesses that want to focus more on their core operations, and less on infrastructure management.

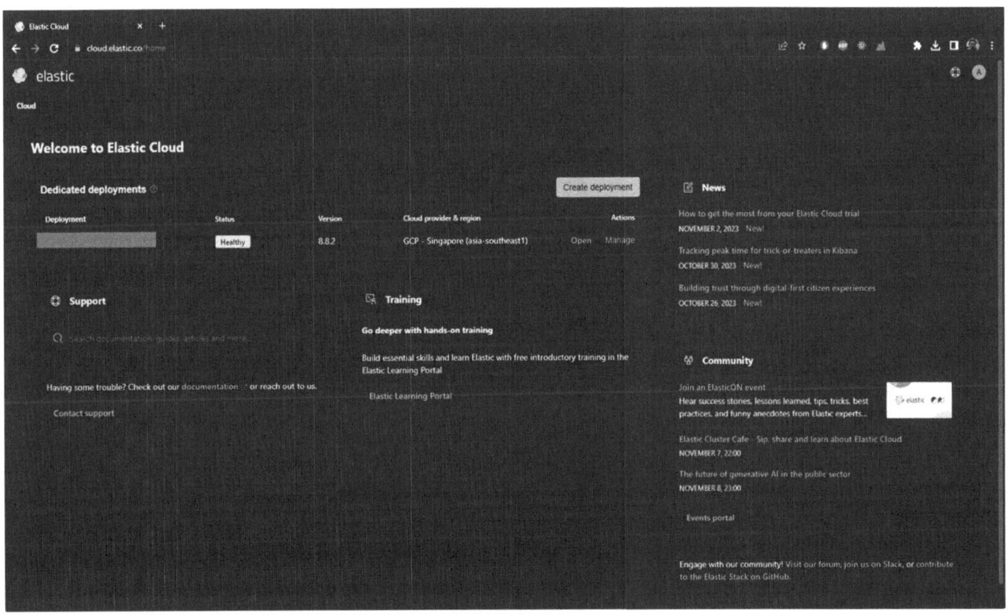

Figure 1.4: *Deploying ELK Stack on Cloud Services*

Figure 1.4 showcases a cloud-based environment for deploying the Elastic Stack. The author has opted for the GCP for running instances of Elasticsearch and Kibana. While GCP is a robust solution for cloud computing, allowing fine control over resource allocation, and offering strong isolation, it is important to note that there are other viable options for setting up your Elastic Stack. You can use Azure, GCP, or any other cloud services of your choice. These alternatives include running on bare metal for performance-critical applications, leveraging containerization with Docker for portability, or utilizing virtual machines for their flexibility and resource management.

- **Method**: Using cloud providers like AWS, Azure, or GCP to host the Elastic Stack.
- **Pros**:
    - Seamless scalability in tune with demands.
    - Outsourcing of hardware and software management.
    - Potential cost savings with pay-as-you-go models.
    - Geographical distribution for better user experiences.
    - Managed services often include updates and security patches.
- **Cons**:
    - Costs can surge if not properly managed.
    - Data transfer fees can add up.
    - Limited control over the underlying infrastructure.
    - Vendor lock-in may dictate future technical decisions.
    - Potential concerns around data privacy and sovereignty.

Docker and Containerization

Containerization with Docker being a prime example, is an approach that packages software and all of its dependencies into a standardized unit for software development. By deploying the Elastic Stack in containers, you achieve an unparalleled level of consistency and speed in deployment. Unlike traditional VMs, containers share the host system's kernel, rather than emulating an entire operating system. This lightweight nature means faster start-up times, and efficient resource utilization. Adopting a containerized approach is well-suited for organizations that lean towards microservices architectures, and seek agility in their development and deployment processes.

- **Method**: Deploying Elastic Stack components within Docker containers, or using orchestration tools like Kubernetes.
- **Pros**:
    - Rapid and consistent deployments.
    - Isolated environments reducing conflicts and dependencies.
    - Efficient use of resources with shared OS kernels.
    - Portability across different platforms and environments.
    - Microservices architecture aligns well with containerization.
- **Cons**:
    - Steeper learning curve for container orchestration.

- Complexity in managing stateful applications.
- Overhead and potential security concerns with container runtime.
- Networking complexities in distributed environments.
- Resource contention, if not properly configured.

The choice of the right method should be grounded in the specific requirements of your project, budgetary considerations, and available technical expertise. Each approach offers unique benefits and potential challenges. For instance, bare metal deployments provide maximum performance and control, but require significant upfront investment and manual management. On the other hand, cloud services offer high scalability and flexibility, but can be costly and might not be suitable for all use cases. Docker and containerization provide a middle ground, offering rapid deployment and scalability, but they require a solid understanding of containerization principles and tools.

Installing the Elastic Stack can be an adventure in its own right. Here, we will provide step-by-step instructions for installing Elasticsearch, Logstash, and Kibana on your system, as well as some initial configurations to get you started.

- **Elasticsearch**: From downloading the package to setting up the initial cluster.
- **Logstash**: Installing the correct version, and configuring your first pipeline.
- **Kibana**: Setting up Kibana to connect to your Elasticsearch cluster and basic configuration.

Next, we will walk you through the installation and configuration of the Elastic Stack components. We will cover the installation of Elasticsearch and Kibana on Ubuntu Server 22.04 LTS, as well as some initial configurations to get you started.

Setting up Lab Environment

In this lab setup for the "*Ultimate Elastic Stack Handbook*," the author has opted for VMWare for running instances of Elasticsearch and Kibana. While VMWare is a robust solution for virtualization, allowing fine control over resource allocation, and offering strong isolation, it is important to note that there are other viable options for setting up your Elastic Stack. You can use VirtualBox, Hyper-V, or any other virtualization software of your choice. These alternatives include running on bare metal for performance-critical applications, leveraging containerization with Docker for portability, or utilizing cloud services for their elasticity and managed services.

For readers looking to replicate a similar environment, VMWare is an excellent tool! So, feel free to explore these other options, based on your preferences, requirements, and available resources.

Hands-On Lab: Building Elasticsearch and Kibana on Ubuntu Server 22.04 LTS

Now, let me guide you through a hands-on lab to build and run Elasticsearch as well as Kibana as daemons on Ubuntu Server 22.04 LTS. The lab environment is shown in *Figure 1.5*.

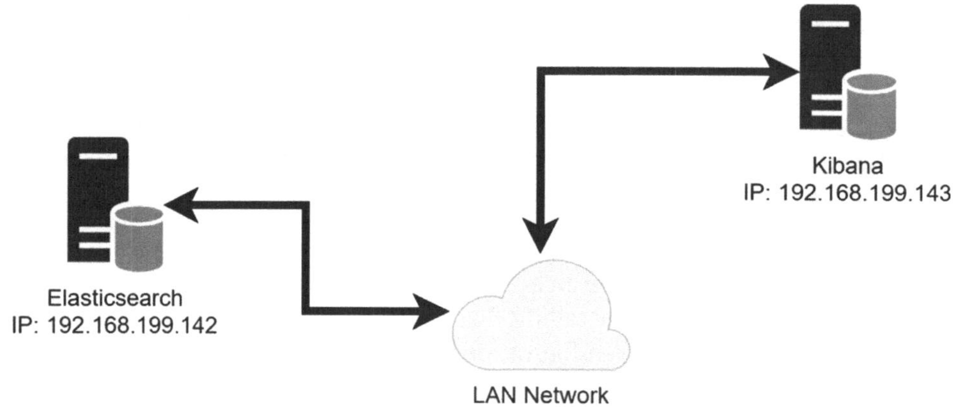

Figure 1.5: *Lab Environment*

Prerequisites:

1. Ubuntu Server 22.04 LTS installed on a VM or physical machine.
2. Sudo privileges or root access.
3. Internet access for downloading packages.

When this book was written, the latest version of Elasticsearch was 8.10.4, and Kibana was 8.10.4. You can check the latest version of Elasticsearch and Kibana at **https://www.elastic.co/downloads/elasticsearch** and **https://www.elastic.co/downloads/kibana**.

Steps to Install Elasticsearch Server

The following steps will guide you through the installation of Elasticsearch on Ubuntu Server 22.04 LTS:

1. **Log into Elasticsearch Server Machine**

   Use the VMWare console or SSH to connect to the Elasticsearch Server Machine.

2. **Install Java Runtime Environment (JRE)**

   Since we are using Elasticsearch and Kibana 8.x, there is no need to install the Java Runtime Environment (JRE). Elasticsearch and Kibana both come bundled with JRE 11.0.12. However, if you are using Elasticsearch and Kibana 7.x, you will need to install JRE 11.0.12.

   If you want to install the default JRE, you can use the following command:

   ```
   sudo apt update
   sudo apt install default-jre
   ```

3. **Import Elasticsearch PGP Key**

   Securely download and install the signing key:

   ```
   wget -qO - https://artifacts.elastic.co/GPG-KEY-elasticsearch |
   sudo gpg --dearmor -o /usr/share/keyrings/elasticsearch-keyring.
   gpg
   ```

4. **Add Elasticsearch Repository**

   You may need to install the apt-transport-https package on Debian before proceeding:

   ```
   sudo apt update
   sudo apt-get install apt-transport-https
   ```

   Save the repository definition to **`/etc/apt/sources.list.d/elastic-8.x.list`**:

   ```
   echo "deb [signed-by=/usr/share/keyrings/elasticsearch-keyring.
   gpg] https://artifacts.elastic.co/packages/8.x/apt stable main" |
   sudo tee /etc/apt/sources.list.d/elastic-8.x.list
   ```

   Make sure you do not have issues with unsigned repositories. Please check that your Elasticsearch PGP Key is imported correctly.

5. **Install Elasticsearch**

   Update your package lists, and install Elasticsearch using the following command:

   ```
   sudo apt update
   sudo apt install elasticsearch
   ```

   During the installation, you will use security configurations that include a generated password for the superuser `elastic`, as shown in *Figure 1.6*. Save this password to sign in to Elasticsearch and Kibana later. You can change the password later.

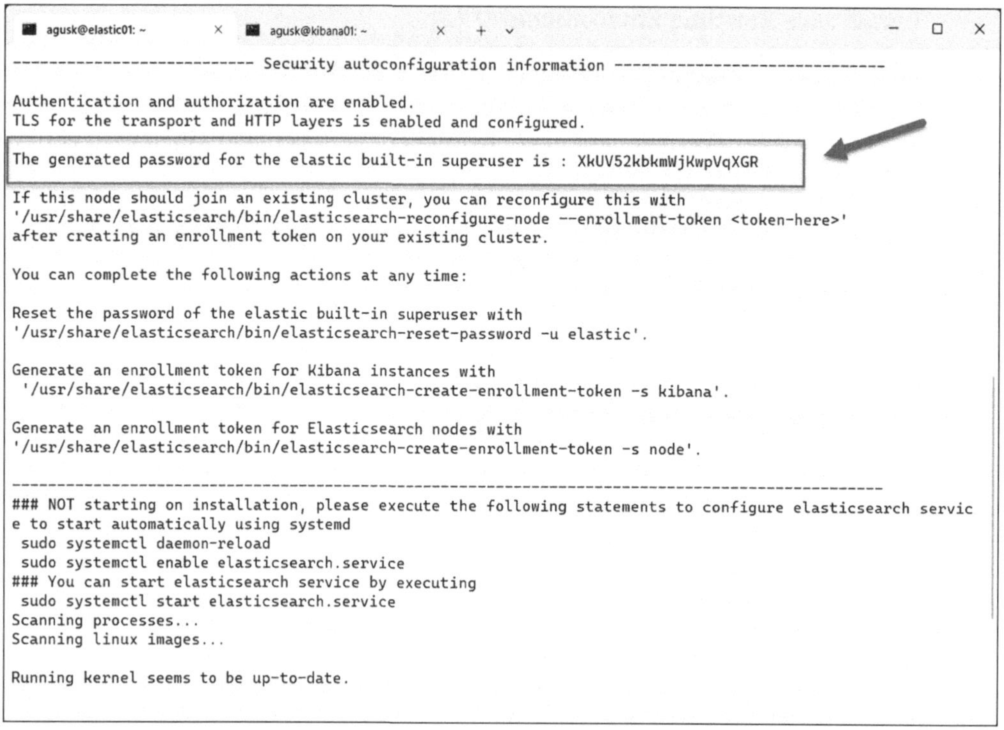

Figure 1.6: *Displaying Passing during Elasticsearch Installation*

6. **Start and Enable Elasticsearch Service**

   Enable Elasticsearch to start on boot, and then start the service using systemd:

   ```
   sudo systemctl enable elasticsearch.service
   sudo systemctl start elasticsearch.service
   ```

   To check the status of the Elasticsearch service, run:

   ```
   sudo systemctl status elasticsearch.service
   ```

   If you see "**`Active: active (running)..`**", it means Elasticsearch is running.

Steps to Install Kibana Server

The following steps will guide you through the installation of Kibana on Ubuntu Server 22.04 LTS.

1. **Log into Kibana Server Machine.**

   Use the VMWare console or SSH to connect to the Kibana Server Machine.

2. **Install Prerequisites.**

   Following the same steps as in Elasticsearch, specifically steps 3 and 4.

3. **Install Kibana**

   Still using the same repository, install Kibana using the following command:

   ```
   sudo apt update
   sudo apt install kibana
   ```

4. **Configure Kibana**

   By default, Kibana listens on localhost only. To allow external access, you need to configure Kibana to listen on all interfaces.

   Edit the Kibana configuration file on **`/etc/kibana/kibana.yml`**:

   ```
   sudo nano /etc/kibana/kibana.yml
   ```

   Uncomment and set the **`server.host`** configuration to **`0.0.0.0`**:

   ```
   server.host: "0.0.0.0"
   ```

5. **Start and Enable Kibana Service**

   Enable Kibana to start on boot, and then start the service:

   ```
   sudo systemctl enable kibana.service
   sudo systemctl start kibana.service
   ```

   To check the status of the Kibana service, run:

   ```
   sudo systemctl status kibana.service
   ```

   If you see "**`Active: active (running)..`**", it means Kibana is running, as shown in *Figure* 1.7. You can see a code (**`..?code=xxxx`**) that you need to enter on Kibana configuration later. Keep this code for later use.

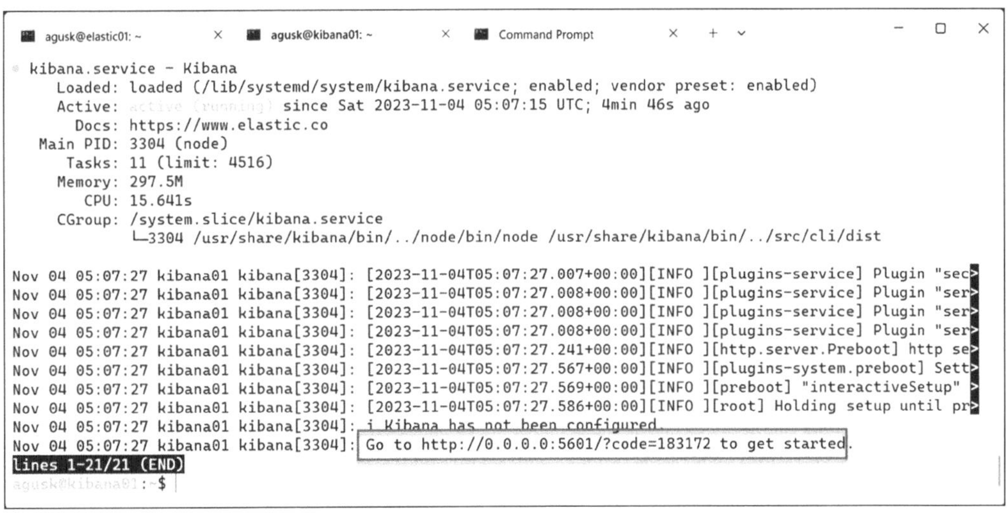

Figure 1.7: *Kibana Service is Running and Displaying a Code*

Steps to Connect Kibana to Elasticsearch

In this section, you will connect Kibana to Elasticsearch. You will need to generate a token from Elasticsearch, and use it to connect to Kibana. The following steps will guide you through the process:

1. **Log into Kibana Server Machine:** Use the VMWare console or SSH to connect to the Kibana Server Machine.

2. **Access Kibana:** Once both services are running, you can access Kibana by navigating to **http://<kibana-server-ip>:5601** from a web browser. You will see the Kibana login page, as shown in *Figure 1.8*. Enter the token generated by Elasticsearch. You can generate the token by running the following command on the Elasticsearch server:

```
sudo /usr/share/elasticsearch/bin/elasticsearch-create-
enrollment-token -s kibana
```

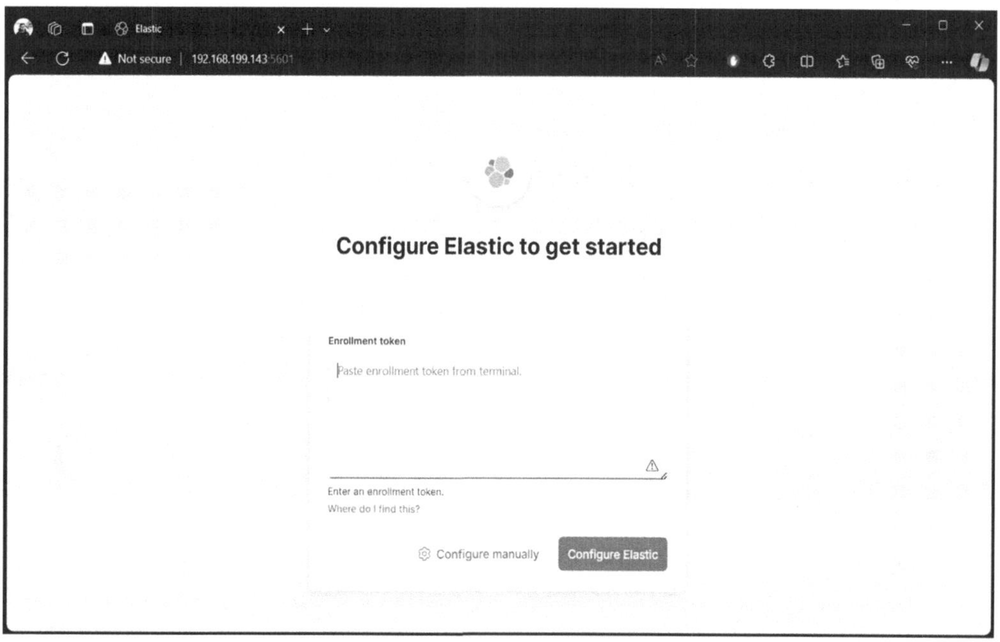

***Figure 1.8**: Configuring Elasticsearch on Kibana*

3. **Code Confirmation:** You may be asked to enter a code from Kibana, as shown in *Figure 1.9*. You can obtain the code by checking messages from the Kibana server service, as demonstrated in *Figure 1.7*.

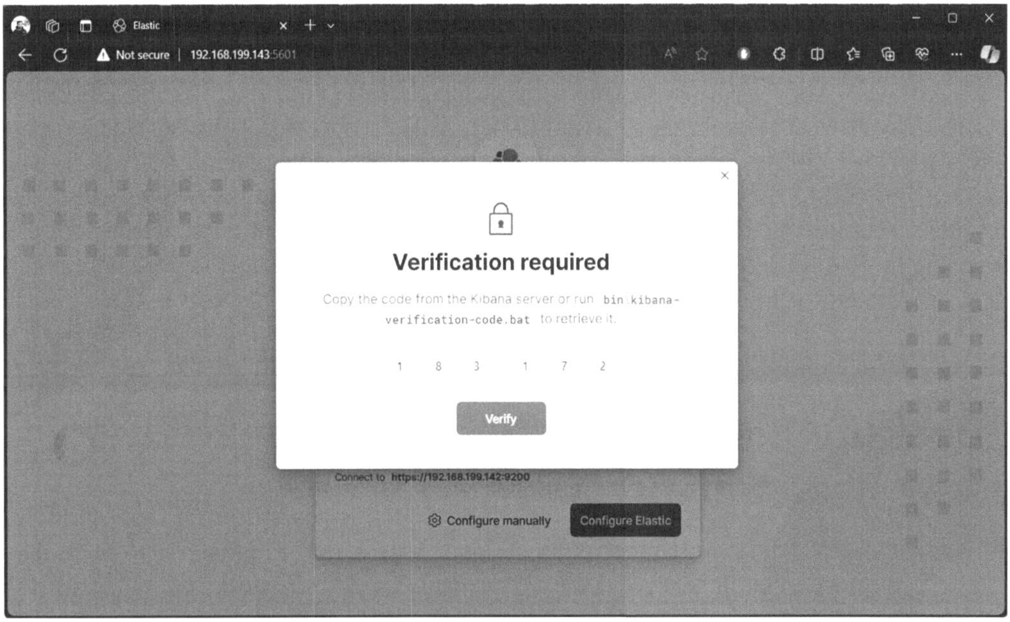

***Figure 1.9**: Enter a Code from Kibana for Confirmation*

4. **Finished:** After completion, you will be redirected to the Kibana home. Enter the username and password for the `**elastic**` user. You can find the password in step 5 of the Elasticsearch installation. You can change the password later.

By following these steps, you will have a basic Elastic Stack setup running on Ubuntu Server 22.04 LTS. Remember, this is a starting point, and for production environments, you should consider additional configurations for security, scalability, and performance tuning.

Verifying Your Installation

Once installation is complete, we must ensure that all the components of the Elastic Stack are communicating correctly, and are ready for use. We will cover how to check each component's status, and some initial tests to confirm that the data is being ingested and indexed.

We will also explore these sub-sections in greater detail in the following pages, providing you with the knowledge and tools to set up your Elastic Stack effectively. So, let us get started on your path to mastering the Elastic Stack.

Before we dive into the script, it is important to understand what we are trying to accomplish. In the realm of network services and web applications, ensuring that critical services such as Elasticsearch and Kibana are operational is key to maintaining system reliability and availability. For those who administer these services, particularly in a Windows environment, PowerShell provides a robust and versatile toolset for system management. The following PowerShell script is designed to check the health and accessibility of Elasticsearch and Kibana services. It sends a simple HTTP request to the respective service endpoints, and checks the response. If the service is active and responsive, you will receive a confirmation message; if not, the script will provide a status indicating that the service is not accessible, or is experiencing issues. This proactive monitoring step can be a fundamental part of a larger automation strategy, ensuring that administrators are alerted to potential issues as soon as they occur, thus allowing for swift remediation.

Next, we create Bash and PowerShell scripts to check Elasticsearch and Kibana status.

Checking Elasticsearch and Kibana Status using Bash Script

Here is a simple Bash script that checks if Elasticsearch and Kibana are up by making an HTTP request to each service. This script uses `curl` to send a request, and then checks the HTTP status code to see if the service is responding correctly.

Make sure to replace **elasticsearch-server-ip** with the IP address of your Elasticsearch server and **kibana-server-ip** with the IP address of your Kibana server. The default ports are used in this script (9200 for Elasticsearch and 5601 for Kibana), but you can change them, if your setup uses different ports.

```
#!/bin/bash

# Elasticsearch variables
ELASTICSEARCH_IP="elasticsearch-server-ip"
ELASTICSEARCH_PORT="9200"
ELASTICSEARCH_URL="http://${ELASTICSEARCH_IP}:${ELASTICSEARCH_
PORT}"

# Kibana variables
KIBANA_IP="kibana-server-ip"
KIBANA_PORT="5601"
KIBANA_URL="http://${KIBANA_IP}:${KIBANA_PORT}"

# Timeout in seconds
TIMEOUT=5

# Function to check service status
check_service() {
  response=$(curl -k -m $TIMEOUT -s -o /dev/null -w '%{http_
code}' -I $1)
  if [ "$response" == "000" ]; then
```

```
    echo "HTTP service at $1 did not respond."
  elif [ "$response" == "401" ]; then
    echo "HTTP service at $1 is running (authentication 
required)."
  elif [ "$response" -ge 200 ] && [ "$response" -lt 300 ]; then
    echo "HTTP service at $1 is reachable and running."
  else
    echo "HTTP service at $1 returned status code $response."
  fi
}

# Check Elasticsearch (with self-signed certificate)
check_service $ELASTICSEARCH_URL

# Check Kibana
check_service $KIBANA_URL
```

Save this script to a file, for example, **check_elk_services.sh**, give it execute permission using **chmod +x check_elk_services.sh**, and run it with **./check_elk_services.sh**. You should see the output as shown in *Figure 1.10*.

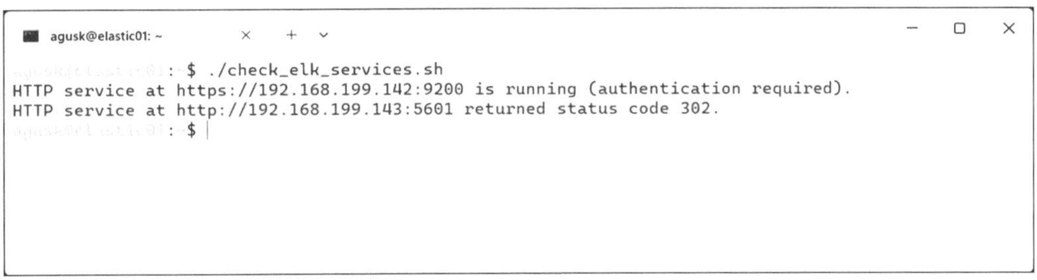

Figure 1.10: *Checking ELK Service Using Bash Scripts*

Checking Elasticsearch and Kibana Status Using PowerShell Script

Here is a simple PowerShell script that checks if Elasticsearch and Kibana are up by making an HTTP request to each service. This script uses **Invoke-WebRequest** to send a request, and then checks the HTTP status code to see if the service is responding correctly.

```
# URLs for Elasticsearch and Kibana
$ElasticsearchUrl = "elasticsearch-server-ip"
$KibanaUrl = "kibana-server-ip" # include port

# Check if the TrustAllCertsPolicy class has already been defined
if (-not ([System.Management.Automation.PSTypeName]'TrustAllCerts
Policy').Type) {
```

```
    add-type @"
        using System.Net;
        using System.Security.Cryptography.X509Certificates;
        public class TrustAllCertsPolicy : ICertificatePolicy {
            public bool CheckValidationResult(
                ServicePoint srvPoint, X509Certificate certificate,
                WebRequest request, int certificateProblem) {
                return true;
            }
        }
"@
}

# Apply the TrustAllCertsPolicy
[System.Net.ServicePointManager]::CertificatePolicy = New-Object
TrustAllCertsPolicy

# Function to check service status
function Check-Service {
    param (
        [string]$url
    )

    try {
        $response = Invoke-WebRequest -Uri $url -Method Head
-UseBasicParsing -TimeoutSec 30 -ErrorAction Stop
        if ($response.StatusCode -eq 401) {
            Write-Host "HTTP service at $url is running
(authentication required)."
        } elseif ($response.StatusCode -ge 200 -and $response.
StatusCode -lt 300) {
            Write-Host "HTTP service at $url is reachable and
running."
        } else {
            Write-Host "HTTP service at $url returned status code
$($response.StatusCode)."
        }
    } catch [Net.WebException] {
        # Output more detailed error info
        if ($_.Exception.Response.StatusCode -eq 401) {
            Write-Host "HTTP service at $url is running
(authentication required)."
        } else {
            Write-Host "A WebException occurred: $_"
            Write-Host "The error message was: $($_.Exception.
Message)"
        }
```

```
        } catch {
            Write-Host "An unexpected error occurred: $_"
        }

    }
    # Check Elasticsearch
    Check-Service -url $ElasticsearchUrl

    # Check Kibana
    Check-Service -url $KibanaUrl
```

Now, make sure to replace **`elasticsearch-server-ip`** and **`kibana-server-ip`** with the actual IP addresses for your Elasticsearch and Kibana instances.

To run this script, you can save it with a **`.ps1`** extension, for instance, **`CheckElkServices.ps1`**. You may need to adjust your PowerShell execution policy to run the script. You can do this by running PowerShell as an administrator, and executing the following command:

```
Set-ExecutionPolicy RemoteSigned
```

Or, if you want to run the script with your current user policy, you can run it with the following command:

```
Set-ExecutionPolicy RemoteSigned -Scope CurrentUser
```

After that, you can run the script by navigating to the directory containing the script and running:

```
.\CheckElkServices.ps1
```

You should see the output as shown in *Figure 1.11*:

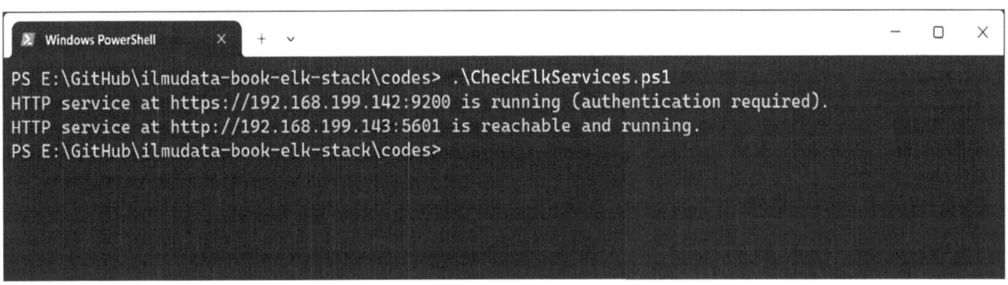

Figure 1.11: *Checking ELK Service Using PowerShell Scripts*

Be aware that if your services require authentication or use non-default ports, you will need to modify the URLs, and potentially add headers or other options to the **`Invoke-WebRequest`** calls to handle those requirements.

In closing our journey through the initial setup and configuration of Elasticsearch and Kibana, has been both challenging and enlightening. We have traversed the nuances of establishing a working environment, learned to adapt our tools to the specifics of network and security settings, and developed a troubleshooting acumen that will undoubtedly serve us in future endeavors. As we prepare to move forward, the experiences documented in this chapter will provide a sturdy foundation from which we can expand our understanding and mastery of these robust search and analytics platforms. Now, we stand on the threshold of deeper discovery, ready to delve into the advanced functionalities that lie in the chapters ahead.

Conclusion

As we reach the conclusion of our first chapter, you have laid down the first stones of your Elastic Stack foundation. We have traveled through the rich history and evolution of this powerful suite of tools which has grown from a simple search engine into an expansive ecosystem capable of handling complex, real-time data processing, and analysis tasks.

You have discovered the key benefits and use cases of the Elastic Stack which are as varied as the industries it serves. From processing and visualizing log data to powering search engines, from monitoring application health to safeguarding networks as part of an SIEM system, the versatility of the Elastic Stack is clear.

We have also navigated the critical preparatory steps, detailing the hardware, software, and cluster configurations necessary to get you started. Thus, whether you are planning a small deployment, or gearing up for a large-scale, distributed environment, you now have the knowledge to plan appropriately.

Following the systematic installation and configuration instructions, you should now have a working Elastic Stack environment. Your Elasticsearch is quietly humming, ready to index the data; Logstash is prepared to process and filter the incoming data stream; and Kibana is waiting to cast your data in visual splendor.

Finally, we have looked at how to verify your installation, ensuring that all the systems are go, and you are ready to take the next steps into the world of data exploration with Elastic.

In the upcoming chapter, we are going to take a comprehensive look under the hood of Elasticsearch, the core engine of the Elastic Stack. *Chapter 2, Deep Dive: Elasticsearch*, will equip you with a robust understanding of its distributed nature, exploring essential concepts such as indexing, search, data modeling, and cluster management. You will also learn the best practices for scaling your setup, ensuring high availability, and securing your data. Hence, whether it is fine-tuning performance or harnessing advanced features for complex queries, the next chapter is your guide to becoming proficient with the powerhouse, that is "*Elasticsearch*".

Points to Remember

- **Installation Options**: Elasticsearch and Kibana can be installed on various platforms such as bare metal servers, virtual machines, or cloud services. Each option comes with its own set of advantages and limitations.
- **Hardware Requirements**: It is important to consider the hardware prerequisites for running an Elastic Stack, which include sufficient CPU, memory, and storage to ensure performance and stability.
- **Virtualization Platforms**: The lab setup demonstrated uses a virtual machine environment which is a common and versatile approach for setting up an Elastic Stack. Various virtualization platforms such as VMware, VirtualBox and Hyper-V can be employed, each with its specific configurations and features, to host Ubuntu Server 22.04 LTS instances for running Elasticsearch and Kibana. The choice of virtualization software can be tailored as per the user's preference, system compatibility, and performance considerations.
- **Network Configuration**: Proper network settings, including NAT port forwarding in VMware, are crucial to ensure that the services are accessible from the host machine or external networks.
- **Ubuntu Firewall Settings**: On the Ubuntu Server, configuring the firewall (UFW) to allow traffic on the ports used by Elasticsearch (default 9200) and Kibana (default 5601) is necessary for remote connectivity.
- **Kibana Configuration**: To enable remote access to Kibana, modifying the `kibana.yml` file to set the `server.host` to "`0.0.0.0`", allows it to listen on all interfaces, not just "`localhost`".
- **Service Management**: Both Elasticsearch and Kibana should be set up to run as services (daemons), ensuring they start on boot, and can be managed with systemd commands.
- **Security Considerations**: While enabling remote access, it is crucial to consider security implications and implement measures such as secure passwords, encryption (SSL/TLS), and access control.
- **Testing Connectivity**: After configuration, verifying that Elasticsearch and Kibana are correctly installed and accessible through their respective IP addresses as well as ports is essential to confirm a successful setup.
- **Lab Documentation**: Documenting the steps taken during the installation and configuration processes in a lab environment, as shown in *Figure 1.2*, can help in troubleshooting and replicating the setup in future scenarios.
- **Interface Familiarity**: Understanding the layout and capabilities of the Kibana interface, as displayed in *Figure 1.2*, is beneficial for efficient navigation, and making the most of the Elastic Stack's features.

Multiple Choice Questions

1. What is the primary function of Elasticsearch in the ELK stack?
    a. To visualize data.
    b. To process and transform data.
    c. To index, search, and analyze data.
    d. To collect logs from various sources.
2. Which Ubuntu version was recommended for setting up Elasticsearch and Kibana in the lab environment?
    a. Ubuntu 20.04 LTS
    b. Ubuntu 18.04 LTS
    c. Ubuntu 22.04 LTS
    d. Ubuntu 16.04 LTS
3. What is the correct way to configure Kibana to enable remote access?
    a. Change the **`server.host`** configuration to "**`localhost`**".
    b. Change the **`server.host`** configuration to "**`0.0.0.0`**".
    c. Change the **`server.host`** configuration to the specific hostname.
    d. Remote access is enabled by default.
4. When configuring the network on VMware to allow external access to a virtual machine, what feature needs to be set up?
    a. DHCP Reservation
    b. NAT Port Forwarding
    c. Bridge Networking
    d. VLAN Tagging
5. Before running Elasticsearch and Kibana as daemons, what step is important to ensure that they can communicate over the network?
    a. Installing a web server.
    b. Configuring the virtual machines with static IP addresses.

c. Setting the time zone on the server.

d. Opening the necessary ports on the Ubuntu firewall.

Answers

1. c
2. c
3. b
4. b
5. d

Questions

1. Describe the process of setting up Elasticsearch on an Ubuntu 22.04 LTS virtual machine. What are the key steps involved from installation to running it as a daemon?
2. How does Kibana integrate with Elasticsearch, and what are the necessary configurations needed to ensure that they communicate effectively in a virtualized lab environment?
3. Discuss the advantages and potential drawbacks of using virtual machines such as VMware, VirtualBox, or Hyper-V, for deploying an ELK stack, compared to using bare-metal installations.
4. Explain the importance of Network Address Translation (NAT) when configuring a virtual machine to host parts of the ELK stack. How does NAT facilitate access to the services from outside the host machine?
5. What considerations should be taken into account, when opening ports in the Ubuntu firewall for Elasticsearch and Kibana? Provide a rationale for the importance of each consideration.
6. Can you describe how to enable remote access to Kibana in a virtualized environment? Why is it necessary to change certain configurations for remote access?
7. Illustrate the steps necessary to ensure that both Elasticsearch and Kibana are set to start on boot within an Ubuntu virtual machine. Why is this step crucial for maintaining the availability of the ELK stack?
8. What role does the **`server.host`** configuration play in Kibana, and what are the implications of setting it to "**`0.0.0.0`**"?

9. Compare and contrast the benefits of using a virtualized environment for the ELK stack against deploying it in a cloud environment. What are the key factors that would influence a decision between these two options?

10. Reflect on the process of setting up port forwarding in a virtual environment. Why is this step necessary, and what could be the potential security implications of misconfiguring port forwarding?

Key Terms

- **ELK Stack**: A collection of three open-source products – Elasticsearch, Logstash, and Kibana – used for searching, analyzing, and visualizing log data in real-time.
- **Elasticsearch**: A distributed, RESTful search and analytics engine capable of addressing a growing number of use cases.
- **Kibana**: A visualization dashboard for Elasticsearch designed to allow users to create bar graphs, pie charts, and histograms.
- **Ubuntu Server 22.04 LTS**: A long-term support version of Ubuntu, tailored for servers and cloud environments.
- **Virtual Machine (VM)**: A software computer that, like a physical computer, runs an operating system and applications.
- **VMware**: A virtualization and cloud computing software provider, known for products such as VMware Workstation and ESXi.
- **VirtualBox**: Oracle's free, open-source virtualization software that allows you to run multiple guest operating systems.
- **Hyper-V**: A virtualization product from Microsoft allowing users to create virtual machines on x86-64 systems.
- **Daemon**: A background process that runs on the system, often without direct user interaction.
- **NAT (Network Address Translation)**: A method of remapping IP addresses by modifying network address information.
- **Firewall**: A network security system that monitors and controls incoming and outgoing network traffic, based on predetermined security rules.
- **Remote Access**: The ability to get access to a computer or a network from a remote distance.
- **Server.host**: A configuration setting in Kibana that specifies the host to which the server will bind.
- **Port Forwarding**: A technique used to redirect a communication request from one address, and port number combination to another.

- **IP Address**: A numerical label assigned to each device connected to a computer network that uses the Internet Protocol for communication.
- **Daemon Service**: A type of daemon that starts up during the boot process, and runs in the background, performing tasks without user intervention.
- **Configuration File**: A software file used to configure the settings and parameters of a specific program or hardware device.
- **Bare Metal**: Physical servers with no need for underlying virtualization.
- **Cloud Environment**: A set of hardware, networks, storage, services, and interfaces that combine to deliver aspects of computing as a service over the Internet.

CHAPTER 2

Deep Dive: Elasticsearch

Introduction

As we venture into the heart of the Elastic Stack, Elasticsearch stands as the cornerstone of this powerful suite of tools. This chapter will take a granular look at Elasticsearch, unraveling its intricate design, and showcasing the robust features that have made it an indispensable asset in the realms of search and data analytics. Hence, whether you are a developer, a data scientist, or an IT professional, understanding the mechanics and capabilities of Elasticsearch is pivotal for harnessing the full potential of the Elastic Stack.

Elasticsearch is more than a mere search engine; it is a distributed, RESTful search and analytics engine capable of addressing a multitude of use cases. Its versatility stems from the underlying architecture that balances performance with simplicity. As we delve deeper, you will uncover the principles of its distributed nature, learn how it ensures high availability, and how it scales to handle petabytes of data, while maintaining lightning-fast search responses.

At its core, Elasticsearch operates on the concept of indexing documents, and providing near real-time search capabilities. The beauty of this system lies in its ability to not just search text, but also to analyze and aggregate vast amounts of diverse data. This chapter will decode the complex, yet elegant way Elasticsearch processes data – starting with the basics of indexing, and moving through to the nuanced intricacies of text analysis, field mappings, and query DSL.

Moreover, the operational aspect of Elasticsearch cannot be overlooked. We will explore the practical side of managing an Elasticsearch cluster, covering critical topics such as shard allocation, cluster health monitoring, and backup strategies. By equipping you with this knowledge, you will be able to not only implement Elasticsearch solutions, but also ensure their resilience and stability.

As we begin our deep dive, keep in mind that Elasticsearch is continually evolving, with a vibrant community and a dedicated team of developers contributing to its growth.

The concepts and techniques you learn here will lay the groundwork for your mastery of this powerful search engine, enabling you to build, manage, and optimize systems that can transform the way organizations handle, and gain insights from their data. So, let us embark on this intellectual journey into Elasticsearch, the engine that drives the Elastic Stack's capabilities to new heights.

Structure

In this chapter, we will discuss the following topics:

- Elasticsearch Dev Tools on Kibana
- Index Lifecycle Management
- Hands-On Lab: Index Lifecycle Management in Elasticsearch Using Kibana Dev Tools
- Understanding Document IDs in Elasticsearch
- Advanced Querying Techniques
- Hands-On Lab: Uploading NDJSON File to Elasticsearch Using Dev Tools
- Hands-On Lab: Elasticsearch Querying Techniques Using Dev Tools
- Hands-On Lab: Simulating Joining Queries in Elasticsearch
- Optimizing for Search Speed and Relevance
- Data Modeling and Schema Design
- Hands-On Lab: Data Modeling and Schema Design in Elasticsearch
- Understanding Elasticsearch Geolocation Data
- Hands-On Lab: Working with Geolocation Data in Elasticsearch
- Working with Binary Data in Elasticsearch

Elasticsearch Dev Tools on Kibana

Elasticsearch Dev Tools in Kibana offers a powerful interface for interacting with your Elasticsearch cluster. It provides capabilities for running searches, executing administrative operations, and debugging issues, all from within a user-friendly console. This hands-on lab will guide you through the basics of getting started with Dev Tools, and executing a few fundamental operations.

Introduction to Dev Tools

Dev Tools in Kibana leverages the Console, a feature resembling a command-line interface that accepts Elasticsearch queries in the form of RESTful requests. It provides auto-completion of commands and indices, syntax highlighting, and direct execution of queries with quick access to documentation.

Getting Started with Dev Tools

Step 1: Accessing Dev Tools

1. Open your Kibana interface in a web browser.
2. Click the "`Dev Tools`" icon on the left-hand navigation panel as shown in *Figure 2.1*.
3. You will see two panels: The left panel is where you type your requests, and the right panel displays the responses from Elasticsearch. You can see an example in *Figure 2.2*.

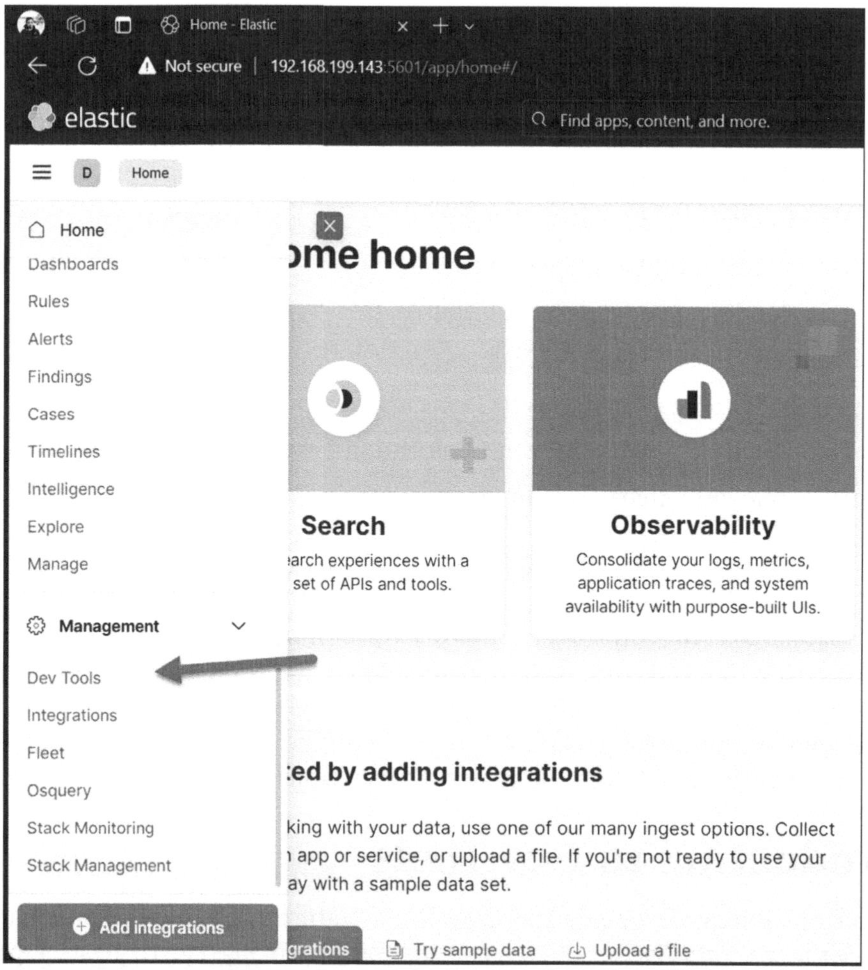

***Figure 2.1**: Dev Tools Menu on Kibana Portal*

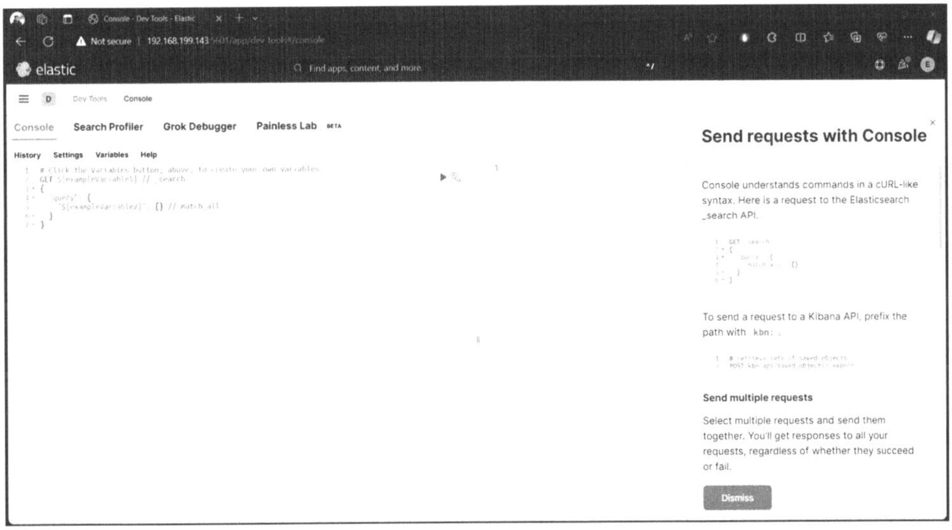

***Figure 2.2**: A Form of Dev Tools Application*

Step 2: Basic Commands

Before running complex queries, familiarize yourself with a few basic commands:

- To get information about your Elasticsearch cluster:
  `GET /`

1. Click the green triangle (**`play`**) button to execute the command. You can also press *Ctrl + Enter* (*Cmd + Enter on Mac*) to execute the command.
2. After executing the command, you will see the response in the right panel. The response will look similar to *Figure* 2.3.

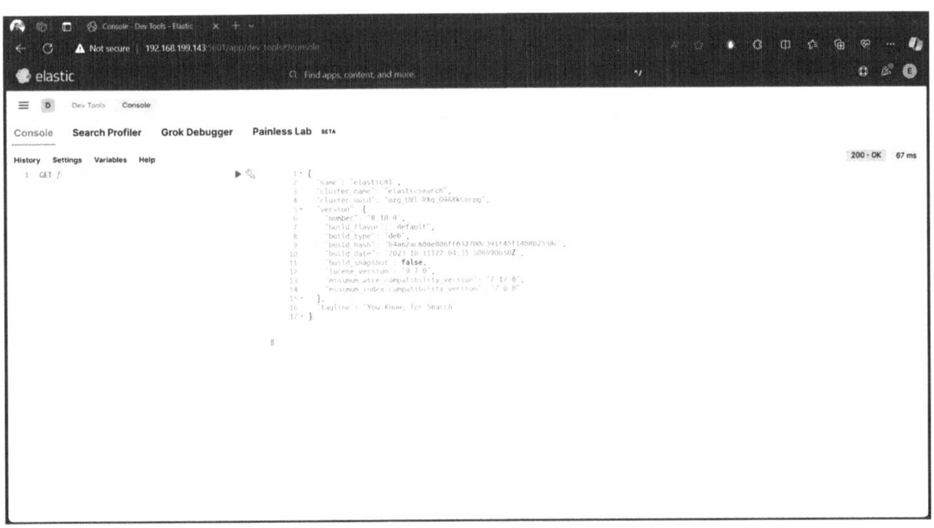

***Figure 2.3**: Getting Elasticsearch Cluster Information*

Next, let us try a few more commands.

- To list all indices in your cluster:
  ```
  GET /_cat/indices
  ```
- To check the health of your cluster:
  ```
  GET /_cluster/health
  ```

Run these commands in the left panel, and press the green triangle (play) button to execute.

HTTP Request Methods in Elasticsearch's Dev Tools

When interfacing with Elasticsearch through Kibana's Dev Tools, understanding the purpose and use of different HTTP request methods is crucial. Following is an explanation of each request method, and its relevance in the context of Elasticsearch operations:

GET

The **GET** method is used to retrieve information from an Elasticsearch cluster. It is a read-only operation, which means it does not change any data in the cluster. In Dev Tools, you would use **GET** to fetch data from an index, check the status of nodes, retrieve cluster health, or see the details of a specific document.

Example:

```
GET /_cat/indices
```

This request would list all indices in the cluster.

PUT

The **PUT** method is used to create new resources, or replace the existing ones. In Elasticsearch, **PUT** is often used to create a new index, update index settings, or create/update a document in an index.

Example:

```
PUT /my-index-000001
      {
        "settings": {
          "number_of_shards": 1
        }
      }
```

This would create a new index with the specified settings.

POST

The **POST** method is typically used to perform operations that can change the state of the server. In Elasticsearch, **POST** is used to add a new document to an index, when you do not specify an ID (Elasticsearch will auto-generate an ID), update a document, or perform searches.

Example:

```
POST /my-index-000001/_doc
{
  "title": "Ultimate Elastic Stack Handbook"
}
```

This would add a new document to **my-index-000001**.

You can verify that the document was added by running the following command:

```
GET /my-index-000001/_search
```

You should see the document you just added in the response, along with the auto-generated ID (**_id**) for the document. For instance, if the document ID is **7i18sYsBBDr4QfYX4Kdm**, we can retrieve the document by running the following command:

```
GET /my-index-000001/_doc/7i18sYsBBDr4QfYX4Kdm
```

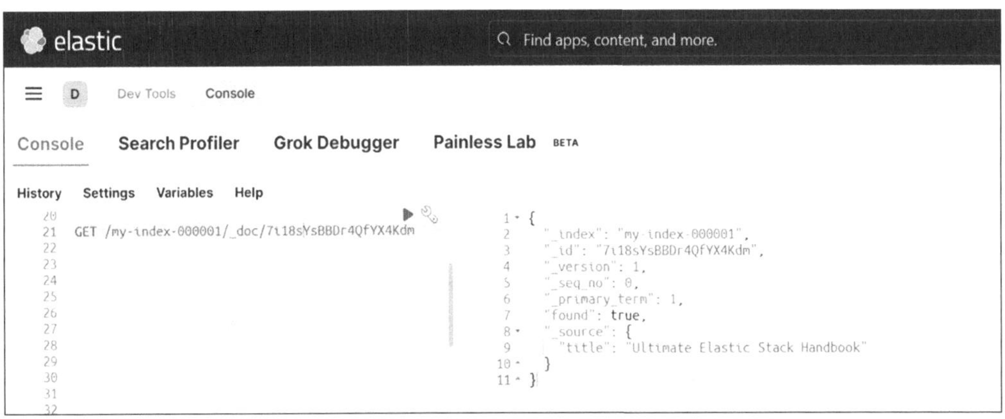

***Figure 2.4**: Getting a Document by ID*

HEAD

The **HEAD** method is used to retrieve the headers from a given endpoint. It is like **GET**, but it does not return the body of the response. It is mainly used to check for the existence of a resource (such as an index or a document) without retrieving the actual data.

Example:

```
HEAD /my-index-000001/_doc/1
```

This would check if a document with the ID **`1`** exists in **`my-index-000001`**. If no document exists with that ID, the response will have a status code of **`404`** (Not Found). If a document exists, the response will have a status code of **`200`** (OK).

In our previous example, we created a document with the ID **`7i18sYsBBDr4QfYX4Kdm`**. If we run the following command, we will get a response with the status code **`200,`** and the headers for the document:

```
HEAD /my-index-000001/_doc/7i18sYsBBDr4QfYX4Kdm
```

DELETE

The **`DELETE`** method removes resources from the cluster. In the context of Elasticsearch, **`DELETE`** is used to delete indices, remove documents from an index, or delete an entire index.

Example:

```
DELETE /my-index-000001
```

This request would delete the index named **`my-index-000001`**.

PATCH (less common in Elasticsearch)

The **`PATCH`** method is used to apply partial modifications to a resource. However, it is not commonly used in Elasticsearch because this typically uses the **`POST`** method to perform partial updates to documents.

In essence, these HTTP methods are integral to RESTful operations within Elasticsearch, enabling developers and administrators to interact with the cluster's data and configuration in a standardized way. Proper use of each method ensures the cluster's data integrity and efficient operation.

Tips for Effective Use of Dev Tools

- **Use Auto-Complete**: Dev Tools provides suggestions for fields and commands as you type.
- **Reference the Documentation**: Direct links to Elasticsearch documentation are available in Dev Tools for quick reference.
- **Save Your Work**: You can save commands; you might want to reuse later.

Summary

The Dev Tools Console in Kibana is a versatile and indispensable tool for anyone working with Elasticsearch. By following this hands-on lab, you now have the basic knowledge to create indices, index documents, execute searches, and perform clean-up operations. As you become more comfortable with these foundations, you can explore more complex queries and Elasticsearch functionalities, making Dev Tools an integral part of your Elasticsearch journey.

In this book, we will use Dev Tools to demonstrate various Elasticsearch concepts and techniques. The following chapters will delve into the details of Elasticsearch, providing you with the knowledge to build robust and efficient search as well as analytics solutions.

Index Lifecycle Management

At the heart of Elasticsearch's robustness and efficiency in handling data lies a critical feature: Index Lifecycle Management (ILM). This powerful component ensures that your indices are optimized, managed, and stored effectively throughout their existence. The lifecycle of an index in Elasticsearch is a journey through various stages – each with its own purpose and management strategies. Understanding ILM is essential for anyone looking to utilize Elasticsearch to its fullest potential, whether you are maintaining a lean search architecture or orchestrating a vast data lake for complex analytics.

We can manage the lifecycle of an index in Elasticsearch through the ILM API. This API allows us to define policies that automate the transition of an index through its various stages. These policies can be applied to multiple indices, allowing for centralized management of the entire cluster. *Figure* 2.5 illustrates the lifecycle of an index in Elasticsearch.

We can use Kibana to manage the lifecycle of an index in Elasticsearch. You can access the ILM feature in Kibana by clicking the "Index Management" icon on the left-hand navigation panel, as shown in *Figure* 2.5.

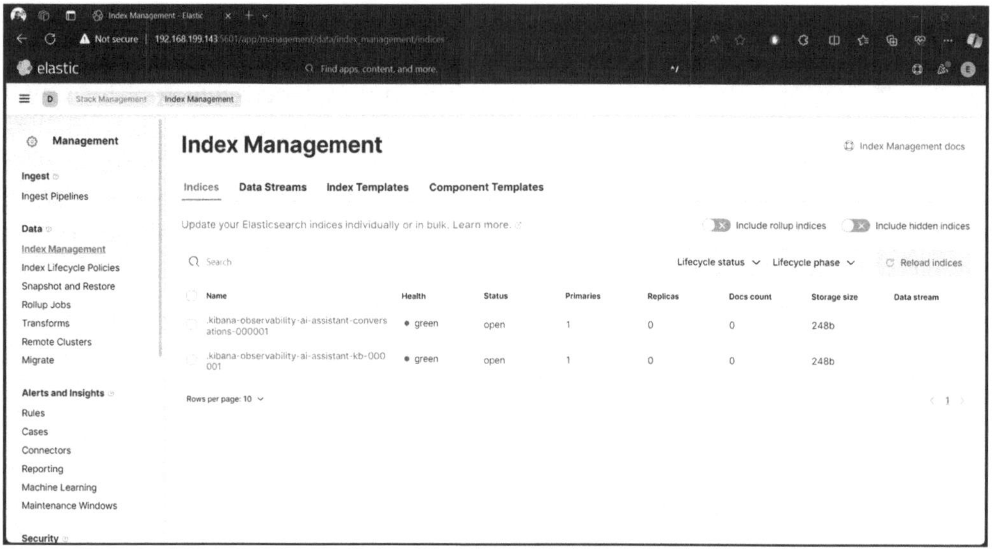

***Figure* 2.5**: *Managing Elasticsearch Index via Kibana Portal*

Creation and Ingestion

The lifecycle begins with the creation of an index, which is typically designed to store a specific type of document, such as logs, product listings, or customer data. During the ingestion phase, documents are indexed – meaning that they are processed, stored, and made searchable. It is a time of growth, where the emphasis is on the rapid and efficient handling of the incoming data. Here, you will learn how to define index settings and mappings to optimize the indexing process, and ensure that your data is structured in a way that supports your search and analysis needs.

Rollover and Growth

As indices grow in size and age, their performance and cost-effectiveness can wane. To maintain efficiency, Elasticsearch's ILM introduces the concept of rollover – a process that creates a new index, when the current one reaches a specified size, age, or document count. This strategy keeps indices at an optimal size for search performance, and helps with segmentation, making data management more practicable. This section will guide you through setting up rollover criteria, and initiating the rollover process, an essential technique for handling time-series data like logs or metrics.

Hot-Warm-Cold-Frozen Phases

After the rollover, indices are often moved through the hot-warm-cold-frozen phase model, each representing a different storage and accessibility profile. '`Hot`' indices are actively written to, and frequently accessed. '`Warm`' indices are less frequently accessed, but still need to be searchable. '`Cold`' indices are rarely accessed, and can be stored on less expensive hardware. Finally, '`frozen`' indices are seldom queried, and are archived in a highly compressed format, minimizing costs. Here, we will dissect how to automate the transition between these phases, aligning with your organization's access patterns and budget constraints.

Retention and Deletion

Data retention policies play a vital role in ILM, determining how long data remains in the system before it is deleted or archived. In this part of the lifecycle, it is important to balance the value of historical data against the cost and performance of storage. Elasticsearch provides tools to automate data retention according to your policies. This segment will delve into configuring and applying retention policies that automatically delete or archive data to comply with storage limitations, legal requirements, and business needs.

Snapshot and Restore

While not strictly a phase, snapshotting is an integral part of ILM. Snapshots provide a means to backup and restore data, ensuring that you can recover from hardware failure, data corruption, or user error. In this section, we will look at how to create snapshots of your indices, and how to restore from a snapshot as well as strategies for snapshot lifecycle management, which coordinates the creation and deletion of snapshots according to a schedule.

In summary, Index Lifecycle Management in Elasticsearch is a multifaceted toolset that helps manage the flow of data from ingestion to deletion. Through ILM, Elasticsearch empowers users to automate the mundane yet critical tasks of index administration, ensuring that performance is maintained, costs are controlled, and data remains compliant and secure. The following subsections will delve into each stage of ILM in detail, providing you with the knowledge to implement a robust data lifecycle strategy.

Hands-On Lab: Index Lifecycle Management in Elasticsearch Using Kibana Dev Tools

In this lab, you will learn how to use Elasticsearch's ILM feature to automate index management tasks such as creating, ingesting data into, rolling over, and eventually, deleting indices. We will cover the lifecycle from hot to warm, cold, and frozen phases, and how to set up policies that dictate the transition and retention of data through these stages.

We will continue from where we left off in the previous ILM setup, and now integrate snapshot as well as restore operations into our index management process.

Prerequisites

- Running Elasticsearch cluster.
- Kibana installed, and connected to the Elasticsearch cluster.
- Basic familiarity with Elasticsearch, and Kibana's Dev Tools console.

Part 1: Creation and Ingestion

Step 1: Define an Index Template

An index template in Elasticsearch is a way to tell the cluster how to configure new indices, when they are created. Templates are necessary for managing settings, mappings, and other index-specific configurations in a reusable manner. When an index is created, Elasticsearch will apply the template that matches the index pattern, thereby ensuring that all new indices conform to a predefined set of rules.

Templates are particularly useful, when working with time-series data, logs, or any situation where indices are created regularly, and need a consistent configuration. Without templates, you would have to manually set up mappings, settings, and aliases, each time you create a new index, which is prone to errors and inconsistencies.

The goals for defining an index template are as follows:

1. **Consistency**: Ensure that all indices matching the pattern have the same structure, settings, and behaviors. This is crucial for systematic querying, aggregation, and analysis across similarly structured data.
2. **Automated Configuration**: Automate the process of index creation with the desired settings such as the number of shards and replicas, refresh intervals, and mappings. This saves time, and reduces manual overhead as well as the potential for configuration errors.
3. **Optimized Mapping**: Define mappings in the template to control how different fields are indexed and stored. This can include data types, analyzer settings for text fields, and format definitions for dates and numbers.
4. **Scalability and Performance**: Establish index settings that are tuned for the scale and performance needs of the application, like specifying shard and replica counts, which can improve search performance, and increase resilience to failures.

5. **Maintenance and Evolution**: Manage the evolution of the index structure more easily. If you need to change the configuration, you can update the template and all new indices will inherit the changes, ensuring gradual and manageable schema evolution.

By achieving these goals, you set a solid foundation for your indices, allowing you to focus on the more complex tasks of data ingestion, search optimization, and query design, with the confidence that your underlying index structures are set up consistently and efficiently.

Let us walk through the process of defining an index template in Elasticsearch:

1. Open Kibana, and navigate to Dev Tools.
2. Create an index template that includes settings and mappings necessary for your data:

```
PUT _index_template/lab_index_template
{
  "index_patterns": ["lab-data-*"],
  "template": {
    "settings": {
      "number_of_shards": 1,
      "number_of_replicas": 1
    },
    "mappings": {
      "properties": {
        "timestamp": {
          "type": "date"
        },
        "value": {
          "type": "double"
        }
        // Define other properties relevant to your data
      }
    }
  }
}
```

Step 2: Create an ILM Policy

In this step, you will create an ILM policy, a set of rules that automate the management of indices through their life from inception to deletion. The ILM policy defines how indices should be handled as they grow and age; it specifies when they should roll over to a new index, move to less expensive storage, or be deleted to conserve resources. The policy is composed of phases – Hot, Warm, Cold, and Delete – each configured with actions and triggers, based on the index's age, size, or other custom criteria.

Creating an ILM policy helps in managing data systematically, optimizing storage, and ensuring that data retention conforms to compliance and business requirements.

Let us define an ILM policy that specifies the lifecycle of your indices:

```
PUT _ilm/policy/lab_data_policy
{
  "policy": {
    "phases": {
      "hot": {
        "min_age": "0ms",
        "actions": {
          "rollover": {
            "max_age": "7d",
            "max_size": "5GB"
          }
        }
      },
      "warm": {
        "min_age": "10d",
        "actions": {
          "readonly": {}
        }
      },
      "cold": {
        "min_age": "30d",
        "actions": {
          "freeze": {}
        }
      },
      "delete": {
        "min_age": "90d",
        "actions": {
          "delete": {}
        }
      }
    }
  }
}
```

Part 2: Rollover and Growth

Step 3: Apply the ILM Policy to an Index

In this crucial step, you will link the previously defined ILM policy to an index, or an index alias. Applying the ILM policy to an index automates the execution of the lifecycle rules, you have set out in your policy, dictating how and when the index should transition through various phases – hot, warm, cold, and delete. This process effectively binds the index to a set of behaviors that will manage its life cycle such as rollovers, shrinkage, freezing, and eventual deletion. This step is fundamental to ensuring that your indices are optimized for performance and cost throughout their existence, and are cleaned up in accordance with your data governance standards.

Let us create an initial index, and apply the ILM policy:

```
PUT /lab-data-000001
{
  "aliases": {
    "lab-data": {
      "is_write_index": true
    }
  },
  "settings": {
    "index.lifecycle.name": "lab_data_policy",
    "index.lifecycle.rollover_alias": "lab-data"
  }
}
```

Step 4: Index Some Documents

Simulate data ingestion by indexing some documents:

```
POST /lab-data/_doc
{
  "timestamp": "2023-11-05T12:00:00Z",
  "value": 100
}
```

Repeat the preceding POST request as necessary to simulate continuous data ingestion.

To verify that the documents are indexed, run the following command:

```
GET /lab-data/_search
```

Figure 2.6 shows the response from Elasticsearch, after indexing a few documents.

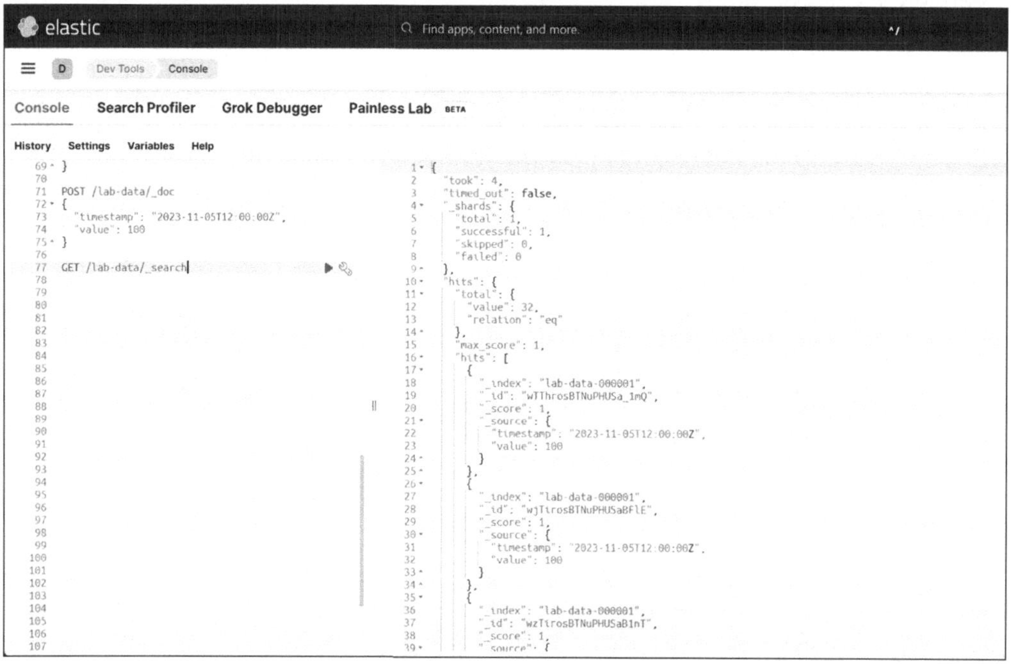

Figure 2.6: *Getting Documents*

Part 3: Hot-Warm-Cold-Frozen Phases

Step 5: Monitoring the Transition

Monitor the index as it transitions through the lifecycle phases:

```
GET lab-data-*/_ilm/explain
```

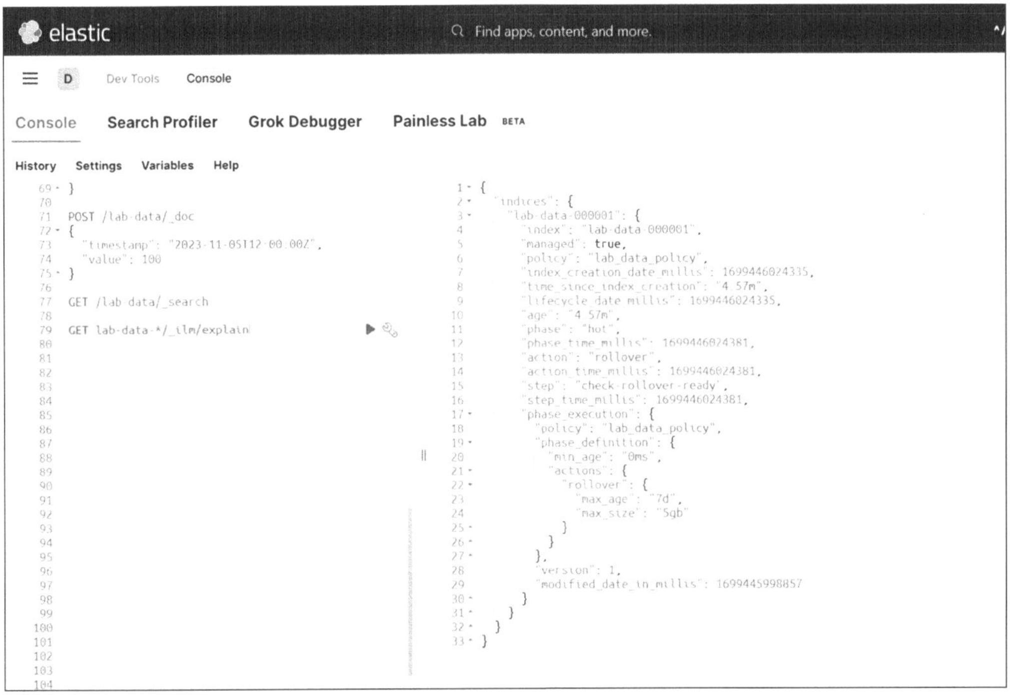

***Figure 2.7**: Getting ILM Information*

After sending the request, you will see the response in the right panel. The response will look similar to *Figure 2.7*. The response you received from the Elasticsearch cluster is an explanation of the current status of the index **`lab-data-000001`** with regard to its ILM. Here is a breakdown of the key components of the response:

- "**`indices`**": This is a list of the indices that the ILM explain API call has information about.
- "**`lab-data-000001`**": This is the name of the index for which the ILM status is being reported.
- "**`managed`**": This is set to **`true`**, indicating that the index is under the management of an ILM policy.
- "**`policy`**": This indicates the name of the ILM policy (**`lab_data_policy`**) that is applied to the index.
- "**`index_creation_date_millis`**": This represents the timestamp in milliseconds, since the epoch when the index was created. The index was created on this cluster approximately 4.57 minutes ago.
- "**`time_since_index_creation`**": This is a human-readable format of the time elapsed, since the index was created again, stating it has been approximately 4.57 minutes.

- "**lifecycle_date_millis**": This represents the start time of the index lifecycle in milliseconds since the epoch, which is essentially the same as the index creation time.
- "**age**": This is a human-readable format of the time elapsed since the lifecycle of the index began, which is the same as the time since the index was created.
- "**phase**": This indicates the current phase of the ILM policy that the index is in. "hot" is the phase intended for new and actively updated data.
- "**phase_time_millis**": This is the timestamp in milliseconds, when the index entered the current phase.
- "**action**": This represents the current action that is being performed as part of the lifecycle policy. The "**rollover**" action indicates that Elasticsearch is evaluating, whether the conditions to rollover the index have been met or not.
- "**action_time_millis**": This is the timestamp in milliseconds, when the current action began.
- "**step**": This indicates the specific step within the action that is currently being executed, which is "**check-rollover-ready**" in this case. This step is where Elasticsearch checks, if the index meets the criteria defined for a rollover (like **max_age** or **max_size**).
- "**step_time_millis**": This is the timestamp in milliseconds, when the current step began.
- "**phase_execution**": This provides details about the execution of the current phase, including:
- "**policy**": The name of the policy being executed.
- "**phase_definition**": The specific configuration for the current phase (here, it specifies that rollover should happen after 7 days, or if the index size exceeds 5 GB).
- "**version**": The version of the ILM policy.
- "**modified_date_in_millis**": The last modification date and time of the ILM policy.

In summary, this response tells you that the index **lab-data-000001** is managed by an ILM policy named **lab_data_policy**. The index is currently in the "hot" phase, and the rollover action is being evaluated to determine, if the index should be rolled over, based on its age or size.

Part 4: Retention and Deletion

Step 6: Verify Deletion Policy

After the time has passed, verify indices are deleted according to the policy:

```
GET /_cat/indices/lab-data-*?v&s=index
```

This command lists the indices, and you should not see any indices older than the deletion phase's **`min_age`**.

Certainly! We will incorporate steps for Snapshot, and Restore in the context of the ILM process in Elasticsearch using Kibana Dev Tools.

Part 5: Snapshot Lifecycle Management

Step 7: Define a Snapshot Lifecycle Policy

You need to define a snapshot repository in Elasticsearch with the name **`my_snapshot_repo`**. This is where the snapshots created by the SLM policy will be stored. The repository could be a shared filesystem, an S3 bucket, Azure Blob Storage, Google Cloud Storage, or any other supported type.

To create the repository, you would send a **`PUT`** request to Elasticsearch with the necessary settings for the chosen repository type. For example, to create a filesystem repository, you would use a request like this:

```
PUT /_snapshot/my_snapshot_repo
{
    "type": "fs",
    "settings": {
    "location": "/path/to/your/backup"
    }
}
```

Replace **`"/path/to/your/backup"`** with the actual file path to your backup directory.

On Ubuntu, you would typically use a path that resides within a directory where Elasticsearch has permission to read and write data. For instance, you might use a subdirectory within **`/var/lib/elasticsearch`**, which is a common location for Elasticsearch data, or you could create a new directory specifically for snapshots.

Here is an example of how you might set up a snapshot directory:

1. **Create a New Directory**: Open your terminal, and run the following command to create a new directory:

   ```
   sudo mkdir -p /var/lib/elasticsearch/snapshots
   ```

2. **Set Appropriate Permissions**: Make sure that the Elasticsearch user has read and write permissions for this directory. You can set the ownership to the Elasticsearch user with:

   ```
   sudo chown -R elasticsearch:elasticsearch /var/lib/elasticsearch/
   snapshots
   ```

   This command changes the ownership of the directory to the **`elasticsearch`** user and group which should be the user running the Elasticsearch service.

3. **Configure `path.repo` on Elasticsearch**: Next, you need to configure the **`path.repo`** setting in Elasticsearch to allow the use of this directory as a snapshot repository. Open the Elasticsearch configuration file in a text editor:

   ```
   sudo nano /etc/elasticsearch/elasticsearch.yml
   ```

   Add the following line to the end of the file:

   ```
   path.repo: ["/var/lib/elasticsearch/snapshots"]
   ```

   Save and close the file.

   You may restart Elasticsearch to apply the changes:

   ```
   sudo systemctl restart elasticsearch.service
   ```

4. **Configure the Elasticsearch Repository Path**: When creating your snapshot repository in Elasticsearch, you would then specify the path as:

   ```
   PUT /_snapshot/my_snapshot_repo
   {
     "type": "fs",
     "settings": {
       "location": "/var/lib/elasticsearch/snapshots"
     }
   }
   ```

Make sure to execute these commands with appropriate permissions, and double-check that your Elasticsearch configuration allows for this directory to be used as a snapshot repository.

After setting up the directory, and ensuring the correct permissions, you can then use the preceding PUT request to define the snapshot repository in Elasticsearch.

Next, we will define a policy that automatically creates snapshots of our indices, before the deletion phase:

```
PUT _slm/policy/lab_data_snapshot_policy
{
  "schedule": "0 30 1 * * ?",
  "name": "<lab-data-snap-{now/d}>",
  "repository": "my_snapshot_repo",
  "config": {
    "indices": ["lab-data-*"]
  },
  "retention": {
    "expire_after": "30d",
    "min_count": 5,
    "max_count": 50
  }
}
```

This request configures an SLM policy named **`lab_data_snapshot_policy`** to automatically create daily snapshots of indices matching the pattern **`lab-data-*`** at 1:30 AM, and store them in the **`my_snapshot_repo`** repository. The snapshots are named with a date-stamped pattern for easy identification. The policy ensures a minimum of 5 snapshots that are always retained, while capping the maximum at 50, with any snapshots older than 30 days' subject to deletion, unless this would drop the total below 5.

To retrieve information about an existing Snapshot Lifecycle Management (SLM) policy in Elasticsearch, you can use the GET API to request details about the policy. For your specific **`lab_data_snapshot_policy`**, you would issue the following request in the Kibana Dev Tools console or via any tool that can send requests to the Elasticsearch REST API:

```
GET _slm/policy/lab_data_snapshot_policy
```

This will return information about the specified SLM policy, including its configuration details, and the current status.

The response you receive should contain data about when the policy was last executed, any snapshots that have been taken according to this policy, and the next scheduled execution time, among other details. You can see an example of this response in *Figure 2.8*.

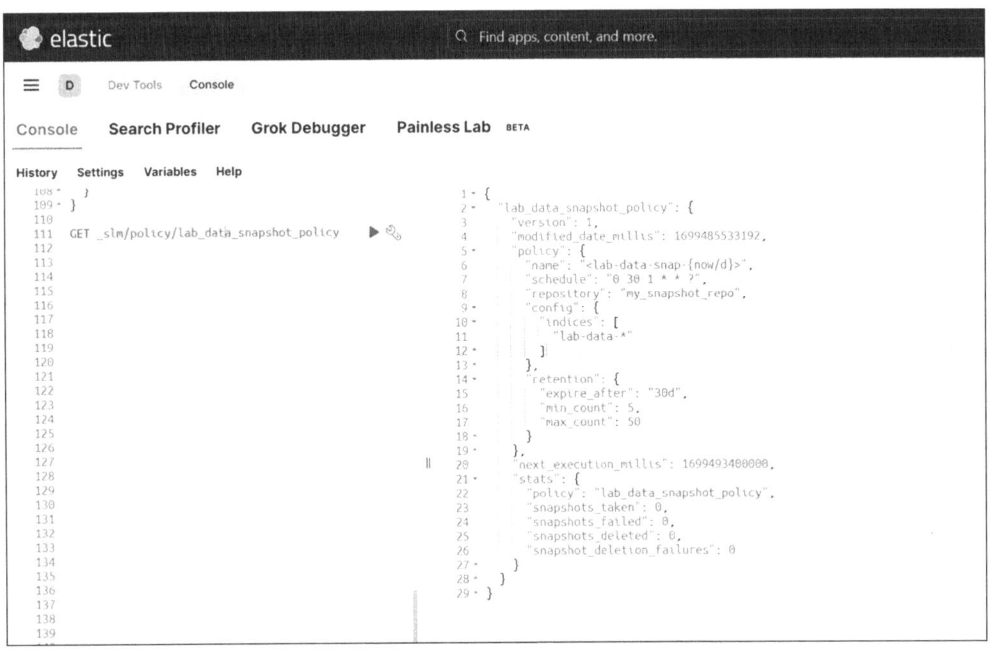

Figure 2.8: *Getting Snapshot Policy Information*

Step 8: Execute Snapshot Lifecycle Policy

Execute the snapshot policy to ensure that it is correctly set up:

```
POST _slm/policy/lab_data_snapshot_policy/_execute
```

Figure 2.9 shows the response you should receive from the Elasticsearch cluster. The response indicates that the snapshot policy was executed successfully, and that a snapshot named **`lab_data_snapshot_policy`** was created.

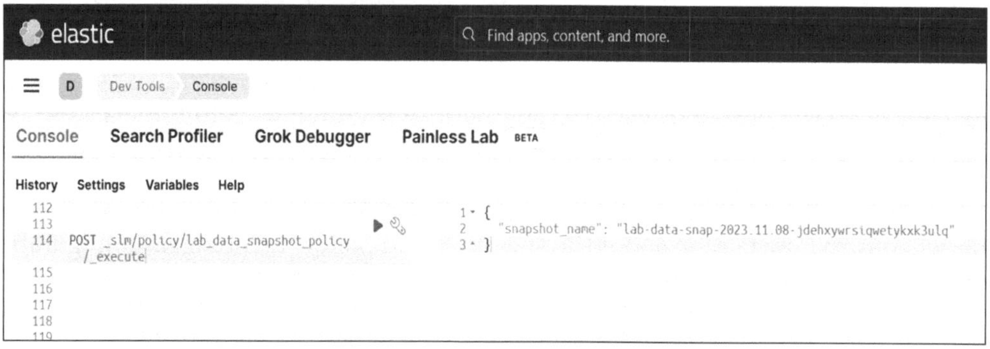

Figure 2.9: *Executing an SLM on Elasticsearch*

Step 9: Update ILM Policy to Include Snapshot before Deletion

We refine our existing ILM policy to add a crucial data protection step. This enhancement instructs Elasticsearch to automatically create a backup snapshot of an index, just before it is scheduled to be deleted as part of the ILM's "**`delete`**" phase. Thus, by integrating snapshot creation into our ILM policy, we ensure that a recoverable copy of the data is preserved, allowing us to safeguard against accidental data loss, and providing a point of recovery if the data needs to be restored in the future. This step is vital for maintaining data durability, and adds a layer of resilience to our data retention strategy.

Let us modify the existing ILM policy to include a snapshot step, before the delete action:

```
PUT _ilm/policy/lab_data_policy
{
  "policy": {
    "phases": {
      "hot": {
        "min_age": "0ms",
        "actions": {
          "rollover": {
            "max_age": "7d",
            "max_size": "5GB"
          }
```

```
          }
        },
        "warm": {
          "min_age": "10d",
          "actions": {
            "readonly": {}
          }
        },
        "cold": {
          "min_age": "30d",
          "actions": {
            "freeze": {}
          }
        },
        "delete": {
          "min_age": "90d",
          "actions": {
            "wait_for_snapshot": {
              "policy": "lab_data_snapshot_policy"
            },
            "delete": {}
          }
        }
      }
    }
  }
```

Step 10: Verify the Snapshot Creation

Check the snapshots created by the SLM policy:

```
GET /_snapshot/my_snapshot_repo/_all
```

After sending the request, you will see the response in the right panel. The response will look similar to *Figure* 2.10. You can see that the snapshot named **`lab-data-snap-<snapshot>`** was created by the SLM policy. Keep in mind that the snapshot name will be different in your case. Save the snapshot name for the next step. For instance, our snapshot name is **`lab-data-snap-2023.11.08-jdehxywrsiqwetykxk3ulq`**.

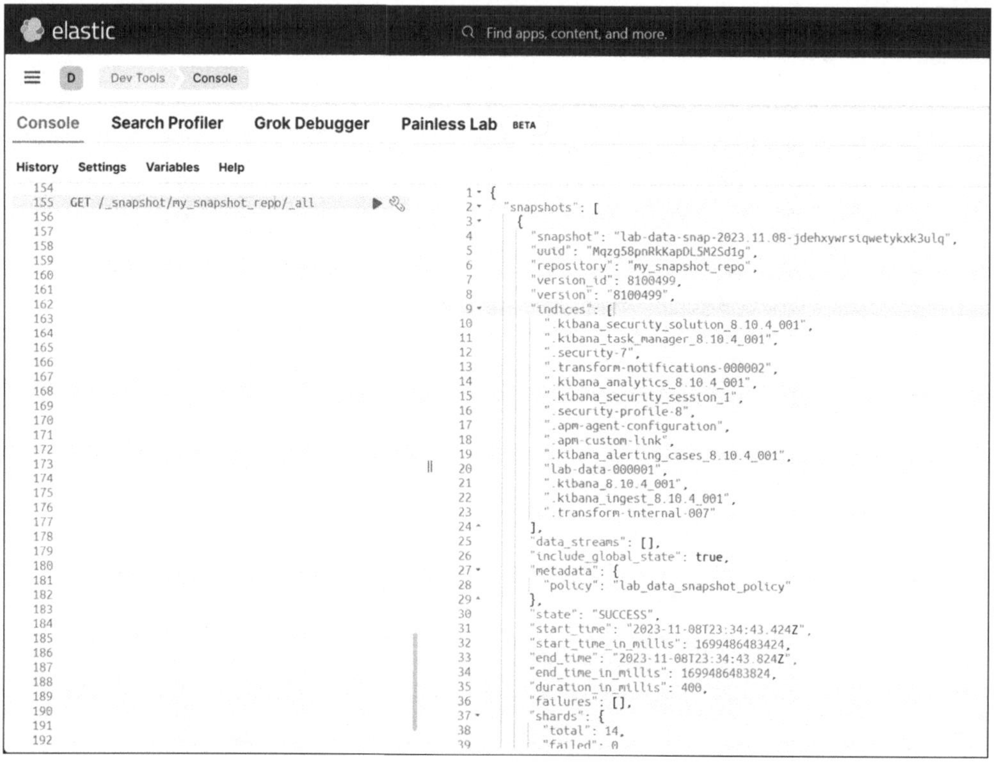

***Figure 2.10**: Getting a Snapshot Repo on Elasticsearch*

Part 6: Restore from Snapshot

Step 11: Restoring Data

To simulate a restore process, first manually delete an index (preferably in a safe, controlled environment):

```
DELETE /lab-data-000001
```

Next, verify that the index is deleted:

```
GET /_cat/indices/lab-data-*
```

You should see a response, indicating that the index is no longer present.

Then, restore the index from a snapshot:

```
POST /_snapshot/my_snapshot_repo/lab-data-snap-<snapshot>/_
restore
{
  "indices": "lab-data-000001",
  "include_global_state": false
}
```

Make sure to replace **`<snapshot>`** with the actual snapshot name that contains the index you want to restore. Since our snapshot name is **`lab-data-snap-2023.11.08-jdehxywrsiqwetykxk3ulq`**, we would use **`lab-data-snap-2023.11.08-jdehxywrsiqwetykxk3ulq`** in the preceding request:

```
POST /_snapshot/my_snapshot_repo/lab-data-snap-2023.11.08-jdehxy-
wrsiqwetykxk3ulq/_restore
{
  "indices": "lab-data-000001",
  "include_global_state": false
}
```

After sending the request, you can verify that the index is restored by running the following command:

```
GET /_cat/indices/lab-data-*
```

You should see a response, indicating that the index is present.

Wrap-Up

In this lab, you have walked through setting up an ILM policy for managing the lifecycle of indices in Elasticsearch. You have also learned how to:

- Define an index template with settings and mappings.
- Create an ILM policy with hot, warm, cold, and delete phases.
- Apply the ILM policy to an index.
- Ingest data into the index.
- Monitor the index as it transitions through the lifecycle stages.
- Verify that the policy is appropriately deleting indices.
- Create a snapshot lifecycle policy.
- Execute the snapshot lifecycle policy.
- Update the ILM policy to include a snapshot step, before deletion.
- Verify that the snapshots are created.
- Restore an index from a snapshot.
- Verify that the index is restored.
- Verify that the index is deleted, after the retention period.

To get the most out of this lab, it is encouraged to adjust the **`min_age`** settings for each phase to shorter intervals to observe the transitions quickly, as waiting for days or months is not practical in a learning environment. Also, repeat the data ingestion step multiple times, or automate it to better simulate a production environment's continuous data flow.

Remember to monitor the snapshot repository's storage, as it will grow with each snapshot. Adjust retention settings as needed to balance between having sufficient backups, and managing disk space.

Keep in mind that taking snapshots, and restoring from them can be resource-intensive operations. Schedule them during low-usage times when possible, and monitor your cluster's performance during these operations.

Understanding Document IDs in Elasticsearch

Elasticsearch provides a unique identifier for each document stored in an index. This identifier is known as the Document ID. When you index a document, you can either provide your own custom ID, or let Elasticsearch generate one for you. The choice between using a custom ID, or an auto-generated ID has implications for performance, indexing, and application design.

Auto-generated IDs

- **Elasticsearch generates a unique ID**: When a document is indexed without specifying an ID, Elasticsearch will automatically generate a random 20-character string as the document ID.
- **High performance**: Auto-generated IDs are optimized for performance in Elasticsearch because they are guaranteed to be unique across the cluster, and are generated in a way that is friendly to the underlying Lucene segments.
- **Use case**: Auto-generated IDs are ideal, when the uniqueness of the document is defined by its content, rather than an external identifier, or when you do not have a natural document identifier.

Custom IDs

- **User-defined uniqueness**: When you index a document, you have the option to specify your own ID. This can be any string that uniquely identifies the document such as a UUID or a natural key derived from the document's content.
- **Potential for collisions**: When using custom IDs, it is the developer's responsibility to ensure that they are unique. If you index a document with an ID that already exists, the new document will overwrite the existing one.

- **Impact on indexing speed**: Indexing with custom IDs can be slower than using auto-generated IDs because Elasticsearch must first check if a document with that ID already exists in the index.
- **Use case**: Custom IDs are suitable when you want to maintain consistency with an external system that uses a specific ID scheme or when documents are naturally identified by certain attributes, such as a social security number or an email address.

When to Use Custom IDs

- **Integration with external systems**: When documents are associated with IDs from an external database or system, it makes sense to use these IDs within Elasticsearch to keep the systems synchronized.
- **Document updates and upserts**: If you need to frequently update or upsert documents, having a custom ID allows you to easily reference the document, without needing to look up an auto-generated ID.
- **Deterministic behavior**: Custom IDs allow you to reindex the same data, and get the exact same document IDs, which is not possible with auto-generated IDs.

When to Use Auto-generated IDs

- **No natural identifier**: If there is no obvious attribute that can serve as a unique identifier for your documents, it is simpler and more efficient to let Elasticsearch handle ID generation.
- **Best performance**: When maximum write performance is a priority, and there are no external constraints requiring a specific ID scheme, auto-generated IDs will provide the best indexing performance.

Best Practices

- **Decide early**: Choose between custom and auto-generated IDs early in the design of your application, as changing the scheme later can be complex.
- **Consistency**: Use the same ID generation strategy consistently across all documents in an index to avoid confusion and errors.
- **Avoid unnecessary updates**: Be aware that using custom IDs can lead to unintended overwrites, if the uniqueness of IDs is not properly managed.

Summary

Whether to use custom or auto-generated IDs in Elasticsearch depends on your specific requirements and use cases. Auto-generated IDs offer the best performance, and are ideal when no external systems influence the ID scheme. Custom IDs provide control and consistency with external identifiers, but require careful management to ensure uniqueness, and can impact indexing performance.

Advanced Querying Techniques

Elasticsearch's querying capabilities are what truly set it apart as a search and analytics engine. Beyond the basic match queries, a rich landscape of advanced querying techniques allows for nuanced data interrogation and complex search operations. This section dives into the advanced querying techniques that enable users to extract precise information, identify patterns, and derive insights from their data in Elasticsearch.

Boolean Queries

At the core of advanced querying lies the Boolean Query. It allows for the combination of multiple queries using boolean logic – such as **`must`**, **`should`**, **`must_not`**, and **`filter`**. This gives you the precision to construct queries that can match various criteria simultaneously, boosting relevant documents, or excluding the irrelevant ones. We will explore the balance between query precision and performance, teaching you how to construct complex Boolean queries that are both efficient and effective.

In Elasticsearch, Boolean queries allow you to combine multiple queries in a logical manner. Here is a summary of the different types of Boolean queries, and their purposes:

`must`

Purpose: The **`must`** clause behaves like a logical AND. All queries within this clause must match for the document to be included in the results. It contributes to scoring.

`should`

Purpose: The **`should`** clause is equivalent to a logical OR. At least one of the **`should`** queries must match for the document to be included in the results. If there are also **`must`** clauses, then they **`should`** clauses act as optional constraints that influence scoring, but are not mandatory for matching.

`must_not`

Purpose: The **`must_not`** clause is used to exclude documents that match the specified query. It behaves like a logical NOT. The queries in this clause must not match for the document to be included in the results. This clause does not contribute to scoring.

filter

Purpose: The **filter** clause is used to filter the results, without affecting the score. It behaves like a logical AND. All queries within this clause must match, but they do not influence scoring, which makes **filter** faster and cacheable.

Example of a Boolean Query

Here is an example of a Boolean Query that combines these clauses:

```
GET /_search
{
  "query": {
    "bool": {
      "must": [
        { "match": { "title": "Elasticsearch" }}
      ],
      "should": [
        { "term": { "tag": "search" }},
        { "term": { "tag": "distributed" }}
      ],
      "must_not": [
        { "range": { "date": { "gte": "2023-01-01" }}}
      ],
      "filter": [
        { "term": { "status": "published" }}
      ]
    }
  }
}
```

In this example, documents must match the **title** query, should match at least one of the **tag** queries, must not be dated on or after **2023-01-01**, and must have a status of **published**. The **must** and **should** clauses will influence the relevancy score of the documents, while the **must_not** and **filter** clauses will not.

Full-text Search Enhancements

Elasticsearch provides a full-text search capability that goes well beyond simple keyword matching. Techniques such as phrase matching, proximity searches, and the use of synonyms expand the matching criteria to understand the context and closeness of terms within the text. Additionally, we will delve into the use of analyzers and tokenizers that break down complex text into searchable elements, enhancing the quality of the search results.

Aggregation for Data Analysis

Querying in Elasticsearch is not only about finding documents; it is also about summarizing your data. Aggregations are a powerful way to process and analyze your data, providing capabilities for building summaries or extracting statistics. From simple count operations to advanced bucketing and metrics, aggregations help turn your data into actionable insights. This section will cover a range of aggregation techniques, including terms, histograms, and significant terms, and will demonstrate how to nest these aggregations to perform sophisticated data analysis.

Scoring and Relevance Tuning

Understanding how Elasticsearch scores and ranks query results is vital for fine-tuning relevance. Scoring algorithms such as TF/IDF and BM25, determine how closely results match the query terms. This section will dive into the mechanics of scoring, and how to influence it with functions such as field-level boosts, the **`function_score`** query, and the **`script_score`** query which allow for custom scoring models, based on your specific requirements.

Autocomplete and Suggestions

Real-time search experiences often require features such as autocomplete and search suggestions to enhance user interaction. Elasticsearch facilitates this through features like the **`completion suggester`** and **`search_as_you_type`** field types. Here, we will discuss implementing intelligent autocomplete systems that can provide feedback to users as they type, leveraging Elasticsearch's fast and efficient suggestion capabilities.

Geo-Searches and Proximity Queries

Location-based data can be critical for many applications, and Elasticsearch supports geo-queries out of the box. Whether you are searching for documents within a certain distance from a point or within a geographic shape like a polygon, Elasticsearch has you covered. This subsection will explain how to index geo-points and geo-shapes, and how to use geo-queries to find results based on location.

Joining Queries

While Elasticsearch is not a relational database, it does provide mechanisms to perform join-like operations. Parent-child relationships and nested document structures can be queried in ways that approximate SQL joins. We will guide you through the process of setting up parent-child relationships and nested objects as well as crafting queries that can efficiently retrieve related data across different document types.

Cross-Cluster Search

For organizations operating in multi-cluster environments, cross-cluster search is a critical capability. This feature allows a query to span across multiple Elasticsearch clusters, treating them as a single unified data source. This segment will explore how to configure and execute cross-cluster searches, providing strategies for querying and aggregating data across geographically distributed clusters.

By mastering these advanced querying techniques, you will be able to leverage the full power of Elasticsearch to answer complex questions and perform intricate search tasks. The following subsections will provide a deep dive into each of these techniques, complete with practical examples and best practices to enhance your querying skills.

Hands-On Lab: Uploading NDJSON File to Elasticsearch Using Dev Tools

Before we dive into querying practices in Elasticsearch, it is imperative that we populate our Elasticsearch cluster with relevant data. For the upcoming exercises, we will use a dataset containing product information. This dataset is formatted as an NDJSON (Newline Delimited JSON) file, `product_data.ndjson`, which will be provided in the source code of the book. Uploading this data will set the stage for the next lab, where we will perform a variety of search and query operations.

Understanding NDJSON Format

NDJSON stands for **Newline Delimited JSON**. It is a convenient format for storing or streaming structured data that may be processed one record at a time. Each line in an NDJSON file is a valid JSON object, but unlike regular JSON, line breaks are used to separate objects, not commas or array brackets. This format is especially useful for bulk operations in Elasticsearch.

Prerequisites

- Have Elasticsearch and Kibana installed and running.
- Ensure that you have the `product_data.ndjson` file which contains the product data to be uploaded. This file is available in the source code of the book.

Step-by-Step Guide

1. **Access Kibana Dev Tools**:
   a. Open your browser, and navigate to the Kibana interface.
   b. Click the "**`Dev Tools`**" icon on the left-hand navigation bar.
2. **Prepare the Data**:
   a. Locate the **`product_data.ndjson`** file from the source code of the book.
   b. Open the file with a text editor to review the data structure.
   c. Make sure that the data is in the correct NDJSON format:
   d. Each JSON object should be in a single line.
   e. There should be no commas between objects.
   f. Ensure that no trailing commas are within any JSON objects.
3. **Upload the NDJSON File:**
   a. In Kibana Dev Tools, you will utilize the bulk API endpoint to upload your data.
   b. Copy the content of your **`product_data.ndjson`** file.
   c. In the Dev Tools console, enter the following command:

```
POST /_bulk
{paste the copied content here}
```

- Paste the NDJSON content after **`POST /_bulk`**, as shown in *Figure 2.11*.
- Press the "**`play`**" button or *Ctrl* + *Enter* to execute the request.

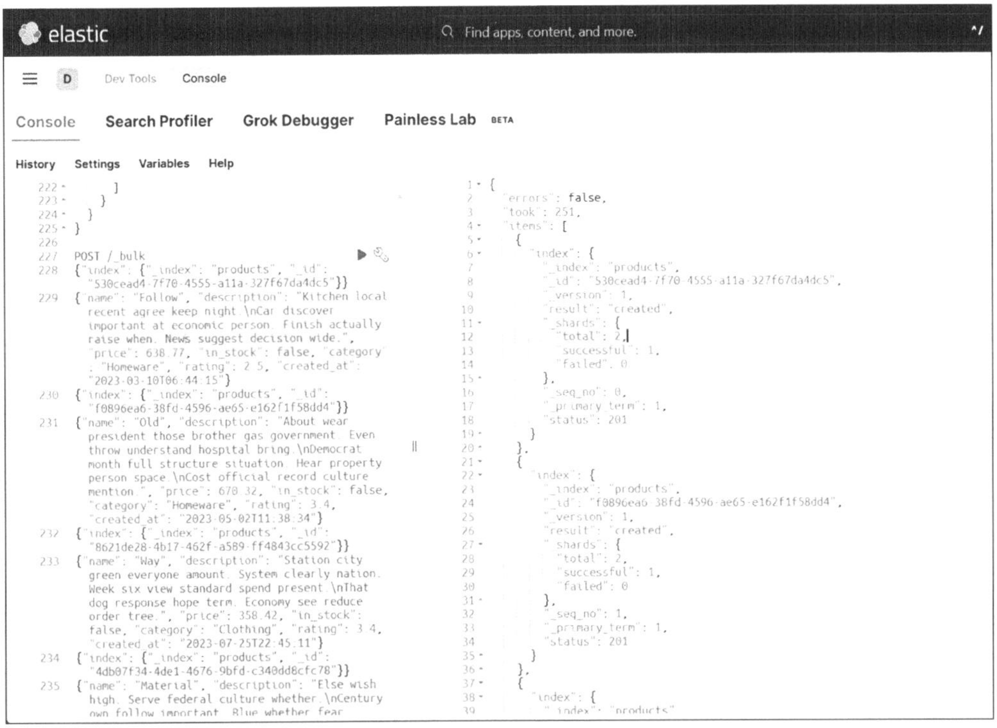

***Figure 2.11**: Uploading NDJSON Content*

4. **Verify Upload**:

   a. After the bulk operation, Elasticsearch will return a response, indicating success or failure for each document.

   b. To check if the data was correctly indexed, perform a search query:

   ```
   GET /products/_search
   {
      "query": {
         "match_all": {}
      }
   }
   ```

   This will return a subset of the documents from the **`products`** index.

5. **Error Handling**:

   - If there are errors in the response, check the NDJSON file for formatting issues.
   - Correct any errors in the file, and repeat the upload process.

6. **Clean Up (Optional):**
   - If this was a test, and you want to remove the data, you can delete the index:
     ```
     DELETE /products
     ```
   - Execute the preceding command in the Dev Tools console to delete the **`products`** index.

Summary

You have now completed the hands-on lab for uploading an NDJSON file to Elasticsearch, using Kibana Dev Tools. This process is essential for managing bulk data operations, and is a foundational skill for any Elasticsearch practitioner.

Hands-On Lab: Elasticsearch Querying Techniques Using Dev Tools

Having successfully uploaded our **`product_data.ndjson`** in the previous lab, we are now equipped to explore a range of Elasticsearch querying techniques. This hands-on lab will guide you through the execution of Boolean Queries, Full-Text Search, Aggregations, and Techniques for Scoring and Relevance Tuning.

Lab Steps

1. **Boolean Queries**
   - **Objective**: Combine multiple queries in a logical fashion (AND, OR, NOT).
   - **Task**: In Dev Tools, execute a Boolean query to find products that have a **`price`** greater than 20, and are in the **`electronics`** category.
   - **Request**:
     ```
     GET /products/_search
     {
       "query": {
         "bool": {
           "must": [
             { "term": { "category": "electronics" } },
             { "range": { "price": { "gt": 20 } } }
           ]
         }
       }
     }
     ```

Another example of a Boolean Query is as follows. This hypothetical query searches for products within the "**Electronics**" category, with a price greater than or equal to 500, that are not out of stock, and preferably with a rating of 2 or more. Adjust the fields and values in the query to suit your actual data, and what you wish to search for.

```
GET /products/_search
{
    "query": {
        "bool": {
        "must": [
            { "match": { "category": "Electronics" } },
            { "range": { "price": { "gte": 500 } } }
        ],
        "must_not": [
            { "term": { "in_stock": false } }
        ],
        "should": [
            { "range": { "rating": { "gte": 2 } } }
        ]
        }
    }
}
```

2. **Full-text Search**
   - **Objective**: Perform a search on text fields that will analyze the query string.
   - **Task**: Search for products that have a description containing the word, "**education**".
   - **Request**:

```
GET /products/_search
{
  "query": {
    "match": {
      "description": "education"
    }
  }
}
```

You can see the response output in *Figure 2.12*.

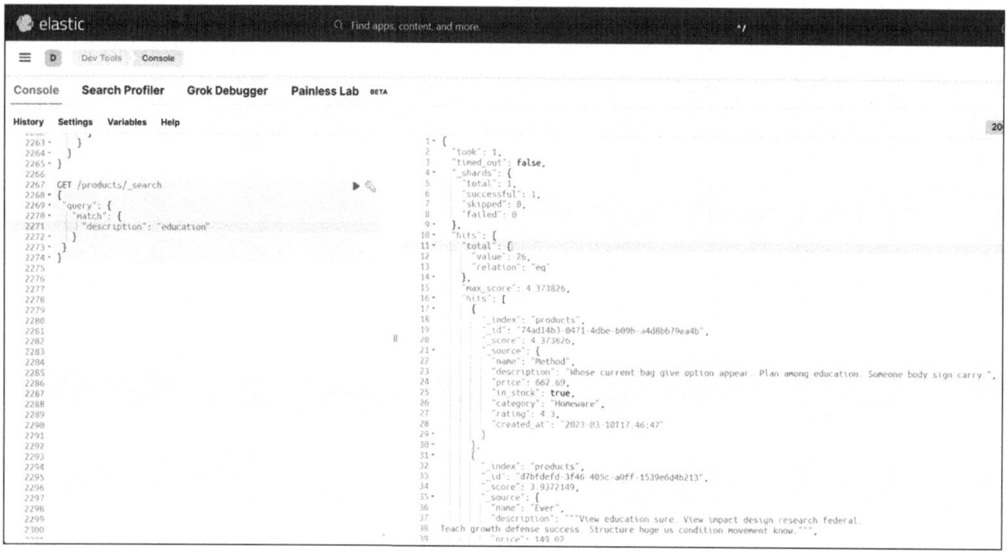

Figure 2.12: Response Output for Full-text Search

3. **Aggregation**

   - **Objective**: Summarize your data as metrics, statistics, or other analytics.
   - **Task**: Aggregate products by **category**, and get the average price per category.
   - **Request**:

```
GET /products/_search
{
  "size": 0,
  "aggs": {
    "categories": {
      "terms": { "field": "category.keyword" },
      "aggs": {
        "average_price": {
          "avg": { "field": "price" }
        }
      }
    }
  }
}
```

4. **Scoring and Relevance Tuning**

   - **Objective**: Adjust the relevance score of search results.
   - **Task**: Search for products using a **match** query that boosts the relevance score for products in the **electronics** category.

- **Request**:

```
GET /products/_search
{
  "query": {
    "bool": {
      "should": [
        { "match": { "description": "smartphone" } },
        { "boosting": {
          "positive": { "term": { "category":
"electronics" } },
          "negative": { "term": { "category": "clothing"
} },
          "negative_boost": 0.5
        }}
      ]
    }
  }
}
```

Summary

In this lab, you have learned how to execute complex queries in Elasticsearch using Kibana's Dev Tools. You have combined conditions with Boolean logic, performed a full-text search, aggregated data for insights, and tuned the relevance of your search results. These querying techniques are crucial for making the most of Elasticsearch's powerful search capabilities, and for gaining actionable insights from your data. Remember, the actual queries you run may vary depending on the structure of your **`product_data.ndjson`**, and the precise nature of your data.

Hands-On Lab: Simulating Joining Queries in Elasticsearch

Introduction

In this lab, we will simulate the joining queries in Elasticsearch by creating a parent-child relationship between two types of documents: **`product`** and **`review`**. We will define the mappings to establish the relationship, index some sample documents, and then perform queries that demonstrate how to retrieve data from this relational structure using Elasticsearch's join capabilities.

Prerequisites

- Elasticsearch and Kibana are installed and running.

- Basic familiarity with Elasticsearch and Kibana Dev Tools.

Step 1: Create Index with Relationship Mapping

First, we will create a new index with a mapping that includes a **join** field to establish the parent-child relationship.

1. **Define the mapping for the index**:

```
PUT /product_reviews
{
  "mappings": {
    "properties": {
      "name": { "type": "text" },
      "description": { "type": "text" },
      "price": { "type": "float" },
      "category": { "type": "keyword" },
      "rating": { "type": "float" },
      "created_at": { "type": "date" },
      "relationship": {
        "type": "join",
        "relations": {
          "product": "review"
        }
      }
    }
  }
}
```

2. Execute the preceding mapping in Kibana Dev Tools to create the index.

Step 2: Indexing Parent and Child Documents

Now, let us index some parent **product** documents and child **review** documents.

1. **Index a parent document**:

```
POST /product_reviews/_doc
{
  "name": "Amazing Gadget",
  "category": "Electronics",
  "price": 99.99,
  "created_at": "2023-11-04T06:15:32",
  "relationship": { "name": "product" }
}
```

Then, retrieve the documents to verify that they were indexed correctly:

```
GET /product_reviews/_search
```

Copy a document ID from the response, and use it to index a child document in the next step.

2. **Index a child document**:

   - **Note**: To index a child document, you need to specify the ID of the parent document in the routing parameter. For instance, if the ID of the parent document is **1**, you would use **routing=<parent_doc_id>** in the request.

   ```
   POST /product_reviews/_doc?routing=<parent_doc_id>
   {
     "review": "This is a great product!",
     "rating": 4.5,
     "created_at": "2023-11-05T10:00:00",
     "relationship": {
       "name": "review",
       "parent": "<parent_doc_id>"
     }
   }
   ```

Step 3: Perform Joining Queries

After indexing the documents, we can use the **has_child** and **has_parent** queries to retrieve related documents.

1. **Query products with reviews (has_child):**

   ```
   GET /product_reviews/_search
   {
     "query": {
       "has_child": {
         "type": "review",
         "query": {
           "match_all": {}
         }
       }
     }
   }
   ```

2. **Query reviews and include the related product information (has_parent):**

   ```
   GET /product_reviews/_search
   {
     "query": {
       "has_parent": {
         "parent_type": "product",
   ```

```
          "query": {
            "match_all": {}
          }
        }
      }
    }
```

After sending the requests, you should see responses similar to those shown in *Figure 2.13*.

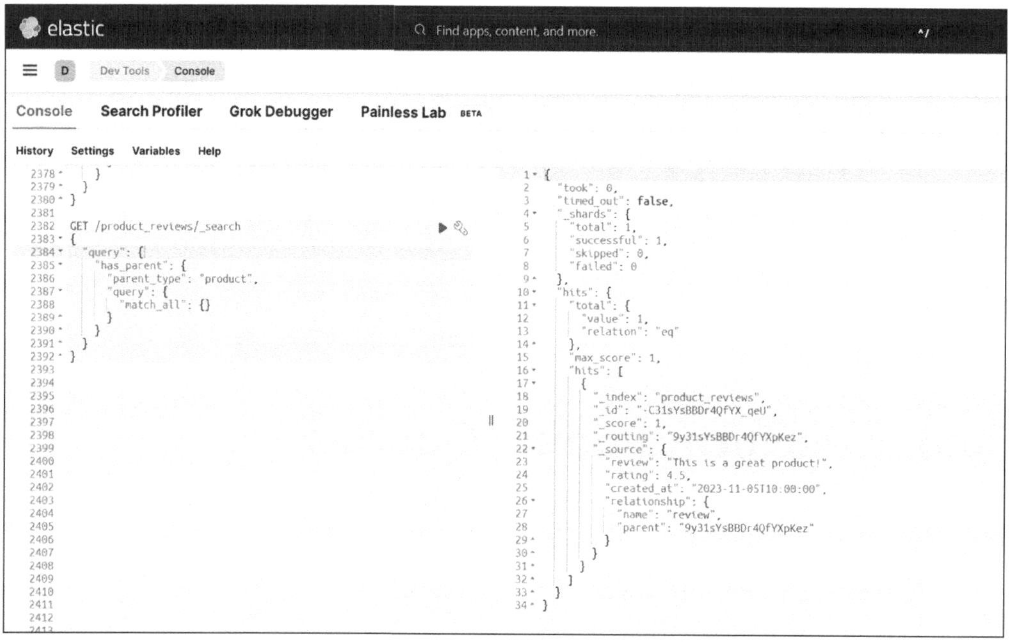

Figure 2.13: *Querying Reviews Included Its Parent*

Summary

This lab demonstrated how to create parent-child relationships within a single index in Elasticsearch, and how to perform queries that simulate joins by retrieving documents, based on these relationships. These querying techniques are necessary for applications that require relational data structures within a NoSQL environment like Elasticsearch.

Next Steps

Explore further by indexing more documents and experimenting with different types of join queries. Try using more complex queries within the **`has_child`** and **`has_parent`** clauses, and observe how Elasticsearch handles these relational queries.

Optimizing for Search Speed and Relevance

The performance of an Elasticsearch cluster is measured not just by the speed with which it returns results, but also by the relevance of those results to the user's query. Optimizing for both speed and relevance requires a nuanced understanding of Elasticsearch's internals, and the careful tuning of various components. This section outlines the strategies for achieving peak performance in both areas.

Optimizing for Speed

Efficient Indexing

- **Selective Indexing**: Only index the data you need. Carefully consider each field's `index` setting to determine, if it should be searchable.
- **Sharding Strategy**: Optimize the number of shards for your index. Too few can lead to hotspots; too many can increase overhead. The "`shrink`" and "`split`" index APIs can adjust the shard count post-creation.
- **Index Templates**: Use index templates to ensure that settings and mappings are consistently applied to new indices.

Query Performance Tuning

- **Filtered Context**: Use a filtered context for queries that do not require scoring to improve cache utilization.
- **Search Types**: Use the most appropriate search type for your use case (for example, `query_then_fetch` vs. `dfs_query_then_fetch`).
- **Source Filtering**: Limit the `_source` field returned by the query to only the fields you need.

Performance Monitoring and Tools

- **Slow Log**: Monitor slow query logs to identify and optimize slow queries.
- **Profile API**: Use the Profile API to understand how queries are executed, and identify performance bottlenecks.

Optimizing for Relevance

Fine-Tuning Text Analysis

- **Custom Analyzers**: Design custom analyzers to improve text analysis and search quality.

- **Synonyms**: Use synonyms to capture the variety of expressions that mean similar things.
- **Stop Words**: Define stop words to exclude common words that carry less meaning in search.

Scoring and Ranking

- **Field-Level Boosts**: Use field-level boosts to give more weightage to matches in more important fields.
- **Custom Scoring**: Employ the `function_score` query to incorporate custom scoring logic, based on your application's needs.
- **BM25 Parameters**: Adjust the BM25 algorithm parameters to better suit the nature of your content and search requirements.

Result Set Refinement

- **Highlighting**: Use highlighting to show users why a document was matched.
- **Rescoring**: Implement rescoring to refine the top N search hits.
- **Search Templates**: Leverage search templates to maintain complex queries, and improve maintainability.

Balancing Speed and Relevance

Query Optimization

- **Multi-Search API (`msearch`)**: Combine multiple search requests into a single API call to reduce round-trip times.
- **Bool Query Optimization**: Simplify boolean queries to avoid deep nesting which can slow down query performance.

Caching Strategies

- **Shard Request Cache**: Enable the shard request cache for frequent identical searches.
- **Query Cache**: Use the query cache wisely for static data or slow-changing indices to improve performance.

Infrastructure Considerations

- **Hardware**: Choose the right balance of CPU, RAM, and I/O capacity to support both fast querying and relevance calculations.
- **Elasticsearch Version**: Stay updated with the latest version of Elasticsearch as performance improvements, and new features are continuously added.

Monitoring and Iterative Improvements

Optimization is not a one-off task, but a continuous process. Regularly monitor your cluster's performance using Kibana's monitoring features, tweak your configurations, and keep abreast of new Elasticsearch features that can offer additional performance benefits. Regularly revisiting the indexing strategy, query patterns, and relevance feedback mechanisms will ensure that your Elasticsearch cluster remains both fast and precise, providing users with the best possible search experience.

Data Modeling and Schema Design

Data modeling and schema design are foundational to effectively leveraging Elasticsearch. The way data is modeled and the schema is designed can significantly influence both the performance of the Elasticsearch cluster, and the relevance of search results. In this section, we delve into the best practices for structuring your data, and crafting your schema in Elasticsearch to ensure optimal efficiency and searchability.

Understanding Elasticsearch Data Modeling

Elasticsearch, being a NoSQL database, does not enforce strict schemas like relational databases. However, thoughtful data modeling is crucial for maintaining performance, and achieving precise search results.

Document-Oriented Modeling

- **Denormalization**: Elasticsearch operates most efficiently on denormalized data. While relational databases normalize data across tables, Elasticsearch prefers consolidating related data into a single document.
- **Nested Objects**: When modeling relationships, use nested types to preserve the connection between elements that belong together, while taking advantage of Elasticsearch's ability to index nested objects and arrays.

Schema Design Considerations

- **Explicit Mappings**: Define explicit mappings for your data to control how Elasticsearch interprets the type of each field.
- **Field Types**: Choose appropriate field types (`text`, `keyword`, `date`, `geo_point`, and more) based on the content, and how users will search.
- **Analyzers and Tokenizers**: Select or create custom analyzers and tokenizers that accurately process your text data for search.

Best Practices in Schema Design

Index Design

- **Single vs. Multiple Indices**: Decide whether to use a single index for all documents or multiple indices, based on access patterns, security, and scaling needs.
- **Sharding and Replicas**: Determine the number of primary shards and replicas for your indices, based on data volume and query load.

Optimizing Field Mappings

- **Avoid Unnecessary Fields**: Do not index fields that you will not search or aggregate.
- **Multi-Fields**: Use multi-fields to index a field in different ways (for example, raw and analyzed text).

Performance Considerations

- **Index Time vs. Query Time**: Strike the right balance between what you compute at index time (for example, analyzers and normalizers) versus query time (for example, scripts).
- **Compression and Storage**: Utilize index settings for compression to optimize storage, especially for logging or time-series data.

Strategies for Schema Evolution

Your schema is not set in stone. As your application evolves, your Elasticsearch schema might need to evolve as well.

Reindexing

- **Reindex API**: Use the Reindex API to migrate data to a new index with an updated schema.

Alias Management

- **Index Aliases**: Employ index aliases to seamlessly transition between old and new index versions without downtime.

Data Modeling for Specific Use Cases

Elasticsearch is versatile, and can support a variety of use cases, each with its own data modeling needs.

- **Text Search**: Focus on text analysis, considering the use of synonyms, stemming, and custom analyzers.

- **Aggregations**: Optimize numeric and keyword fields for aggregation operations, and understand the memory implications.
- **Geo-Search**: Model geo data using **`geo_point`** and **`geo_shape`** types for efficient geo-queries.
- **Time-Series Data**: Use the rollover pattern for time-series data to maintain performance over time.

Validation and Testing

Once your data model and schema are designed, validation and testing are vital.

- **Automated Testing**: Implement automated testing to validate the schema against a subset of your data.
- **Real-World Query Performance**: Test with real-world queries and data volumes to ensure that the schema performs under the expected conditions.

Summary

Data modeling and schema design in Elasticsearch are as much an art as a science. The flexibility of Elasticsearch demands a thoughtful approach to how data is structured, and how the schema is crafted. By applying the principles outlined in this section, you can build a robust Elasticsearch schema that scales efficiently, handles your search requirements, and provides a foundation for powerful and fast search experiences. Keep in mind that as your data and requirements evolve, your schema may need to be revised, demanding continuous monitoring and adjustments.

Hands-On Lab: Data Modeling and Schema Design in Elasticsearch

Data modeling and schema design are critical when working with Elasticsearch to ensure efficient query performance and relevancy. This hands-on lab will guide you through the process of designing a schema for an Elasticsearch index tailored to specific querying needs.

Objective: Create an Elasticsearch index with an optimized schema for a blogging platform where users can post articles, comment on them, and like them.

Prerequisites:

- Access to an Elasticsearch cluster.
- Kibana or another interface to interact with Elasticsearch.

Part 1: Understanding Requirements

- Articles can be written by authors that contain a title, content, a list of tags, and a publication date.
- Comments can be added to articles by users, and include the comment text as well as the user's details.
- Users can like an article, but the count of likes needs to be updated frequently.

Part 2: Designing the Index Mapping

Create the **`blog`** index with the appropriate mappings:

- Define properties for article fields: **`title`**, **`content`**, **`tags`**, and **`publication_date`**.
- Use nested objects for comments to keep them within the context of an article.
- Use a simple integer field for likes to facilitate easy updates.

```
PUT /blog
{
  "mappings": {
    "properties": {
      "title": { "type": "text" },
      "content": { "type": "text" },
      "tags": { "type": "keyword" },
      "publication_date": { "type": "date" },
      "likes": { "type": "integer" },
      "comments": {
        "type": "nested",
        "properties": {
          "user": {
            "properties": {
              "name": { "type": "text" },
              "id": { "type": "keyword" }
            }
          },
          "comment_text": { "type": "text" },
          "comment_date": { "type": "date" }
        }
      }
    }
  }
}
```

Part 3: Indexing Documents

Index an example article with comments and likes:

We will use the following document as an example to index into the **`blog`** index. You can use the Dev Tools console in Kibana to execute the request:

```
POST /blog/_doc
{
  "title": "The Importance of Data Modeling",
  "content": "In this article, we will explore the importance of
data modeling...",
  "tags": ["Data", "Modeling", "Elasticsearch"],
  "publication_date": "2023-11-05T12:00:00",
  "likes": 150,
  "comments": [
    {
      "user": {
        "name": "Jane Doe",
        "id": "user_123"
      },
      "comment_text": "Great article, very informative!",
      "comment_date": "2023-11-06T08:00:00"
    }
  ]
}
```

Part 4: Querying the Data

Search for articles by tag:

We will use the following query to search for articles that contain the tag, "Elasticsearch". You can use the Dev Tools console in Kibana to execute the request:

```
GET /blog/_search
{
  "query": {
    "match": {
      "tags": "Elasticsearch"
    }
  }
}
```

Copy the document ID from the response, and use it in the next query.

Part 5: Updating Like Counts

Update the likes count for an article:

Change the **doc_ID** to the ID of the document you indexed in Part 3.

```
POST /blog/_update/<doc_ID>
{
  "script" : {
    "source": "ctx._source.likes += params.count",
    "lang": "painless",
    "params" : {
      "count" : 1
    }
  }
}
```

Part 6: Analyzing and Reporting

Create a query to list articles with the most likes:

```
GET /blog/_search
{
  "size": 5,
  "sort": [
    {
      "likes": {
        "order": "desc"
      }
    }
  ]
}
```

Part 7: Cleanup (Optional)

Delete the blog index after the lab (optional):

```
DELETE /blog
```

Summary

In this lab, you designed and implemented an Elasticsearch schema for a blogging platform, indexed a sample document, and performed various queries. This practice illustrated the importance of understanding the data, and how it will be queried to design an effective schema for Elasticsearch.

Understanding Elasticsearch Geolocation Data

Elasticsearch provides powerful features to handle geolocation data, allowing users to perform location-based searches and analyses. This capability is widely used in applications ranging from mapping services to location-aware recommendations.

Geolocation Data Types

Elasticsearch offers two primary data types for geolocation:

- **geo_point**: This type is used to represent a geographic location, using latitude and longitude values.
- **geo_shape**: This type is for more complex geometries such as polygons, multipolygons, and other shapes.

Indexing Geolocation Data

Before you can query geolocation data, you must index it properly with the correct data type.

```
PUT /my_locations
{
  "mappings": {
    "properties": {
      "position": {
        "type": "geo_point"
      },
      "area": {
        "type": "geo_shape"
      }
    }
  }
}
```

Geo-Queries

Elasticsearch provides several types of geo-queries:

- **Geo-Point Queries**: These include **geo_distance** (finds documents within a certain radius of a point), **geo_bounding_box** (finds documents within a rectangle), and **geo_polygon** (finds documents within a polygon).

- **Geo-Shape Queries**: These are used for querying **geo_shape** fields, and can handle more complex shapes and relations like **intersects**, **contains**, and **disjoint**.

Geo-Aggregations

Aggregations can be used to group documents by geolocation, for example, to create buckets of documents that fall within certain distances from a point.

Example Use Cases

- **Local Search**: Finding businesses within a certain radius of a user's location.
- **Mapping**: Displaying a set of geographic points on a map.
- **Logistics**: Tracking and querying the locations of vehicles or shipments.

Challenges with Geolocation Data

Handling geolocation data comes with its set of challenges, such as:

- **Precision**: Geolocation data requires high precision, and there are trade-offs between precision as well as storage requirements.
- **Query Performance**: Geo-queries can be resource-intensive, especially for large datasets and complex shapes.
- **Data Normalization**: Ensuring consistency in the representation of location data.

Summary

Geolocation data in Elasticsearch opens up numerous possibilities for location-based searching and analysis. By using **geo_point** and **geo_shape** types, as well as the various geo-queries and aggregations provided by Elasticsearch, developers can build sophisticated location-aware applications.

Hands-On Lab: Working with Geolocation Data in Elasticsearch

Introduction

Elasticsearch supports various geo data types, and one of the common use cases is to store, index, and query the geolocation data. This hands-on lab will guide you through the process of indexing geolocation data, and running geo-queries to find documents based on location.

Prerequisites

- Elasticsearch cluster up and running.
- Kibana or another tool to interact with Elasticsearch (such as cURL or Postman)

Step 1: Set Up a Geolocation-Enabled Index

First, you will need an index that can store geolocation data. Then you will define a **geo_point** field in your index mapping.

```
PUT /places
{
  "mappings": {
    "properties": {
      "name": {
        "type": "text"
      },
      "location": {
        "type": "geo_point"
      }
    }
  }
}
```

Step 2: Indexing Geolocation Data

Index some documents with geolocation data. The **location** field must contain latitude and longitude values.

```
POST /places/_doc/1
{
  "name": "Brandenburger Tor",
  "location": { "lat": 52.516274, "lon": 13.377704 }
}

POST /places/_doc/2
{
  "name": "Französischer Dom",
  "location": { "lat": 52.5145, "lon": 13.3921 }
}
```

Step 3: Basic Geo-Queries

Perform a query to find places within a certain distance of a point. This example finds places within 10km of Branden burger Tor.

```
GET /places/_search
{
  "query": {
    "geo_distance": {
      "distance": "10km",
      "location": { "lat": 52.516274, "lon": 13.377704 }
    }
  }
}
```

Step 4: Advanced Geo-Queries

Elasticsearch also supports more advanced geo-queries such as finding documents within a bounding box or a polygon.

Bounding Box Query:

Find documents within a rectangular area.

```
GET /places/_search
{
  "query": {
    "geo_bounding_box": {
      "location": {
        "top_left": { "lat": 52.6, "lon": 13.3 },
        "bottom_right": { "lat": 52.4, "lon": 13.2 }
      }
    }
  }
}
```

Polygon Query: Find documents within a custom polygon shape. We can use the **geo_shape** query to find documents within a polygon shape. The polygon must be closed, meaning the last point should be the same as the first point.

```
GET /places/_search
{
  "query": {
    "geo_shape": {
      "location": {
        "shape": {
          "type": "polygon",
          "coordinates": [[
            [13.377, 52.516],  // Point west of Brandenburg Gate
            [13.378, 52.516],  // Point east of Brandenburg Gate
            [13.378, 52.517],  // Point northeast of Brandenburg
Gate
```

```
            [13.377, 52.517],  // Point northwest of Brandenburg
Gate
            [13.377, 52.516]   // Closing the polygon with the
initial point
          ]]
        },
        "relation": "within"
      }
    }
  }
}
```

Step 5: Aggregations with Geo-Data

You can also perform aggregations based on geolocation data such as grouping places by geographical areas.

```
GET /places/_search
{
  "size": 0,
  "aggs": {
    "berlin": {
      "geo_distance": {
        "field": "location",
        "origin": { "lat": 52.516274, "lon": 13.377704 },
        "ranges": [
          { "to": 5000 },
          { "from": 5000, "to": 10000 },
          { "from": 10000 }
        ]
      }
    }
  }
}
```

Summary

This lab walked you through setting up a geolocation-capable index, indexing geolocation data, running basic and advanced geo-queries, as well as performing geo-aggregations. You can expand on these basics to build complex location-based applications and services.

Remember to clean up any resources you have used during the lab, if they are no longer needed.

Working with Binary Data in Elasticsearch

Elasticsearch does not inherently store binary files; however, it can index binary content that has been encoded as a Base64 string. This is primarily done using the `binary` field type in an Elasticsearch index.

Here is a basic guide for handling binary data in Elasticsearch:

Understanding the Binary Field Type

Elasticsearch includes a `binary` field type which is a Base64 encoded string. This field type is not stored by default which means it will not be retrievable from _ source. To store the binary data, your application will need to convert it into a Base64 encoded string, before sending it to Elasticsearch.

Use Cases for Binary Data in Elasticsearch

- **Storing encoded files**: Small files like thumbnails, can be encoded to Base64, and stored directly in Elasticsearch. This is not recommended for large files due to performance and size constraints.
- **Ingest attachment plugin**: This plugin is used for extracting file contents (such as PDFs, and Office documents) and indexing those contents as text. The binary file itself is not stored, but its contents are extracted and indexed.

Steps to Index the Binary Data

1. **Convert to Base64**: Convert your binary data into a Base64 encoded string, using your preferred programming language.
2. **Mapping**: Define a field in your Elasticsearch index mapping as a `binary` type.
3. **Indexing**: Send the Base64 encoded string to Elasticsearch as the value for the binary field.
4. **Retrieval**: When retrieving the document, you will get the Base64 encoded string back which your application will then need to decode, if you want to use the original binary format.

Example

Here is a quick example of how you might define a mapping with a binary field, and then index a document:

1. Define the mapping:

```
PUT /my_binary_index
{
  "mappings": {
    "properties": {
      "my_binary_field": {
        "type": "binary"
      }
    }
  }
}
```

2. Index a document:

```
PUT /my_binary_index/_doc/1
{
  "my_binary_field": "U29tZSBiYXNlNjQgYmluYXJ5IGJsb2I="
}
```

The Base64 string here is just an example, and would correspond to the Base64 representation of your binary data.

To retrieve the document, you would use the following request:

```
GET /my_binary_index/_doc/1
```

Considerations

- **Performance**: Encoding, decoding, and transferring large binary files can be resource-intensive.
- **Size**: Elasticsearch has a default maximum field size of 100KB for Base64 encoded fields, which you can increase by setting **`index.mapping.total_fields.limit`** in your index settings. Still, large binary files are not ideal for storage in Elasticsearch.
- **Use Case Fit**: Consider whether Elasticsearch is the right tool for storing binary data. In many cases, it is better to store actual binary files in a dedicated file store like Amazon S3, while using Elasticsearch to index metadata and textual content related to those files.

For actual binary file storage and full-text search on file contents, it is common to use a workflow where files are stored in a dedicated service (like a blob store) and only metadata as well as extracted text are indexed in Elasticsearch. The Ingest Attachment Processor plugin can automatically extract text from binary documents at the index time.

Conclusion

Throughout Chapter 2, we have taken a comprehensive journey through the various facets of Elasticsearch, gaining a deeper understanding of its core functionalities, and how to effectively work with data within this powerful search and analytics engine.

We began by setting up and configuring Elasticsearch, ensuring a proper understanding of index creation, data insertion, and snapshot repositories for backup and recovery. As we progressed, we delved into the nuances of document and index management, mastering the art of CRUD operations, and learning how to handle common errors and exceptions.

Our exploration included a detailed look at the Elasticsearch query DSL, where we exercised a range of queries – from Boolean to full-text search, aggregations, and even geospatial queries – gaining insights into the intricacies of data retrieval and analytics. Alongside this, we investigated the subtleties of data modeling and schema design, appreciating the significance of creating efficient mappings, and understanding the impacts on performance and relevance.

One of the highlights was the practical application of these concepts, where we generated and manipulated random data sets using Python, employed bulk operations for data ingestion, and conducted various searches and aggregations, using the Dev Tools in Kibana.

Error diagnosis and resolution played a crucial role in our discussions, as we navigated through potential pitfalls, and learned to interpret Elasticsearch's error messages to fine-tune our queries and index operations.

Through hands-on exercises, we became familiar with Elasticsearch's robust capabilities, including handling nested and relational data structures, which mimicked the behavior of traditional SQL joins through parent-child relationships and nested queries.

As we conclude this chapter, we take with us a solid foundation in Elasticsearch's capabilities for data handling and querying, equipped with the knowledge to apply these skills in real-world scenarios.

In the upcoming chapter, we will embark on an exciting exploration of the various integrations available with Elasticsearch. *Chapter 3, Deep Dive: Integrations*, will open up a new dimension of possibilities as we learn how to enhance and extend the capabilities of Elasticsearch by integrating it with different tools and platforms.

Stay tuned as we dive into the next chapter, where the convergence of Elasticsearch with other technologies enables us to create comprehensive and sophisticated systems tailored to a wide array of use cases.

Points to Remember

When working with Elasticsearch and related technologies, here are some key points to remember:

- **Index Structure:** Understand the relationship between an index, type, and document, and how indexing works in Elasticsearch.
- **Data Types and Mapping**: Familiarize yourself with various data types, and the importance of mapping in indexing performance as well as search relevance.
- **CRUD Operations**: Master the Create, Read, Update, and Delete operations, as they are fundamental to working with documents in Elasticsearch.
- **Query DSL**: Deepen your knowledge of the Elasticsearch Query Domain Specific Language for performing and optimizing various search operations.
- **Boolean Logic**: Boolean queries are powerful in combining multiple search criteria. Understand how to use `must`, `should`, `must_not`, and `filter` clauses.
- **Full-Text Search Capabilities**: Utilize full-text search features such as match, multi-match, and query string queries to exploit the full potential of Elasticsearch's search capabilities.
- **Aggregations**: Leverage the aggregation framework to summarize data, and extract insights from your documents.
- **Analyzers and Tokenizers**: Analyzers and tokenizers are crucial for text processing and search; know when and how to use them effectively.
- **Handling Relationships**: Learn how to handle relationships within documents, using nested queries and parent-child relationships.
- **Bulk Operations**: Use bulk API for batch operations to efficiently index or delete multiple documents in a single request.
- **Snapshot and Restore**: Understand how to implement snapshot, and restore functionality for backup and disaster recovery.
- **Error Handling**: Practice reading and understanding error messages to troubleshoot and resolve issues quickly.
- **Performance Tuning**: Monitor performance metrics, and optimize indexing as well as search performance accordingly.
- **Security**: Implement security best practices, including authentication, authorization, and encryption where necessary.
- **Elasticsearch Integrations**: Explore how to integrate Elasticsearch with other tools in the Elastic Stack such as Kibana for visualization, Logstash for data processing, and Beats for data shipping.

- **Updates and Migrations**: Stay informed about updates to Elasticsearch, and how to handle migrations.
- **Geospatial Data**: Utilize the geo-capabilities of Elasticsearch to handle and query geospatial data effectively.
- **Scripting**: Use Elasticsearch's scripting capabilities for custom scoring, filtering, and more complex operations.
- **Cluster Health and Management**: Regularly check the health of your Elasticsearch cluster, and understand the importance of settings like shard allocation, node roles, and cluster scaling.
- **Documentation**: Always refer to the official Elasticsearch documentation for the most up-to-date and accurate information.

Keeping these points in mind will help you to work more effectively with Elasticsearch, and build robust, scalable search as well as analytics solutions.

Multiple Choice Questions

1. What does CRUD stand for in Elasticsearch?

    a. Create, Read, Update, and Delete.

    b. Connect, Retrieve, Unlink, and Detach.

    c. Cluster, Replica, Update, and Distribute.

    d. Create, Report, Update, and Deploy.

2. Which of the following is NOT a core component of the Elastic Stack?

    a. Elasticsearch

    b. Logstash

    c. Kibana

    d. Spark

3. Which query will you use to find documents that contain terms within a certain range in Elasticsearch?

    a. Term Query

    b. Match Query

    c. Range Query

    d. Boolean Query

4. What is the purpose of an analyzer in Elasticsearch?
    a. To optimize the cluster performance.
    b. To convert text into tokens or terms.
    c. To store data in a compressed format.
    d. To secure the Elasticsearch cluster.
5. Which of the following is a correct use of the bulk API in Elasticsearch?
    a. To search for multiple documents in a single request.
    b. To perform multiple indexing, or delete operations in a single request.
    c. To increase the number of shards of an index.
    d. To monitor the health of the Elasticsearch cluster.

Answers

1. a
2. d
3. c
4. b
5. b

Questions

1. Explain the process of setting up a snapshot repository in Elasticsearch, and discuss the importance of snapshots in data backup strategies.
2. Describe the steps involved in creating a Snapshot Lifecycle Management (SLM) policy in Elasticsearch, and its role in automating snapshot creation.
3. Discuss the "**`PUT`**" and "**`DELETE`**" HTTP methods in the context of Elasticsearch's REST API. Provide examples of how they are used to manage indices.
4. Summarize the concept of Boolean Queries in Elasticsearch. How do they enhance searching capabilities, and what are some common Boolean operators?
5. Describe the process of generating and uploading JSON-formatted data into Elasticsearch using Python scripts. Why is the NDJSON format preferred for bulk operations?

6. Elaborate on the importance of data modeling and schema design in Elasticsearch. How does it affect indexing performance and query efficiency?
7. Discuss the role of document IDs in Elasticsearch. What are the trade-offs between using auto-generated IDs and custom IDs?
8. Explain the use of geolocation data in Elasticsearch. How can geospatial queries enhance data analytics?
9. Evaluate the challenges and limitations, when working with geo-polygon queries in Elasticsearch. How has the shift to the "`geo_shape`" query addressed these issues?
10. Reflect on the content of *Chapter 2*, and discuss the key points that should be remembered when working with Elasticsearch. How do these points prepare a user for the integrations discussed in *Chapter 3*?

Key Terms

Here is a list of key terms that encapsulate the main concepts and tools discussed in this chapter:

- **Elasticsearch**: A distributed, RESTful search and analytics engine capable of addressing a growing number of use cases.
- **Snapshot**: A backup taken from a running Elasticsearch cluster.
- **Snapshot Repository**: A location that stores Elasticsearch snapshots such as a shared file system or remote storage services.
- **Snapshot Lifecycle Management (SLM)**: A feature in Elasticsearch that automates the creation, deletion, and management of snapshots.
- **Index Lifecycle Management (ILM)**: Elasticsearch's feature for automating index management according to user-defined policies.
- **HTTP Methods (`GET`, `PUT`, `POST`, `DELETE`)**: The operations used for interacting with the Elasticsearch API to perform actions such as reading, creating, updating, and deleting data.
- **Boolean Queries**: Search queries that use Boolean logic to combine several queries (like `must`, `should`, `must_not`), providing a powerful way to find a precise set of documents.
- **NDJSON (Newline Delimited JSON)**: A convenient format for streaming JSON records, used to bulk import data into Elasticsearch.
- **Data Modeling**: The process of structuring and organizing data which in Elasticsearch helps to define indexes and mappings that affect performance and relevance.

- **Schema Design**: Designing the structure of data within Elasticsearch, including fields and data types.
- **Document ID**: The unique identifier for a document in an Elasticsearch index which can be auto-generated or user-defined.
- **Geolocation Data**: Data that is used to represent geographic locations, utilized in Elasticsearch for spatial search queries.
- **Geo-Polygon Query**: A type of query that finds documents within a geographic area defined by a polygon.
- **Geo-Shape Query**: The improved method in Elasticsearch for querying documents, based on more complex shapes like polygons, circles, and lines.
- **Dev Tools (Kibana Dev Tools Console)**: An interface within Kibana that allows for direct interaction with the Elasticsearch API through a console.
- **Aggregation**: A feature in Elasticsearch that provides the capability to group and extract statistics from your data.
- **Relevance Scoring**: The method Elasticsearch uses to calculate how well a document matches a query.
- **Data Ingestion**: The process of importing or loading data into Elasticsearch.
- **Mapping**: The schema definition for the fields in an index in Elasticsearch.
- **Nested Objects**: A type of field in Elasticsearch mappings that allows documents to contain nested lists of objects.
- **Parent-Child Relationship**: A specialized way to model relationships between connected documents in different indexes.
- **Geo-Distance Query**: A query that finds documents within a certain radius of a central geolocation point.

CHAPTER 3
Deep Dive: Integrations

Introduction

In the ever-evolving landscape of data management and analysis, the Elastic Stack has emerged as a powerful toolset for handling vast and varied data in real-time. While the previous chapters laid the foundational knowledge of Elastic Stack's core components—Elasticsearch, Logstash, and Kibana—this chapter ventures into the integrative capabilities of the Elastic Stack, a crucial aspect for leveraging its full potential.

Integrations are at the heart of the Elastic Stack's versatility. They enable the stack to connect with various data sources, applications, and platforms, thereby expanding its utility beyond its native environment. In this chapter, we will embark on a comprehensive exploration of Elastic Stack's integration mechanisms. We will delve into how these integrations enhance data ingestion, processing, and visualization capabilities, making the Elastic Stack not just a tool, but a comprehensive solution for diverse data challenges.

Our journey through this chapter will uncover the practicalities of integrating the Elastic Stack with popular databases, cloud services, and log management tools. We will explore case studies and examples that illustrate the transformative impact of these integrations in real-world scenarios. This will not only provide a deeper understanding of each integration's technical aspects, but also offer insights into their strategic applications.

Furthermore, we will address the challenges and best practices in implementing these integrations. From ensuring seamless data flow to maintaining system integrity and security, the nuances of successful integration strategies are vital for any IT professional working with the Elastic Stack.

As we proceed, keep in mind that the power of the Elastic Stack lies not just in its individual components, but in how effectively they can be integrated to work as a cohesive, dynamic system. This chapter aims to equip you with the knowledge and skills to harness this power, paving the way for innovative and efficient data solutions.

Structure

In this chapter, we will discuss the following topics:

- Logstash
- Hands-On Lab: Setting Up Logstash for Data Ingestion with User Permissions
- Hands-on Lab: My First Logstash Pipeline
- Hands-on Lab: Running My First Logstash Pipeline as Service
- Hands-On Lab: Building a Comprehensive Logstash Pipeline
- Elastic Agent
- Hands-On Lab: Monitoring Ubuntu System with Elastic Agent
- Hands-On Lab: Monitoring Windows System with Elastic Agent
- Web Crawler
- Data Connectors
- API Integrations
- Hands-On Lab: CRUD Operations with Elasticsearch API
- Elastic Language Clients
- Hands-On Lab: CRUD Operations in Elasticsearch Using Python Client

Selecting Elastic Integrations

Elastic Integrations is a powerful toolset that enables the Elastic Stack to connect with a wide range of data sources, applications, and platforms. This chapter will explore the various integration points of Elastic Integrations, providing a comprehensive overview of its capabilities and applications. We will also discuss the best practices for selecting and implementing Elastic Integrations, ensuring seamless data flow and optimal performance.

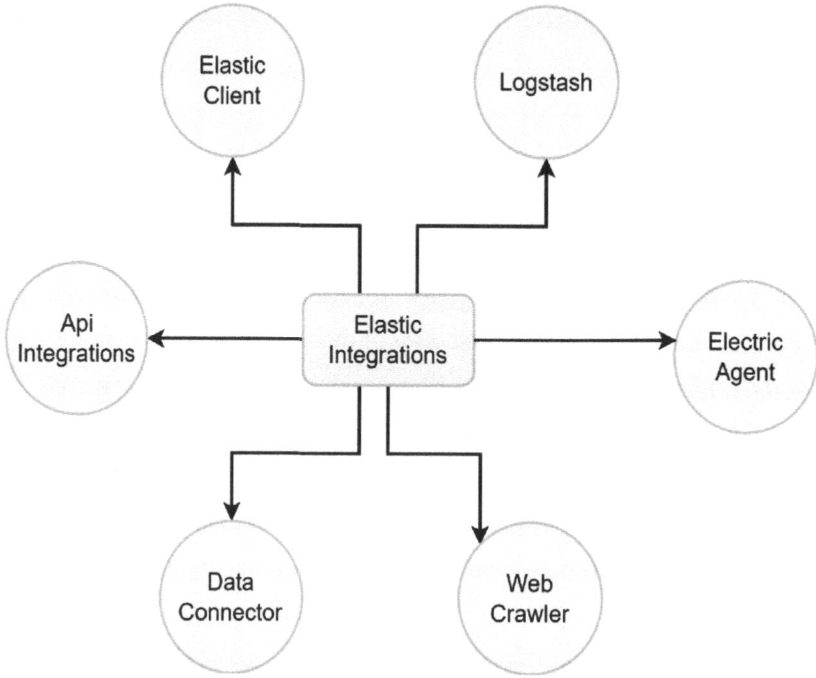

Figure 3.1: *Solution Options for Elastic Integrations*

Figure 3.1 appears to be a diagram illustrating the different components that can be integrated with Elastic Integrations, which is highlighted in green and placed at the center, indicating its central role in the integration process. Surrounding Elastic Integrations are six nodes, each representing a different integration point or component that can connect with Elastic Integrations:

- **Elastic Client**: This suggests a client interface for Elastic Stack, potentially indicating tools or applications that interact with Elasticsearch or other Elastic products.
- **Logstash**: A core component of the Elastic Stack, Logstash is shown as a separate entity that can be integrated, highlighting its role in data processing and pipeline management within the ecosystem.
- **API Integrations**: This likely refers to various APIs that Elastic Integrations can connect with, allowing for data exchange and functionality expansion through third-party services or applications.
- **Electric Agent**: This might be a typo or a specific agent within the user's context. Typically, it could be referring to the Elastic Agent, a single, unified way to add monitoring for logs, metrics, and other types of data to each host.
- **Data Connector**: This represents tools or services that facilitate the transfer of data into the Elastic Stack from various sources, emphasizing the versatility of Elastic Integrations in connecting with different data providers.

- **Web Crawler**: This node indicates the capability of Elastic Integrations to work with tools that automatically browse the web which can be used for indexing and searching web content.

Each of these nodes is a point of interaction or a way in which Elastic Integrations can extend the functionality of the Elastic Stack, implying a network of possible configurations and uses within the broader ecosystem. This figure would be a part of a subsection focused on selecting appropriate Elastic Integrations, guiding the reader through the options available for enhancing their Elastic Stack setup.

Logstash

Logstash is a data processing pipeline that can collect, enrich, and transport data from a myriad of sources to various destinations, all in real-time. This chapter will explore Logstash's core concepts and functionalities, providing insights into its mechanisms, and how they interplay to create powerful data processing pipelines. We will also delve into some of the most commonly used plugins, and demonstrate how they can be leveraged to enhance Logstash's functionality.

Overview and Core Concepts

In the realm of the Elastic Stack, Logstash stands as a pivotal component, orchestrating the flow of data between the source and the Elasticsearch cluster. This chapter delves into the world of Logstash, providing an extensive overview and elucidating its core concepts. Logstash is more than just a data processing tool; it is a powerful pipeline that can collect, enrich, and transport data from a myriad of sources to various destinations, all in real-time.

Logstash's ability to unify data from disparate sources is a key aspect of its functionality. It seamlessly integrates with a multitude of data formats and sources, ranging from simple log files to complex data streams from databases and cloud services. This flexibility makes it an indispensable tool for log and event data management, a cornerstone for monitoring, security, and operational intelligence in modern IT environments.

At the heart of Logstash lies its pipeline architecture, consisting of three primary components: Inputs, filters, and outputs. Inputs define how Logstash receives data, filters describe the processing and transformation of this data, and outputs determine how Logstash forwards the processed data to specified destinations. This chapter will explore each of these components in detail, providing insights into their mechanisms, and how they interplay to create powerful data processing pipelines.

Furthermore, this chapter will introduce the concept of plugins which are integral to extending Logstash's capabilities. Plugins in Logstash enable customization and adaptation, allowing users to tailor their data processing needs precisely. We will delve into some of the most commonly used plugins, and demonstrate how they can be leveraged to enhance Logstash's functionality.

In summary, Logstash is not just a tool but a comprehensive ecosystem for data processing and management. As we explore its core concepts and functionalities, you will gain a deeper appreciation of its role within the Elastic Stack, and its impact on efficient data handling in various IT scenarios.

Advantages and Disadvantages

Logstash is a powerful data processing pipeline that offers several advantages and some disadvantages, depending on the use case and context of its deployment. Here is an overview:

Advantages of Logstash:

- **Versatility in Data Processing**: Logstash can handle a wide variety of data sources, types, and formats, making it highly adaptable to different environments and requirements.
- **Extensibility with Plugins**: With a rich ecosystem of input, filter, and output plugins, Logstash can be extended to meet specific needs. Users can also develop their own plugins for custom use cases.
- **Strong Integration with Elastic Stack**: Logstash is designed to work seamlessly with Elasticsearch and Kibana, providing a robust end-to-end solution for data ingestion, search, and visualization.
- **Real-time Processing**: Logstash can process data in real-time, allowing for timely insights and actions, which is particularly useful in monitoring and alerting scenarios.
- **Filtering and Enrichment**: It offers powerful filtering capabilities, enabling users to transform and enrich data, before it is stored which can significantly improve the relevance and value of the data.
- **Open Source**: Being an open source, Logstash is free to use, which can lower the cost of implementation for businesses, and allows for community-driven improvements and support.

Disadvantages of Logstash:

- **Performance Overhead**: Logstash can be resource-intensive, especially when dealing with large volumes of data or complex processing pipelines. This might necessitate more robust hardware or cloud resources.
- **Complexity**: For newcomers, Logstash's learning curve can be steep due to its complex configuration, and the need to understand its DSL (Domain-Specific Language) for creating pipelines.

- **Deployment and Management**: Setting up and managing a Logstash pipeline requires careful planning and ongoing management which can be a challenge in larger, more dynamic environments.
- **Scalability**: While Logstash can handle a significant amount of data, scaling it out can be complex, and may require additional tools or solutions like Elasticsearch's ingest nodes or alternative log shippers.
- **Startup Time**: Logstash has a comparatively slow startup time which can be a disadvantage in environments where rapid scaling or quick redeployments are common.
- **Error Handling**: Logstash can sometimes be unforgiving with data parsing errors or unexpected input, which may result in data loss or require additional error handling mechanisms.

In summary, Logstash is a feature-rich data processing tool that excels in flexibility and integration within the Elastic Stack, but may present challenges in terms of performance, complexity, and scalability. The decision to use Logstash should be weighed against these factors, and the specific requirements of the deployment scenario.

Use Cases and Applications

Logstash is a versatile tool that can be applied to various use cases across different industries. Here are some common scenarios where Logstash is particularly useful:

- **Centralized Logging**: Logstash is often used to aggregate logs from multiple sources, normalize them into a consistent format, and then send them to a central place like Elasticsearch for storage and analysis. This is useful for organizations with complex infrastructures that generate logs in various formats.
- **Security and Compliance Monitoring**: It can process and analyze logs from security devices, applications, and systems to detect anomalies, potential breaches, and compliance violations in real-time. This helps security teams respond to threats more quickly.
- **Application Performance Monitoring (APM)**: By collecting and processing metrics and logs from applications and services, Logstash enables APM by providing insights into application performance, and helping to uncover issues that affect user experience.
- **Event Data Enrichment**: Logstash can enrich data by adding additional information from external sources, or by using its own filters. For instance, it can add geographical information to IP addresses or resolve user identifiers to actual user names.

- **Stream Processing**: For real-time analytics, Logstash can process streaming data from IoT devices, applications, or online services, allowing for immediate insights and actions, based on the latest data streams.
- **Data Transformation and Preparation**: In situations where data needs to be transformed before it is stored or analyzed (like converting formats, adding timestamps, or anonymizing personal data), Logstash can be configured to handle these transformations.
- **Complex Data Pipelines**: Logstash pipelines can be created to handle complex data processing tasks such as filtering, mutating, and formatting data from multiple disparate sources, before it reaches the storage destination.
- **Integrating Diverse Data Sources**: Organizations often use Logstash to pull in data from various sources, including databases, message queues, and cloud services, to be indexed in Elasticsearch, thereby creating a more integrated data environment.
- **Business Intelligence (BI)**: By preprocessing data and feeding it into analytics platforms, Logstash supports BI initiatives by ensuring that the data is in the right shape and format for analysis and reporting.
- **Email Processing**: Logstash can be set up to parse and filter email messages, extract useful information, and store it for future analysis or real-time alerting on specific keywords or patterns.

These use cases highlight the flexibility of Logstash in handling data, and its capacity to serve as a bridge between data generation/collection as well as data storage/analysis, making it a critical component of many data infrastructure setups.

Architecture and Components

Logstash is a data processing pipeline that consists of three primary components: **Input**, **filter**, and **output**. You can see the following diagram for a visual representation of the Logstash architecture, and its components.

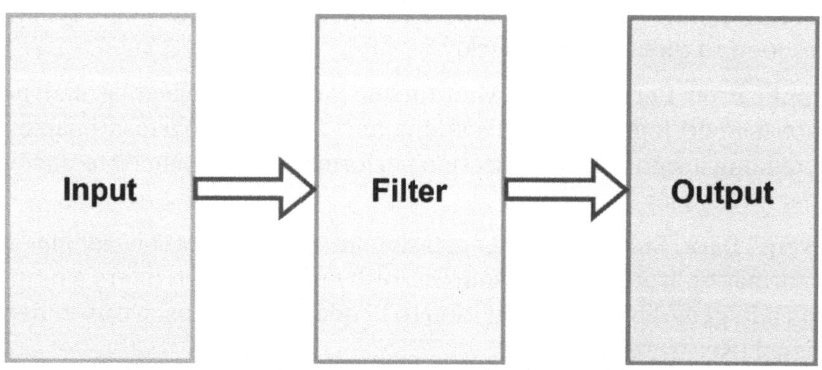

***Figure 3.2**: Architecture and Components for Logstash*

These components work together to create a data processing pipeline that can collect, transform, and send data to various destinations. Each component plays a specific role in the data processing pipeline of Logstash.

Let us now take a closer look at each component:

1. **Input**: This is the first stage of the Logstash pipeline where data is ingested. Input plugins allow Logstash to read from a multitude of sources such as log files, data streams, databases, and cloud services. Common input plugins include file, syslog, HTTP, beats, and many others. The Input stage is responsible for gathering data to be processed, and can be configured to pull in data from different sources simultaneously.

2. **Filter**: After data is ingested by the input component, it moves to the filter stage. Filters are used to transform, enrich, and process the data before sending it to the output. Logstash has a variety of filter plugins that can perform functions such as parsing, mutating, and enriching the data. Filters can be chained together to perform complex data transformations. Common filters include grok for parsing and pattern matching, mutate for changing data fields, and geoip for adding geographical information, based on IP addresses.

3. **Output**: The final stage in the Logstash pipeline is the output component, where processed data is sent to specified destinations. Output plugins define and configure where data should be routed after it has been processed by the input and filter stages. The data can be sent to a variety of outputs such as Elasticsearch, a file, a database, or a messaging queue. Multiple output plugins can be used simultaneously to send the processed data to more than one destination.

Figure 3.2 illustrates the linear flow of data through Logstash, starting from collection (Input), moving through processing (Filter), and culminating in storage or further action (Output). This modular architecture allows for high flexibility in processing various types of data, and is one of the reasons Logstash is so powerful in a wide array of data ingestion, and processing scenarios. Each component is designed to be highly configurable, enabling custom pipelines tailored to specific needs and environments.

Setting Up Logstash

Logstash can be installed on a variety of operating systems, including Linux, Windows, and macOS. It can also be deployed in the cloud, using Docker or Kubernetes. The installation process is straightforward, and can be completed in a few simple steps. You can find detailed instructions for installing Logstash on different platforms in the official documentation, **https://www.elastic.co/downloads/logstash**.

For Debian/Ubuntu Linux distributions, assume installing via Linux Package managers, we have Logstash installed on path **`/usr/share/logstash`**. The configuration files are located in **`/etc/logstash/conf.d,`** and the logs are stored in **`/var/log/logstash`**. The Logstash service is managed by systemd, and the configuration file is located at **`/etc/logstash/logstash.yml`**.

Recommendation: Make sure that you install Logstash version to match your Elasticsearch and Kibana versions. For example, if you are using Elasticsearch 8.10.4 and Kibana 8.10.4, you should install Logstash 8.10.4.

Writing Logstash Configuration Files

Logstash configuration files are written in the Logstash Domain Specific Language (DSL). The configuration files are located in the **`/etc/logstash/conf.d`** directory. Each configuration file contains a single pipeline which is a sequence of inputs, filters, and outputs. The configuration files are written in the YAML format that is a human-readable data serialization language. The following is an example of a Logstash configuration file:

Creating a Logstash configuration involves defining inputs, filters, and outputs in a **`.conf`** file. Here is a skeleton structure of a typical Logstash configuration file with explanations for each section:

```
# Input section
input {
  # Define the source of the data
  file {
    path => "/path/to/your/log/file.log"
    start_position => "beginning"
  }
  # Other input plugins can be added here
}

# Filter section
filter {
  # Perform data transformation or enrichment
  # Example: Parse CSV data
  csv {
    separator => ","
    columns => ["column1", "column2", "column3"]
  }

  # Example: Add a field
  mutate {
    add_field => { "new_field" => "value" }
  }
```

```
  # Other filter plugins can be added here
}

# Output section
output {
  # Define where to send the processed data

  # Example: Sending data to Elasticsearch
  elasticsearch {
    hosts => ["http://localhost:9200"]
    index => "example-index-%{+YYYY.MM.dd}"
  }

  # Example: Outputting to the console for debugging
  stdout { codec => rubydebug }

  # Other output plugins can be added here
}
```

Explanation

- **Input Section:**
  - This part defines where Logstash will read the data from.
  - The **`file`** input plugin is used to read data from a file specified in the **`path`**.
  - **`start_position => "beginning"`** tells Logstash to start reading from the beginning of the file.
  - Multiple input sources can be defined in this section.
- **Filter Section:**
  - This section is used for processing and transforming the data.
  - The **`csv`** filter is an example that parses CSV-formatted data.
  - **`columns`** are specified to name the fields for each column in the CSV.
  - The **`mutate`** filter is used to modify the data such as adding a new field.
  - You can chain multiple filters for complex data processing.
- **Output Section:**
  - This defines where the processed data should be sent.
  - The **`elasticsearch`** output plugin sends data to an Elasticsearch cluster.
  - **`hosts`** specifies the Elasticsearch host, and **`index`** defines the index name pattern.
  - The **`stdout`** output with the **`rubydebug`** codec is useful for debugging, as it prints the data to the console.

- Like inputs and filters, multiple outputs can be defined.

This skeleton provides a basic structure for a Logstash configuration. You can customize it by adding different input, filter, and output plugins, depending on your data processing requirements. The Logstash documentation provides a comprehensive list of available plugins, and their configuration options.

Hands-On Lab: Setting Up Logstash for Data Ingestion with User Permissions

In this lab, we will first create a user with the necessary permissions to ingest data into Elasticsearch via Logstash. After setting up the user, we will configure Logstash to process and send data to Elasticsearch.

Prerequisites

- An operational Elasticsearch and Kibana setup.
- Logstash installed on a machine with network access to the Elasticsearch cluster.
- A sample data file to use as an input source for Logstash.
- Administrative access to Kibana to create users, and assign roles.

Step 1: Create a Custom Role and User in Kibana

1. Open Kibana, and go to `Management` > `Stack Management` > `Security` > `Roles`.
2. Click `Create role`, and define the role as shown in *Figure* 3.3:
    - **Name**: `logstash_ingest_role.`
    - Under `Cluster privileges`, add `manage_index_templates`, `monitor`, and `manage_ilm`.
    - Under `Index privileges`, add:
    - **Indices**: `logstash-test-*` or the specific index names/patterns, you plan to use.
    - **Privileges**: `rite`, `read`, `index`, `create_index`, `create_doc`, and `view_index_metadata`.

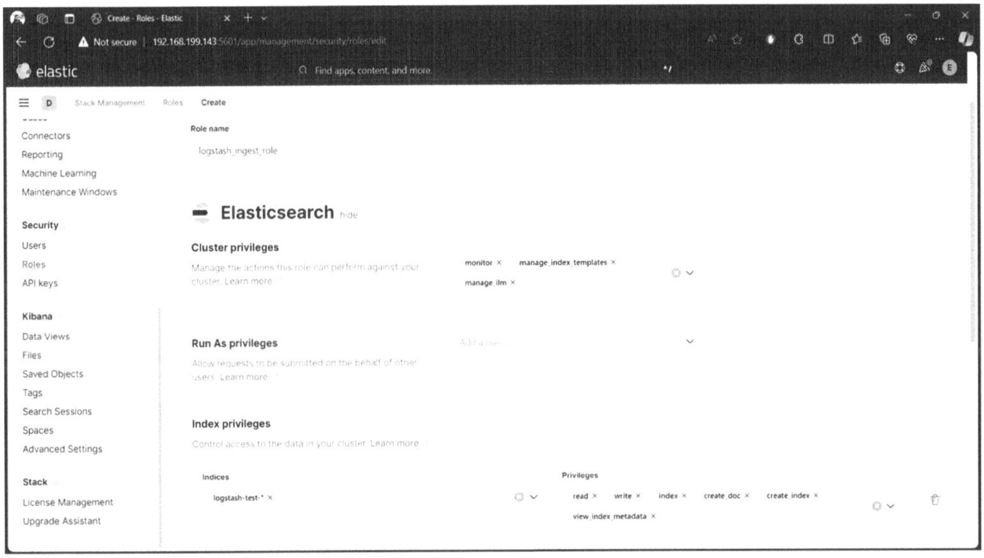

***Figure 3.3**: Creating a Role for Logstash*

3. Save the role.
4. Go to **`Security`** > **`Users`**, and click on **`Create user`** as shown in *Figure 3.4*:
   - **Username**: **`logstash_tester`**
   - **Full name**: **`logstash tester`**
   - **Password**: Choose a secure password, and make a note of it.
   - **Roles**: Assign the **`logstash_ingest_role`** role you just created.
5. Save the new user.

Step 2: Verify Data Ingestion in Elasticsearch

To verify that the data has been ingested:

1. You can open Terminal on **`Elasticserach/Kibana`** server other machine.
2. Make sure that you can access Elasticsearch from the machine where Logstash is installed.
3. Make a query to Elasticsearch, using the credentials of the new **`logstash_tester`**:

```
curl --insecure -u logstash_tester:password -X GET "https://elas-
ticsearch_host:9200/logstash-test-*/_search?pretty"
```

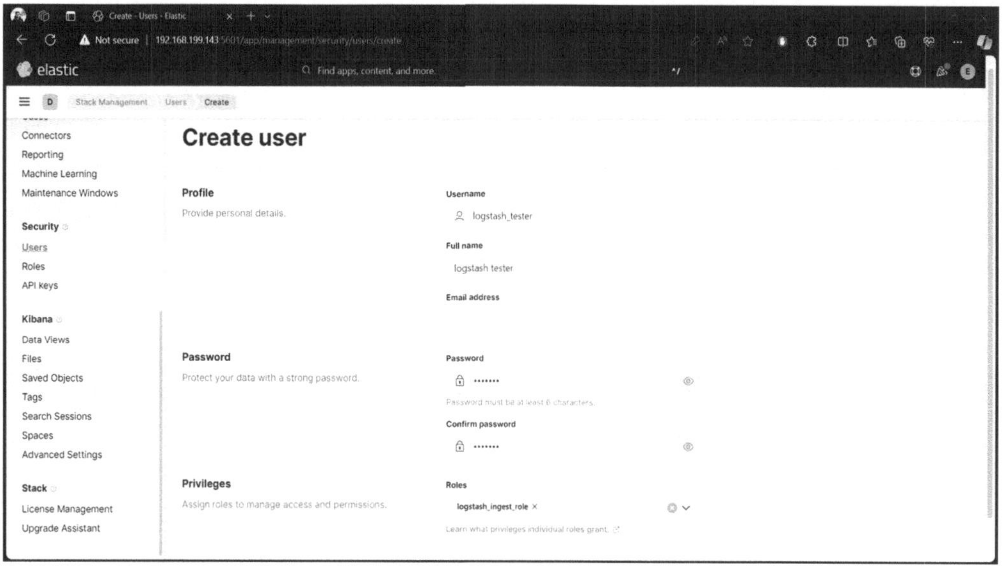

***Figure 3.4**: Creating a Logstash User with `logstash_ingest_role` Role*

1. You can see a response from the server.
2. **`--insecure`** parameter is used to bypass the certificate validation. If you have a valid certificate, you can omit this parameter.
3. Change the **`elasticsearch_host`** to the correct host name or IP address.
4. Change the **`password`** to the password you set for the **`logstash_tester`** user.
5. You should see the JSON response with the data that Logstash has indexed.

By following these steps, you create a secure environment where Logstash has the necessary permissions to ingest data, without having excessive privileges that could potentially be exploited.

Summary

You have completed the lab for setting up a Logstash user with the appropriate permissions to ingest data into Elasticsearch. By creating a dedicated user for Logstash, you have followed security best practices, ensuring that the Logstash pipeline has the minimum required permissions to perform its tasks. This setup provides a foundation for secure and efficient data ingestion workflows, using the Elastic Stack.

Hands-on Lab: My First Logstash Pipeline

In this hands-on lab, we will explore how to set up a Logstash pipeline to send data with the current date and time every 10 seconds to an Elasticsearch server.

This scenario is typical for learning how to schedule tasks within Logstash, and monitor the live feed of data in a production-like environment. We will use two Virtual Machines (VMs) for this setup: **VM1** will host Elasticsearch, which will store and index the data, and **VM2** will have both Logstash and Kibana installed. Logstash will be responsible for data processing and shipping, while Kibana will be used to visualize and test the data flow.

Prerequisites

Before you begin, ensure that you have the following:

1. Installed Logstash on your VM or physical machine.
2. Have a Logstash user with the appropriate permissions to ingest data into Elasticsearch.
3. We user **`logstash_tester`** user with the **`logstash_ingest_role`** role in this lab. You can also use any other user with the appropriate permissions.

Lab Steps

The following steps will guide you through the process of setting up a Logstash pipeline to send data with the current date and time every 10 seconds to an Elasticsearch server.

Step 1: Create Project Directory

a. We will create a directory for the project on **`/demo`** directory.

b. Create a directory for the project, and change to that directory:

```
sudo mkdir /demo
cd demo
```

Step 2: Verify Logstash Permissions

To ensure that Logstash has the appropriate permissions to write to the **`/usr/share/logstash/data`** directory, we will run Logstash as the **`logstash`** user. This will also ensure that the data files created by Logstash are owned by the **`logstash`** user.

a. Make sure that the Logstash user has the appropriate permissions to write to the **`/usr/share/logstash/data`** directory. You can do this by running the following command:

```
sudo chown -R logstash:logstash /usr/share/logstash/data
```

b. Make sure that the Logstash user has the appropriate permissions to write to the **`/demo`** directory. You can do this by running the following command:

```
sudo chown -R logstash:logstash /demo
```

Step 3: Write Logstash Programs

1. Create a configuration file for Logstash (**hello_logstash.conf**) on **/demo** directory. You can use any text editor to create this file. For example, you can use **nano**:

    ```
    sudo -u logstash nano /demo/hello_logstash.conf
    ```

2. We can write the configuration file with the following content:

    ```
    input {
      exec {
        command => "echo 'Current time: $(date)'"
        interval => 10 # Run this command every 10 seconds
      }
    }
    filter {
      # We don't need any filters for this simple scenario.
    }
    output {
      stdout { codec => rubydebug }
      elasticsearch {
        hosts => ["https://192.168.199.142:9200"]
        index => "logstash-test-%{+YYYY.MM.dd}"
        user => "logstash_tester"
        password => "pass123"
        ssl => true
        ssl_certificate_verification => false # Ignore SSL verification
    for self-signed certs
      }
    }
    ```

3. Replace **192.168.199.142** with the actual IP address of your Elasticsearch server. Replace **logstash_tester** and **pass123** with the actual username and password of your Logstash user.

4. This configuration sets up Logstash to execute the **date** command every 10 seconds, and send the output to Elasticsearch.

Code Explanation

The provided Logstash configuration is a simple, yet illustrative example of how to create a Logstash pipeline for data collection, processing, and output. Here is an explanation of each section of the script:

Input Section

```
input {
  exec {
    command => "echo 'Current time: $(date)'"
```

```
    interval => 10 # Run this command every 10 seconds
  }
}
```

a. **input { exec { ... } }**: This section defines the source of the data for Logstash, using the **exec** input plugin.

b. **command => "echo 'Current time: $(date)'"**: Logstash executes this command which outputs the current date and time. The **$(date)** is a shell command that gets substituted with the current date and time.

c. **interval => 10**: This setting specifies that the command should be run every 10 seconds. So, every 10 seconds, Logstash will execute this command, and ingest its output.

Output Section

```
output {
  stdout { codec => rubydebug }
  elasticsearch {
    hosts => ["https://192.168.199.142:9200"]
    index => "logstash-test-%{+YYYY.MM.dd}"
    user => "logstash_tester"
    password => "pass123"
    ssl => true
    ssl_certificate_verification => false
  }
}
```

- **stdout { codec => rubydebug }**: This part of the output section is for debugging. It outputs the processed data to the console in a debug format which is useful for testing and verifying the pipeline's operation.
- **elasticsearch { ... }**: This part configures Logstash to send the processed data to an Elasticsearch cluster.
    - **hosts => ["https://192.168.199.142:9200"]**: Specifies the Elasticsearch host. In this case, it is pointing to an Elasticsearch instance running on IP **192.168.199.142** and port **9200** over HTTPS.
    - **index => "logstash-test-%{+YYYY.MM.dd}"**: Defines the Elasticsearch index pattern where the data will be stored. Logstash will create new indices daily, based on this pattern (example, **logstash-test-2023.03.15**).
    - **user** and **password**: These settings provide the credentials for authenticating with Elasticsearch.
    - **ssl => true**: Enables SSL for secure communication with the Elasticsearch server.

  - **`ssl_certificate_verification => false`**: Disables SSL certificate verification which is often used when connecting to a server with a self-signed certificate. This should be used with caution and typically only in a controlled, secure environment.

In summary, this Logstash configuration creates a simple pipeline that runs a command every 10 seconds to get the current time and date, and then sends this data to both the console (for debugging purposes) and an Elasticsearch index, handling authentication and SSL communication with Elasticsearch.

Step 4: Run Logstash

Run Logstash with the new configuration file:

```
cd /usr/share/logstash/
sudo -u logstash bin/logstash -f /demo/hello_logstash.conf
```

After running Logstash, you should see the program output.

Step 5: Verify Data in Kibana

We cannot see the data in Kibana yet because we have not created an index pattern. We need to create an index pattern in Kibana to view the data that Logstash is sending to Elasticsearch. The following steps will guide you through the process of creating an index pattern in Kibana:

1. Open a web browser, and navigate to Kibana.
2. Go to the **`Stack Management`** section, and click on **`Data Views`** on Kibana section.
3. Click on **`Create data view`**.
4. Fill in the form with the following values as shown in *Figure* 3.5:
    - **Name**: **`logstash-test`**
    - **Index pattern**: **`logstash-test-*`**
    - **Timestamp field**: **`@timestamp`**
5. Save the data view.

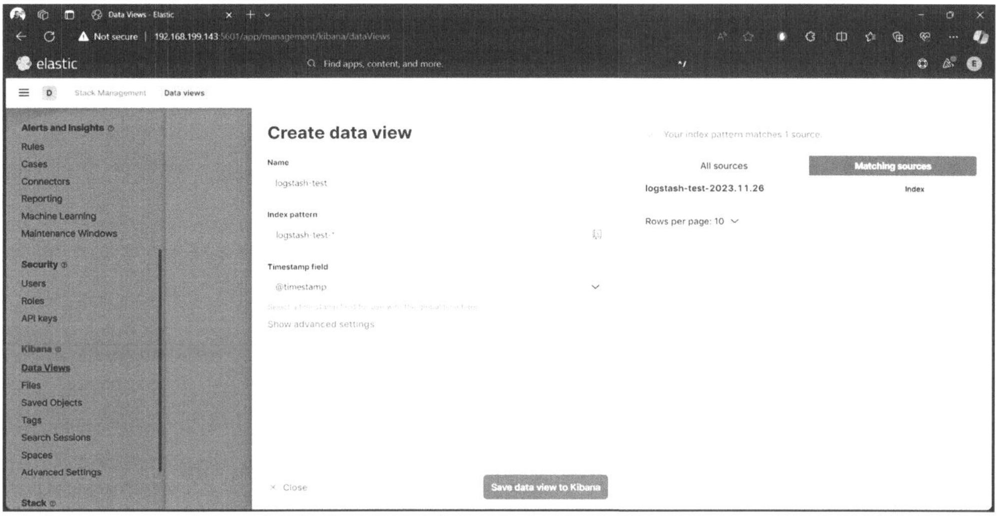

***Figure 3.5**: Create Kibana Data View*

6. Now, go to Kibana **`Discover`** section, and select the **`logstash-test`** data view.
7. You should see documents being created every 10 seconds with the current date and time.
8. Click one of the documents to see the details as shown in *Figure* 3.6:

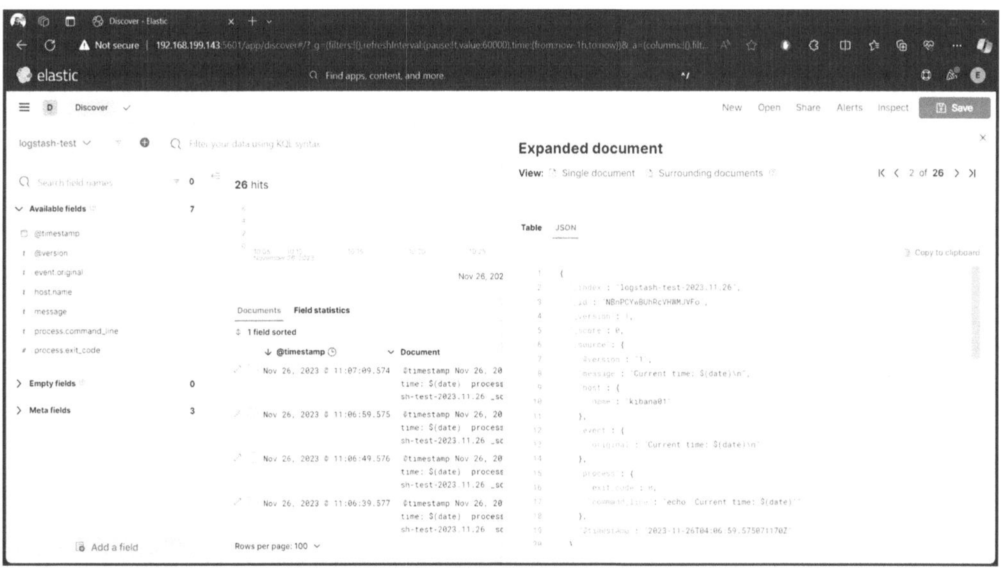

***Figure 3.6**: Show a Detail Document*

9. You can see a document in Table and JSON formats.

Hands-On Lab Notes

- Make sure that the firewalls on VM1 and VM2 are configured to allow traffic on the ports used by Elasticsearch (9200) and Kibana (5601).
- Ensure that time synchronization is set up correctly on both VMs to avoid any time drift issues.
- This setup assumes that Elasticsearch and Kibana are set up with default configurations with no additional security settings like X-Pack security.

How to Test the Setup

1. After starting Logstash, check the Logstash logs for any errors.
2. In Kibana, create an index pattern that corresponds to the one specified in the Logstash output configuration (for example, **`datetime-index-*`**).
3. Navigate to the **Discover** section in Kibana, and select the appropriate index pattern to view the incoming data.
4. Verify that the new data entries with the current date and time appear every 10 seconds.

Summary

Through this lab, you have learned how to set up a basic Logstash pipeline for scheduled data processing, and how to visualize the data using Kibana. This exercise demonstrates the integration between different components of the Elastic Stack, and provides a foundation for building more complex data processing pipelines. You have also practiced testing and verifying the data flow in an Elasticsearch-Kibana setup, a crucial skill for data administrators and engineers working with real-time data processing and monitoring.

Hands-on Lab: Running My First Logstash Pipeline as Service

On the previous lab, we ran Logstash as a command-line program. In this lab, we will run Logstash as a service. This is useful for production environments where Logstash needs to be running continuously. We will use the same setup as the previous lab, where we have two VMs: VM1 will host Elasticsearch, which will store and index the data, and VM2 will have both Logstash and Kibana installed. Logstash will be responsible for data processing and shipping, while Kibana will be used to visualize and test the data flow.

Step 1: Move a Logstash Configuration File

1. We will move the Logstash configuration file from the previous lab to the **/etc/logstash/conf.d** directory. This is the default directory for Logstash configuration files.
2. We copy the configuration file to **/etc/logstash/conf.d** directory:

```
sudo cp /demo/hello_logstash.conf /etc/logstash/conf.d/
```

Step 2: Set Up Logstash as a Service

a. **Linux**:
   i. If you installed Logstash via a package manager (for example, apt, yum), it should already be set up as a service.
   ii. Enable and start the Logstash service:

```
sudo systemctl enable logstash
sudo systemctl start logstash
```

   iii. To use your custom configuration, you may need to edit the Logstash service file, or place your configuration in the default directory (**/etc/logstash/conf.d/**).

b. **Windows**:
   i. Logstash can be set up as a service using NSSM or similar tools that allow running any application as a Windows service.

In this lab, we will use the Linux setup as an example.

Step 3: Verify Logstash Service

a. Check that the Logstash service is running properly, and the data is being ingested into Elasticsearch:

```
sudo systemctl status logstash
```

   Or for Windows, check the service status in the Services management console.

Step 4: Monitor Data in Elasticsearch

a. Use Kibana or direct Elasticsearch queries to monitor the data ingested by Logstash.
b. Go to Kibana **Discover** section, and select the **logstash-test** data view.
c. You should see documents being created every 10 seconds with the current date and time in *Figure* 3.7.

d. Select the **`Last 15 minutes`** in the time range selector to see the latest data.

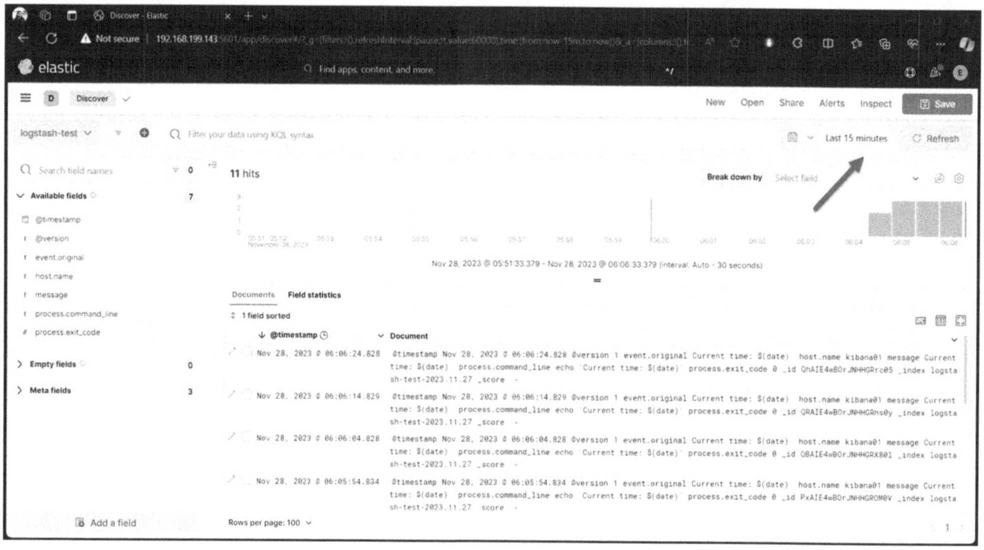

Figure 3.7: *Show Data from logstash-test*

Step 5: Stop Logstash Service

a. Stop the Logstash service:

```
sudo systemctl stop logstash
```

Or for Windows, stop the service in the Services management console.

b. If you want to our Logstash Configuration File, you can remove it from **`/etc/logstash/conf.d`** directory:

```
sudo rm /etc/logstash/conf.d/hello_logstash.conf
```

Plugins, Filters, and Codecs

Logstash is designed around a pluggable framework that makes it highly adaptable to many different use cases and data sources. The core components that leverage this framework are plugins, filters, and codecs, which together enable Logstash to ingest, transform, and load data in a variety of ways.

Plugins

Plugins in Logstash are pieces of code that add specific functionalities to its processing pipeline. There are several types of plugins:

- **Input Plugins**: These plugins are responsible for ingesting data into the

Logstash pipeline from a wide array of sources, including files, streams, databases, and cloud services.

- **Output Plugins**: These plugins send the processed data to various destinations such as Elasticsearch, file systems, databases, message queues, and much more.
- **Filter Plugins**: Filter plugins are used within the Logstash pipeline to manipulate and transform the data as it flows from the input to the output.
- **Codec Plugins**: Codecs are essentially stream filters that can be used in input or output stages to encode or decode data as it enters or exits the pipeline.

Each plugin is designed to be independently developed and maintained which allows for a rich ecosystem where both Elastic and the Logstash community can contribute plugins that extend Logstash's capabilities.

Filters

Filters are a particular type of plugin in Logstash that are used to transform data. They can perform actions such as parsing CSV files, matching and transforming text with regular expressions, enriching data with additional fields, and many more. Some common filter plugins include:

- **Grok**: Breaks down and structures arbitrary text blobs, making them queryable.
- **Mutate**: Allows you to perform general mutations on fields. You can rename, remove, replace, and modify fields in your event.
- **Date**: Used for parsing dates from fields, and then using that date or timestamp as the log's timestamp.
- **GeoIP**: Derives geographical information from an IP address.
- **Aggregate**: Enables the creation of aggregates and summaries, based on Logstash events.

Filters can be chained together to form complex data transformation pipelines.

Codecs

Codecs are a hybrid between input/output plugins and filters, providing a way to encode or decode data as it enters or exits the system. They are typically used to handle data serialization and deserialization, such as converting data to/from JSON, XML, or other formats. Common codecs include:

- **JSON**: For encoding or decoding data in JSON format.
- **Multiline**: Merges multiple line events into a single event, commonly used for stack traces.
- **Plain**: The default codec which outputs data as plain text.

- **RubyDebug**: Outputs data using the Ruby Awesome Print library, useful for debugging.

Codecs simplify the process of getting data into and out of Logstash in the correct format, reducing the need for complex filter configurations, when the primary task is simply encoding or decoding data.

In summary, plugins, filters, and codecs work together to give Logstash its powerful data processing capabilities. They enable Logstash to be highly customizable, allowing it to meet the specific data processing needs of any use case.

Hands-On Lab: Building a Comprehensive Logstash Pipeline

In this advanced hands-on lab, we will create a robust Logstash pipeline that demonstrates the usage of different components - Input, Output, Filter, and Codec. The scenario involves processing web server logs. These logs are in a Common Log Format (CLF) which we will parse, transform, and then send to Elasticsearch for analysis. Additionally, we will use a codec to format the output data.

Objectives

- **Input**: Read log data from a file.
- **Filter**: Parse and enrich log data.
- **Output**: Send the processed data to Elasticsearch.
- **Codec**: Use the `json` codec for formatting data.

Prerequisites

- Logstash and Elasticsearch installed and running.
- Sample web server log file in Common Log Format (for example, Apache server logs).
- Basic understanding of Logstash configuration.

Step 1: Set Up User Permissions

We create a new role and user in Kibana with the appropriate permissions to ingest data into Elasticsearch via Logstash. You can follow the steps in the previous lab to create a new role and user, **Hands-On Lab: Setting Up Logstash for Data Ingestion with User Permissions**.

a. We open Kibana, and go to `Management` > `Stack Management` > `Security` > `Roles`.

b. Click **`Create role`**, and define the role:

- **Name**: **`testbed_role.`**
- Under **`Cluster privileges`**, add **`manage_index_templates`**, **`monitor`**, and **`manage_ilm`**.
- Under **Index privileges**, and add:
    i. **Indices**: **`testbed-*`** or the specific index names/patterns, you plan to use.
    ii. **Privileges**: **`write`**, **`read`**, **`index`**, **`create_index`**, **`create_doc`**, and **`view_index_metadata`**.

c. Save the role.

d. Go to **`Security`** > **`Users`**, and click on **`Create user`**:

- **Username**: **`testbed_tester.`**
- **Full name**: **`testbed tester.`**
- **Password**: Choose a secure password, and make a note of it.
- **Roles**: Assign the **`testbed_role`** role, you just created.

Step 2: Prepare the Sample Log Data

1. Create a sample log file named **`apache_logs,`** and populate it with a few lines of log data in the **`Common Log`** Format.
2. We can download sample log file from **https://raw.githubusercontent.com/elastic/examples/master/Common%20Data%20Formats/apache_logs/apache_logs**.
3. We download the sample log file to **`/demo`** directory.

```
sudo -u logstash wget https://raw.githubusercontent.com/elastic/
examples/master/Common%20Data%20Fo
rmats/apache_logs/apache_logs
```

4. We perform this action as **`logstash`** user to ensure that the file is owned by the **`logstash`** user.

Step 3: Create the Logstash Configuration

a. **Create a configuration file**:

i. Create a configuration file named **`logstash-apache-logs.conf`** in the **`/demo`** directory.

2. We can use any text editor to create this file. For example, we can use **`nano`**:

```
sudo -u logstash nano /demo/logstash-apache-logs.conf
```

b. **Input Configuration**:

Use the **file** input plugin to read from the **apache_logs** file.

```
input {
   file {
     path => "/demo/apache_logs"
     start_position => "beginning"
     sincedb_path => "/dev/null"
   }
}
```

c. **Filter Configuration**:

i. Use the **grok** filter plugin to parse the CLF logs.

ii. Use the **date** filter to parse timestamps.

iii. Add any additional filters as required.

```
filter {
   grok {
     match => { "message" => "%{COMBINEDAPACHELOG}" }
   }
   date {
     match => [ "timestamp", "dd/MMM/yyyy:HH:mm:ss Z" ]
     target => "@timestamp"
   }
}
```

d. **Output Configuration**:

i. Configure the Elasticsearch output.

ii. Apply the **json** codec for formatting.

```
output {
   stdout { codec => rubydebug }
   elasticsearch {
     hosts => ["https://192.168.199.142:9200"]
     index => "testbed-demo-weblog"
     user => "testbed_tester"
     password => "pass123"
     ssl => true
     ssl_certificate_verification => false # Ignore SSL
verification for self-signed certs
   }
}
```

iii. Replace **192.168.199.142** with the actual IP address of your Elasticsearch server. Replace **testbed_tester** and **pass123** with the actual username and password of your Logstash user.

Step 4: Run Logstash

a. Start Logstash with the created configuration file:

```
cd /usr/share/logstash/
sudo -u logstash bin/logstash -f /demo/logstash-apache-logs.
conf
```

b. If you get an error, make sure that the Logstash user has the appropriate permissions to write to the **`/usr/share/logstash/data`** directory. You can do this by running the following command:

```
sudo chown -R logstash:logstash /usr/share/logstash/data
```

Step 5: Explore and Analyze Data in Kibana

a. Open a web browser, and navigate to Kibana.

b. Go to the **`Stack Management`** section, and click on **`Data Views`** on Kibana section.

c. Click on **`Create data view`**.

d. Fill in the form with the following values:

- **Name**: **`testbed-demo-weblog`**
- **Index pattern**: **`testbed-demo-weblog`**
- **Time field**: **`@timestamp`**

e. Save the data view, as shown in *Figure* 3.8.

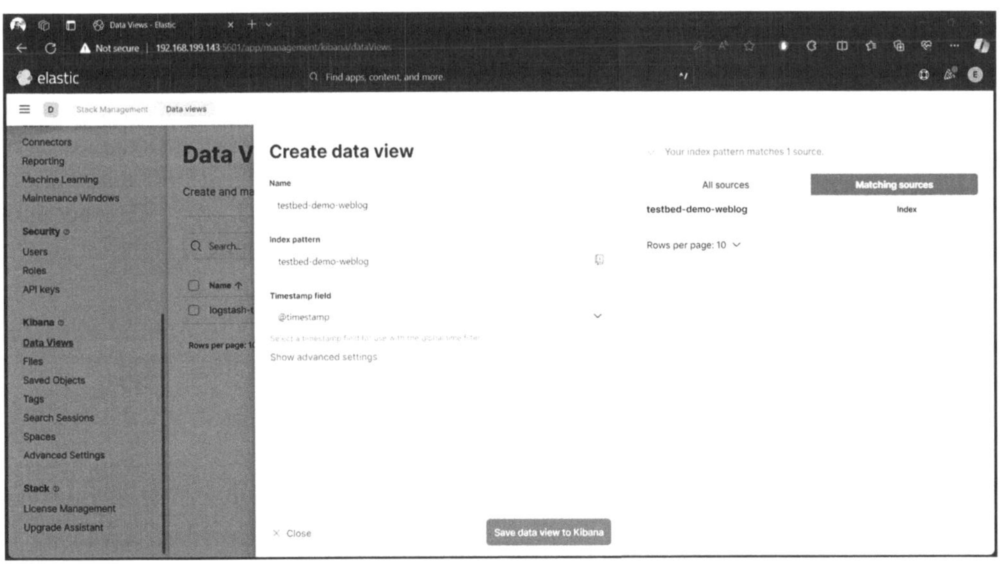

Figure 3.8: *Create Kibana Data View for Testbed-demo-weblog*

f. Now, you can navigate to Kibana **Discover** section, and select the `testbed-demo-weblog` data view.

g. Since log data was written in 2015, you can change the filter time as `Last 15 years`, as shown in *Figure* 3.9.

h. Click one of the documents to see the details.

i. You can see a document in Table and JSON formats.

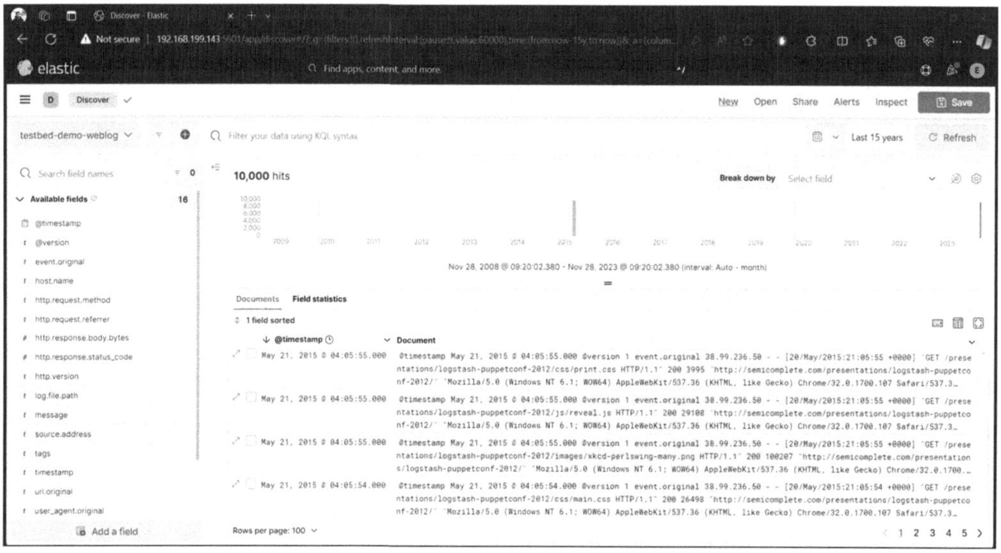

Figure 3.9: *Display Log Data on Kibana Discover*

Summary

This lab demonstrates a comprehensive use of Logstash's capabilities. You have learned how to ingest log data, apply complex filters for parsing and enrichment, and output the processed data to Elasticsearch in a structured format. This scenario is typical in log analysis and monitoring setups, providing valuable insights into web server performance and user behavior.

Advanced Pipelines and Data Processing

Advanced pipelines in Logstash refer to the configurations that enable more complex data processing scenarios. These pipelines are designed to handle a wide variety of use cases, from simple log file ingestion to sophisticated streaming analytics. Here is a description of the features and capabilities that constitute advanced pipelines, and data processing in Logstash:

- **Multiple Pipelines:** Logstash can run multiple pipelines independently. This allows you to isolate data streams and processing logic, which can be beneficial for performance, organization, and reducing the risk of interference between unrelated data flows.

If you have multiple pipelines, you can specify which one to run by using the **`-f`** flag when starting Logstash. For example, if you have two pipelines named **`pipeline1.conf`** and **`pipeline2.conf`**, you can start Logstash with the following command:

```
bin/logstash -f pipeline1.conf -f pipeline2.conf
```

If you want to run as a service, you can specify the pipelines in the Logstash service file. Place your configuration files in the default directory (**`/etc/logstash/conf.d/`**), and then start the Logstash service.

- **Pipeline-to-Pipeline Communication:** Logstash supports the interconnection of pipelines. You can set up an output of one pipeline to be the input to another, creating a complex network of data processing stages. This is useful for breaking down complex processing tasks into manageable, modular chunks.

This feature is particularly useful, when you want to separate concerns or stages in your data processing workflow. Here is how you can set up two interconnected pipelines in Logstash:

Pipeline 1: `pipeline1.conf`

This first pipeline will read data from a source (for example, a file), and then pass it to a second pipeline through a named pipeline output.

```
# pipeline1.conf
input {
  file {
    path => "/path/to/your/data/source.log"
    start_position => "beginning"
    sincedb_path => "/dev/null"
  }
}
filter {
  # Apply necessary filters
}
output {
  pipeline {
    send_to => ["pipeline2"]
  }
}
```

Pipeline 2: `pipeline2.conf`

The second pipeline receives data from the first pipeline, processes it further if needed, and then outputs it to a final destination (for example, Elasticsearch).

```
# pipeline2.conf
input {
  pipeline {
    address => "pipeline2"
  }
}
filter {
  # Further data processing
}
output {
  stdout { codec => rubydebug }
  # Additional outputs like Elasticsearch can be added here
}
```

Setting Up Pipeline-to-Pipeline Communication

1. **Central Configuration**: In your Logstash central configuration file (typically **`pipelines.yml`** - on Ubuntu, you find it on **`/etc/logstash/pipelines.yml`**), define both pipelines and their respective configuration paths:

   ```
   - pipeline.id: pipeline1
     path.config: "/path/to/pipeline1.conf"
   - pipeline.id: pipeline2
     path.config: "/path/to/pipeline2.conf"
   ```

2. **Running Logstash**: Start Logstash normally. It will load both pipelines as defined in the **`pipelines.yml`** file.

Explanation

- In **`pipeline1.conf`**, data is read from a file, processed, and then sent to another pipeline named **`pipeline2`,** using the **`pipeline`** output plugin.
- In **`pipeline2.conf`**, the **`pipeline`** input plugin is used to receive data from **`pipeline1`**. This pipeline can then perform additional processing and output the data to its final destination.
- The **`pipelines.yml`** file is used to configure and run multiple pipelines in Logstash.

Notes

- Ensure that the file paths in the input section and the **`pipelines.yml`** file are correct and accessible.
- The **`sincedb_path => "/dev/null"`** setting in **`pipeline1.conf`** is for demonstration purposes to ensure that Logstash reads from the beginning of the file, each time it starts. In a production environment, this should be managed differently.

- This setup is flexible, and can be extended with more pipelines, filters, and outputs as needed for complex data processing scenarios.

Conditional Logic: Within a pipeline, you can implement conditional logic to route data to different filters or outputs, based on its content. This allows for more sophisticated processing such as applying different processing rules, based on metadata or field values.

Let us create a simple configuration file where the pipeline processes log data differently, based on certain conditions. For this example, we will assume the log data contains a field named **`log_type,`** and we will process the data differently, based on the value of this field.

```
input {
  file {
    path => "/path/to/your/logfile.log"
    start_position => "beginning"
    sincedb_path => "/dev/null"
  }
}
filter {
  grok {
    match => { "message" => "%{COMBINEDAPACHELOG}" }
  }
  # Conditional logic based on the 'log_type' field
  if [log_type] == "error" {
    mutate {
      add_tag => ["error_log"]
    }
  } else if [log_type] == "access" {
    mutate {
      add_tag => ["access_log"]
    }
  }
}
output {
  stdout { codec => rubydebug }
  if "error_log" in [tags] {
    file {
      path => "/path/to/error_logs.log"
    }
  } else if "access_log" in [tags] {
    file {
      path => "/path/to/access_logs.log"
    }
  }
}
```

Explanation

- **Input Section**: Reads data from a specified log file.
- **Filter Section**:
    - The **grok** filter is used to parse the log data. This example uses a common Apache log parsing pattern.
- The **if** statements implement conditional logic, based on the value of the **log_type** field in the log data.
    - If **log_type** is **error**, a tag **error_log** is added to the event.
    - If **log_type** is **access**, a tag **access_log** is added to the event.
- **Output Section:**
    - The **stdout** output is used for debugging, and it will print all the processed log data to the console.
    - Additional conditional outputs to different files, based on the tags added in the filter section.
    - Error logs are written to **error_logs.log**, and access logs are written to **access_logs.log**.

By using conditional logic, you can create more flexible and dynamic pipelines that adapt to different types of data, improving the efficiency and effectiveness of your data processing with Logstash.

- **Persistent Queues:** Logstash offers persistent queues which help protect against data loss by storing the incoming data on disk before processing. This feature enables durability across restarts, and provides a buffer that can absorb bursts of data or allow for planned downtime.

  To enable persistent queues, you need to modify the **logstash.yml** configuration file. You can find it on **/etc/logstash/logstash.yml** in Ubuntu.

  Here is an example of a persistent queue configuration with file-based storage:

  ```
  queue.type: persisted
  path.queue: /var/lib/logstash/queue
  queue.max_bytes: 4gb
  queue.checkpoint.writes: 1024
  queue.page_capacity: 250mb
  ```
- **Dead Letter Queues:** Dead letter queues in Logstash capture events that could not be processed. You can later analyze these events to understand why they failed to process, and to decide whether to drop, fix, or retry processing them.

You can enable dead letter queues by adding the following configuration to the **/etc/logstash/logstash.yml** file:

```
dead_letter_queue.enable: true
dead_letter_queue.max_bytes: 1024mb
dead_letter_queue.flush_interval: 5s
```

- **Plugins for Enrichment:** Logstash has a variety of plugins that can enrich the data as it is processed. This includes looking up data from external sources, adding geographical information to IP addresses, or anonymizing the sensitive data. Enrichment can add significant value to the data, before it lands in its final destination.
- **Worker and Batch Settings:** Advanced Logstash pipelines can be tuned by configuring the number of worker threads, and controlling the size of batches of events that are processed. This can optimize throughput and performance, based on the hardware and workload.
- **Monitoring and Management:** Logstash pipelines can be monitored and managed through a built-in monitoring API, the Kibana interface, or external tools like Elastic Stack Monitoring. You can track performance metrics, and make live changes to the pipeline configurations.
- **Custom Plugin Development:** For scenarios where the existing plugins do not meet the specific requirements, developers can create custom plugins. This provides endless possibilities for what can be achieved within a Logstash pipeline.
- **Advanced Filtering and Grok Patterns:** In more complex data streams, the use of advanced filtering techniques, and custom Grok patterns can parse and structure data in ways that are highly tailored to the needs of the application.
- **Scalability:** Advanced pipelines are designed with scalability in mind. You can scale Logstash horizontally by adding more instances, and you can manage this within a load-balanced environment to handle increased traffic and processing demands.
- In conclusion, advanced pipelines in Logstash offer a robust framework for diverse and complex data processing needs. By utilizing these advanced features, organizations can create resilient, scalable, and highly customized data processing systems that are integral to their operational intelligence, monitoring, and data analytics strategies.

Handling Large Datasets and Scalability

Handling large datasets, and ensuring scalability are critical challenges in data processing that Logstash addresses through a combination of features and architectural considerations. The following is a detailed description of how Logstash manages large datasets, and scales to meet the demands of high-volume data environments:

- **Distributed Processing:** Logstash can be configured in a distributed architecture, where multiple instances of Logstash work in parallel to process the data. This not only provides scalability, but also adds redundancy and reliability to the data processing pipeline.
- **Load Balancing:** Logstash can distribute the data load across multiple instances using load balancing. This ensures that no single instance becomes a bottleneck. Load balancing can be achieved through external tools or services, or by using the built-in load balancing features in certain output plugins like the Elasticsearch output plugin.
- **Pipeline Workers and Batch Sizes:** Logstash allows configuration of pipeline workers (threads) and batch sizes. By tuning these settings, Logstash can optimize the throughput, based on the available CPU cores and memory, thus improving the handling of large datasets.
- **High-Performance Data Processing Plugins:** Logstash's plugin ecosystem includes several high-performance plugins designed for large data sets, such as the Beats input for high-throughput data ingestion or the JDBC input, for efficient database querying.
- **Horizontal Scalability:** Logstash's architecture naturally supports horizontal scaling. You can add more Logstash nodes to your deployment to increase processing power, and because Logstash nodes are stateless, they can scale out without complex coordination.
- **Use of External Queuing Systems:** For very large datasets or high-velocity data, Logstash can be used in conjunction with external queuing systems such as Kafka or RabbitMQ. This allows Logstash to pull data at its own pace, providing an additional layer of buffering and reliability.

  By leveraging these strategies, Logstash is capable of handling large datasets, and can scale to meet the demands of big data processing tasks, ensuring that the data is processed efficiently and reliably at any scale.

Elastic Agent

In this section, we will learn about Elastic Agent, a unified agent that is a part of the Elastic Stack. We will discuss its benefits and architecture, and then, we will walk through the process of deploying and configuring Elastic Agent.

Understanding Elastic Agent: Benefits and Architecture

Elastic Agent is a unified agent that is a part of the Elastic Stack, a suite of free and open tools for data ingestion, enrichment, storage, analysis, and visualization. Elastic Agent simplifies the data integration process, and enhances observability as well as security within an IT environment. Here is an overview of its benefits and architecture:

Benefits of Elastic Agent

- **Unified Data Collection**: Elastic Agent simplifies the process of data collection from various sources like logs, metrics, and traces. It replaces the need for multiple agents, reducing system complexity.
- **Centralized Management**: With Elastic Agent, you can centrally manage and update agent configurations as well as policies through Kibana, the user interface for the Elastic Stack. This central management reduces administrative overhead, and enhances control.
- **Enhanced Security**: It integrates with Elastic Security to provide threat prevention, detection, and response capabilities, ensuring a higher level of security for your systems.
- **Scalability and Flexibility**: Elastic Agent is designed to be scalable and flexible, easily adapting to different environments and scaling as your data needs grow.
- **Improved Observability**: By consolidating various data types, Elastic Agent offers improved observability of your IT environment, providing insights into system performance and health.

Architecture of Elastic Agent

The architecture of Elastic Agent is shown in *Figure* 3.10, and consists of several components:

- **Agent**: The agent itself is installed on the host machine. It is responsible for collecting data, and executing the actions defined in its policy. We have two types of agents: **Standalone** and **Fleet-managed**.
    - **Standalone Agent**: A standalone agent is a single instance of the agent that is not managed by Fleet Server. It is used for small deployments where centralized management is not required.
    - **Fleet-managed Agent**: A Fleet-managed agent is an agent that is managed by Fleet Server. It is used for large deployments where centralized management is required.

- **Integrations**: Elastic Agent uses integrations, which are packages for specific data sources or services, to collect data. These integrations determine what data is collected, and how it is processed.
- **Fleet Server**: In a scalable deployment, Fleet Server is used to manage and distribute agent policies. It acts as a central point for agents to check in, and receive updates.
- **Kibana**: Kibana provides the user interface for managing Elastic Agents. Administrators can create and manage policies, add integrations, and monitor agent status.
- **Elasticsearch**: **The** collected data is sent to Elasticsearch for storage, analysis, and visualization.

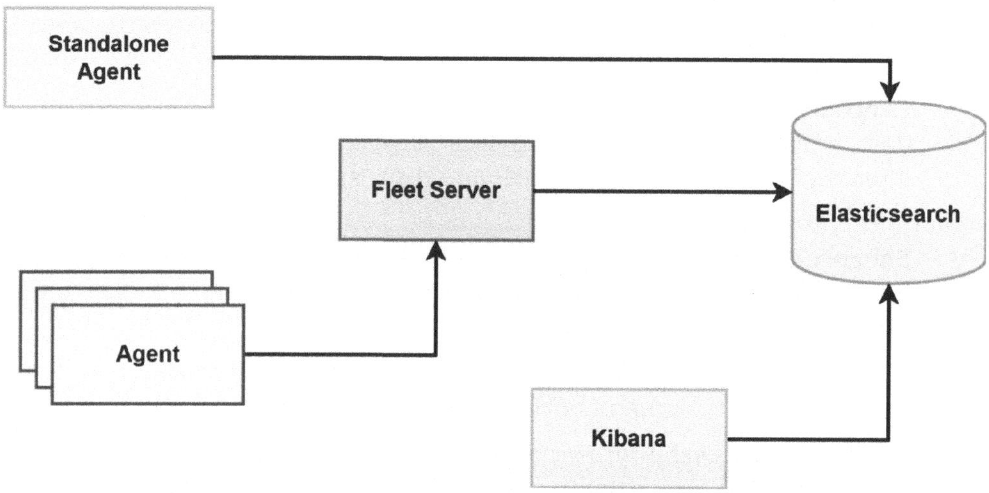

Figure 3.10: *Architecture of Elastic Agent*

In summary, Elastic Agent streamlines data collection, management, and analysis in an Elastic Stack environment, offering benefits such as simplified data integration, centralized management, enhanced security, scalability, flexibility, and improved observability. Its architecture, comprising the agent, integrations, Fleet Server, Kibana, and Elasticsearch, is designed for efficiency and ease of use.

Deploying and Configuring Elastic Agent

Deploying and configuring Elastic Agent involves a series of steps that allow you to effectively integrate it into your IT environment. This process ensures that your systems are set up for efficient data collection, management, and analysis. Here is a guide to help you through the deployment and configuration of Elastic Agent:

Deploying Elastic Agent

1. **System Requirements Check**: Before deploying Elastic Agent, ensure that your system meets the necessary requirements. This includes compatible operating systems, sufficient memory, and network configurations.
2. **Download and Install Elastic Agent**: Download Elastic Agent from the Elastic website. Choose the version that corresponds to your Elastic Stack version. Follow the installation instructions specific to your operating system.
3. **Fleet Server Setup (Optional)**: For centralized management, set up a Fleet Server. This step is crucial for large deployments, and helps in distributing configurations and updates to multiple agents.
4. **Elasticsearch and Kibana Preparation**: Ensure that Elasticsearch and Kibana are properly set up and accessible, as these components are essential for Elastic Agent's operation and management.

Configuring Elastic Agent

1. **Connect to Kibana**: After installation, connect Elastic Agent to Kibana. This step usually involves specifying the Kibana URL and Elasticsearch credentials.
2. **Enroll in Fleet**: If using Fleet, enroll the Elastic Agent in the Fleet. This involves generating an enrollment token in Kibana, and using it to enroll the agent.
3. **Policy Assignment**: Assign or create a policy for the Elastic Agent in Kibana. Policies determine what data the agent will collect, and how it will be processed. You can choose from predefined policies, or create customized ones based on your needs.
4. **Add Integrations**: Select and add integrations to your policy. Each integration is designed for the specific data sources or services such as log files, metrics, or security data.
5. **Policy Configuration**: Configure the details of each integration in the policy. This can include setting log paths, defining metrics to be collected, and other source-specific settings.
6. **Apply and Validate Configurations**: Once you have configured the policies and integrations, apply the configurations. Validate that the agent is properly collecting and sending data to Elasticsearch by checking the data streams in Kibana.
7. **Monitoring and Management**: Regularly monitor the Elastic Agent's performance and health through Kibana. Update policies and configurations as needed.

8. **Scaling Up**: As your needs grow, you can add more Elastic Agents, and manage them through Fleet, ensuring scalable and efficient data collection across your environment.

In summary, deploying and configuring Elastic Agent involves a series of steps that ensure your systems are set up for efficient data collection, management, and analysis. By following this guide, you can successfully integrate Elastic Agent into your IT environment.

Integrating with Beats and Endpoints

Integrating Elastic Agent with Beats and Endpoints is a key step in enhancing the data collection and security capabilities of your Elastic Stack environment. Here is a guide to help you understand and implement this integration effectively:

Understanding Beats and Endpoints

- **Beats Overview**: Beats are lightweight, open-source data shippers that are part of the Elastic Stack. They are used to collect different types of data such as logs (Filebeat), metrics (Metricbeat), network data (Packetbeat), and much more.
- **Endpoint Security**: Endpoint security in the Elastic Stack context refers to protecting endpoint devices such as computers, mobile devices, and servers from cybersecurity threats. Elastic Security integrates endpoint security features to detect and respond to threats.

Integrating Beats with Elastic Agent

1. **Migrating from Beats to Elastic Agent**: If you are already using Beats, consider migrating to Elastic Agent. Elastic Agent can handle all the functions of Beats, simplifying deployment and management.
2. **Setting Up Beats Integrations**: Within the Elastic Agent, select and configure specific Beats integrations depending on the data, you want to collect. For example, use the Filebeat integration for log data or Metricbeat for system metrics.
3. **Customizing Configurations**: Customize your Beats integrations by specifying data sources, log paths, and other relevant settings in the Elastic Agent policy.

Integrating Endpoint Security

1. **Enabling Endpoint Security Integration**: In Kibana, under the Fleet management, enable the Endpoint Security integration. This integration is part of the Elastic Agent, and provides protection against threats.

2. **Configuring Endpoint Protection**: Define the settings for your endpoint protection such as malware prevention, detection rules, and response actions.
3. **Policy Application**: Apply the endpoint security settings to the relevant Elastic Agent policies. This ensures that the configured security measures are implemented on all agents under that policy.

By integrating Beats and endpoint security with Elastic Agent, you can streamline your data collection processes, and enhance the security posture of your IT environment. This integration brings together the strengths of various Elastic Stack components, offering a comprehensive solution for observability and security.

Hands-On Lab: Monitoring Ubuntu System with Elastic Agent

Creating a hands-on lab scenario to monitor an Ubuntu system on a Virtual Machine (VM) using Elastic Agent can be an excellent way to understand the practical aspects of deploying and configuring Elastic Agent in a real-world setting.

Objective

Learn how to deploy and configure Elastic Agent on an Ubuntu VM to monitor system metrics and logs.

Requirements

- A virtualization tool (like VirtualBox or VMware)
- An Ubuntu VM setup
- Access to Elastic Stack (Elasticsearch and Kibana)

For this lab, we use the existing Kibana instances on VM2 as target of Ubuntu System. You can set up your own Ubuntu VM.

Lab Steps

Here is a step-by-step guide to set up the lab:

1. **Install Integrations for System:**
    a. We open Kibana, and click **Integrations** on the left menu, as shown in *Figure* 3.11.
    b. We will see a list of integrations. We can filter the list by typing `system` on the search box in *Figure* 3.12.

c. Click **`System`** on the list.

d. We click **`Install`** on the **`System`** integration.

e. Fill in the form with the following values:

   i. **Name**: **`testbed-integration-demo.`**

   ii. **Policy name**: **`testbed-integration Agent policy.`**

   iii. All other fields are optional.

f. Save the integration.

g. After clicking **`Save`**, we will see a dialog box with the following message: **`System integration added.`**

h. Next, we click **`Add Elastic Agent to your hosts`**.

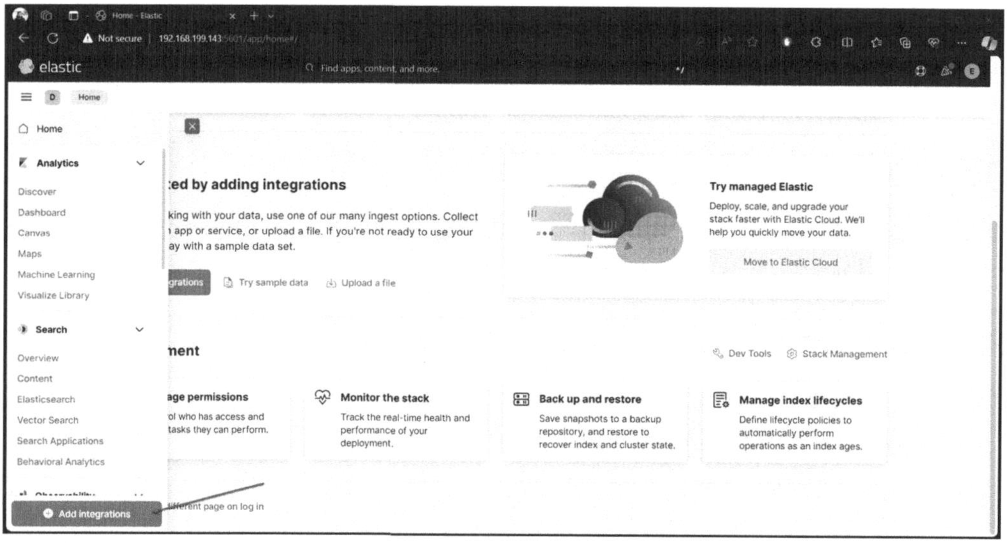

***Figure 3.11**: Integrations Menu on Kibana*

2. **Create Elastic Agent to Target Host**:

   a. After we click **`Add Elastic Agent to your hosts`**, we will see a dialog box with the following message: **`Add Elastic Agent to your hosts.`**

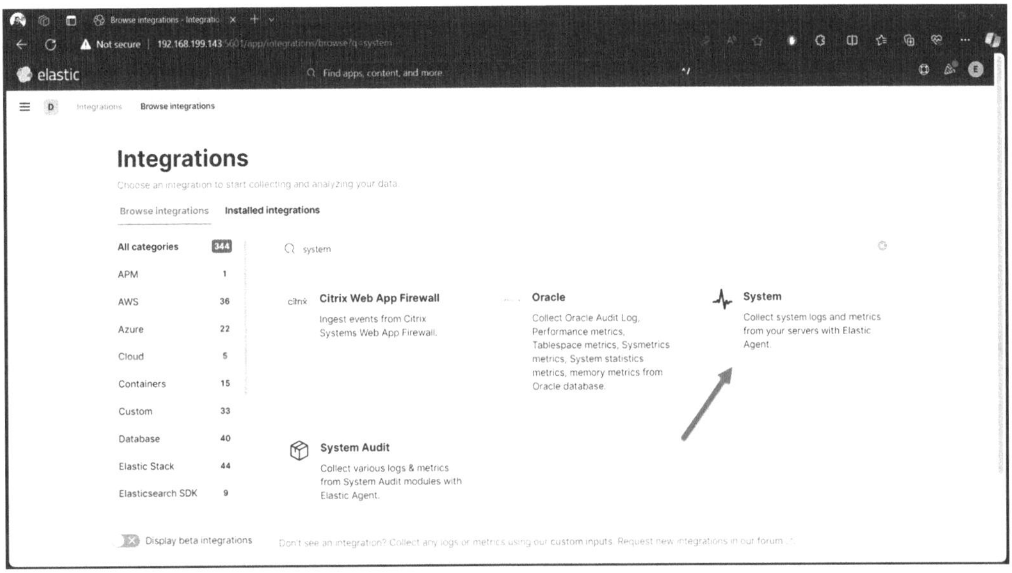

***Figure 3.12**: System Integrations on the List*

b. You will have two options to add Elastic Agent to your hosts:

   i. **Option 1**: Elastic agent with Fleet Server.

   ii. **Option 2**: Elastic agent standalone.

c. For this lab, we will use Elastic agent standalone.

d. Click **`Run standalone`** tab.

e. Copy paste a content of Elastic policy, **`elastic-agent.yml`**, and run it on your Ubuntu VM.

f. Then, scroll down and click **`Download Elastic Agent`**.

g. Copy these commands for Linux Tar and Windows.

   - For Windows installation commands, we will use on next lab.

h. Next, we create Elasticsearch role and user.

3. **Create Elastic Agent Role and User**:

   a. We open Kibana and go to **`Management`** > **`Stack Management`** > **`Security`** > **`Roles`**.

   b. Click **`Create role`**, and define the role:

      i. **Name**: **`elastic_agent_testbed_role.`**

   ii. Under **Cluster privileges**, add **manage_index_templates**, **monitor**, and **manage_ilm**..

   iii. Under **Index privileges**, add:

   iv. **Indices**: **logs-*-***, **metrics-*-***, **traces-*-*** and **synthetics-*-***.

   v. **Privileges**: **auto_configure** and **create_doc**.

c. Save the role.

d. Go to **Security** > **Users**, and click on **Create user**:

   i. **Username**: **testbed_elastic.**

   ii. **Full name**: **testbed elastic.**

   iii. **Password**: Choose a secure password, and make a note of it.

   iv. **Roles**: Assign the **elastic_agent_testbed_role** role, you just created.

4. **Modify elastic-agent.yml File**:

   a. On previous step, we already username **testbed_elastic** and password for Elasticsearch. We will use it on this step.

   b. Open **elastic-agent.yml** file, and modify the following lines:

      i. **username**: Change the **username** value to **testbed_elastic**.

      ii. **password**: Change the **password** value to your user password.

   c. Save the file.

5. **Download and Install Elastic Agent**:

   a. Perform to **ssh** to your Ubuntu server VM.

   b. Install the Elastic Agent using the provided installation commands for Ubuntu. We already copy the commands on previous step.

   c. Since we use Elasticsearch 8.10.4, we should use Elastic Agent 8.10.4.

   d. Here are the commands to download and extract Elastic Agent on Ubuntu:

```
    curl -L -O https://artifacts.elastic.co/downloads/beats/
elastic-agent/elastic-agent-8.10.4-linux-x86_64.tar.gz
    tar xzvf elastic-agent-8.10.4-linux-x86_64.tar.gz
    cd elastic-agent-8.10.4-linux-x86_64
```

   e. After extracted, we will see a directory named **elastic-agent-8.10.4-linux-x86_64**.

f. Copy our modified **`elastic-agent.yml`** file (from previous steps) to the **`elastic-agent-8.10.4-linux-x86_64`** directory.

g. Now, we can run Elastic Agent using the following command:

```
sudo ./elastic-agent install
```

h. Install as service and no Fleet Server.

i. Elastic agent was installed on **`/opt/Elastic/Agent/*`**

j. You can find **`elastic-agent.yml`** file on **`/opt/Elastic/Agent/elastic-agent.yml`**

k. After installed, we can verify the status of Elastic Agent using the following command:

```
sudo ./elastic-agent status
```

6. **View Dashboards in Kibana**:

a. Open Kibana, and go to **`Management`** > **`Integrations`**.

b. On Integrations page, click **`Installed integrations`** tab.

c. Click **`System`** integration.

d. Click **`Assets`** tab.

e. Click **`[Metrics System] Host overview`**.

f. You should see a dashboard as shown in *Figure* 3.13.

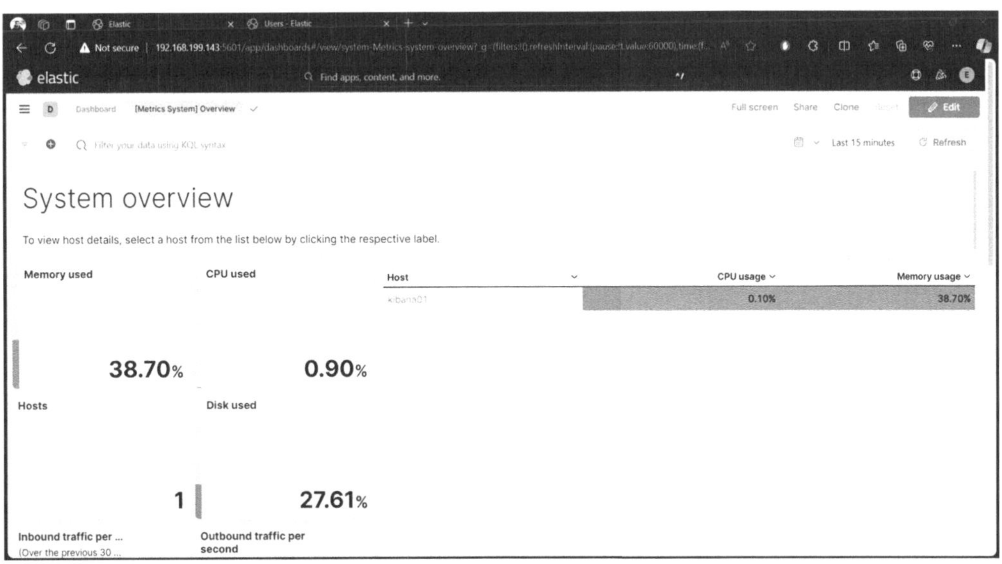

***Figure* 3.13**: *System Integration Dashboard*

g. Click your host name.

h. After that, you should see a dashboard as shown in *Figure* 3.14.

i. You also can explore other dashboards on **`Assets`** tab.

j. We can find all dashboards on **`Dashboards`** menu.

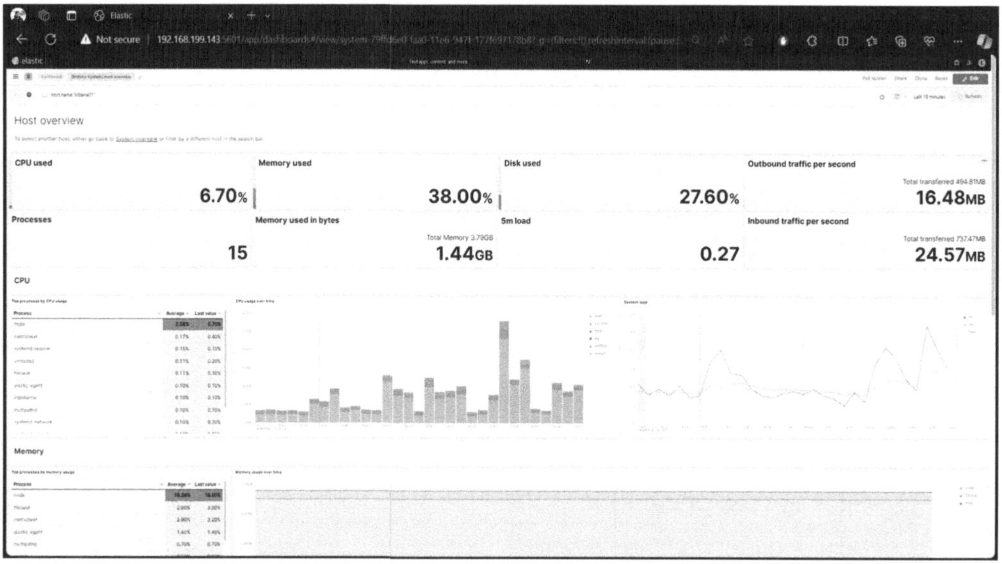

***Figure 3.14**: Status of Elastic Agent*

7. **Uninstall Elastic Agent**:

   a. Open Terminal, and perform to ssh to your Ubuntu server VM.

   b. You can uninstall Elastic Agent using the following command:

   ```
   sudo elastic-agent uninstall
   ```

8. **Uninstall Integrations**:

   a. After all Elastic Agents were uninstalled, we can uninstall integrations.

   b. Open Kibana, and go to **`Management`** > **`Integrations`**.

   c. On Integrations page, click **`Installed integrations`** tab.

   d. Click **`System`** integration.

   e. Click **`Integration policies`** tab.

   f. Click **`Delete integration`** button on the right side.

   g. You also can delete all system assets. Click **`Uninstall System`** on **`Settings`** tab.

   h. If you want to delete all dashboards, you can delete all dashboards on **`Dashboards`** menu.

Upon completion of this lab, you will have hands-on experience in deploying and configuring Elastic Agent on an Ubuntu VM. You will understand how to monitor system metrics and logs, manage agent policies, and troubleshoot the common issues.

Hands-On Lab: Monitoring Windows System with Elastic Agent

This lab extends the previous lab by monitoring a Windows system on a Virtual Machine using Elastic Agent.

Objective

Learn how to deploy and configure Elastic Agent on an Windows to monitor system metrics and logs.

Requirements

- Windows VM setup or Windows host.
- Access to Elastic Stack (Elasticsearch and Kibana).

Make sure that you have completed the previous lab before starting this lab. You also make sure that you have access to Elastic Stack from your Windows host.

Lab Steps

Here is a step-by-step guide to set up the lab:

1. **Download and Install Elastic Agent**:
    a. Open PowerShell as Administrator.
    b. Install the Elastic Agent using the provided installation commands for Windows. We already copy the commands on previous step.
    c. Since we use Elasticsearch 8.10.4, we should use Elastic Agent 8.10.4 for Windows.
    d. Here are the commands to download and extract Elastic Agent on Windows:

```
$ProgressPreference = 'SilentlyContinue'
    Invoke-WebRequest -Uri https://artifacts.elastic.co/down-
loads/beats/elastic-agent/elastic-agent-8.10.4-windows-x86_64.
zip -OutFile elastic-agent-8.10.4-windows-x86_64.zip
```

```
    Expand-Archive elastic-agent-8.10.4-windows-x86_64.zip
-DestinationPath .
    cd elastic-agent-8.10.4-windows-x86_64
```

e. After extracted, we will see a directory named **`elastic-agent-8.10.4-windows-x86_64`**.

f. Copy our modified **`elastic-agent.yml`** file (from previous lab) to the **`elastic-agent-8.10.4-windows-x86_64`** directory.

g. Now, we can run Elastic Agent using the following command:

```
.\elastic-agent.exe install
```

h. Install as service and no Fleet Server.

i. On Windows, we can find Elastic Agent on **`C:\Program Files\Elastic\Agent\*`**

j. After installed, we can verify the status of Elastic Agent using the following command:

```
cd "C:\Program Files\Elastic\Agent\"
.\elastic-agent.exe status
```

2. **View Dashboards in Kibana**:

   a. Open Kibana, and go to **`Management`** > **`Integrations`**.

   b. On Integrations page, and click **`Installed integrations`** tab.

   c. Click **`System`** integration.

   d. Click **`Assets`** tab.

   e. Click **`[Metrics System] Host overview`**.

   f. You should see a dashboard like this:

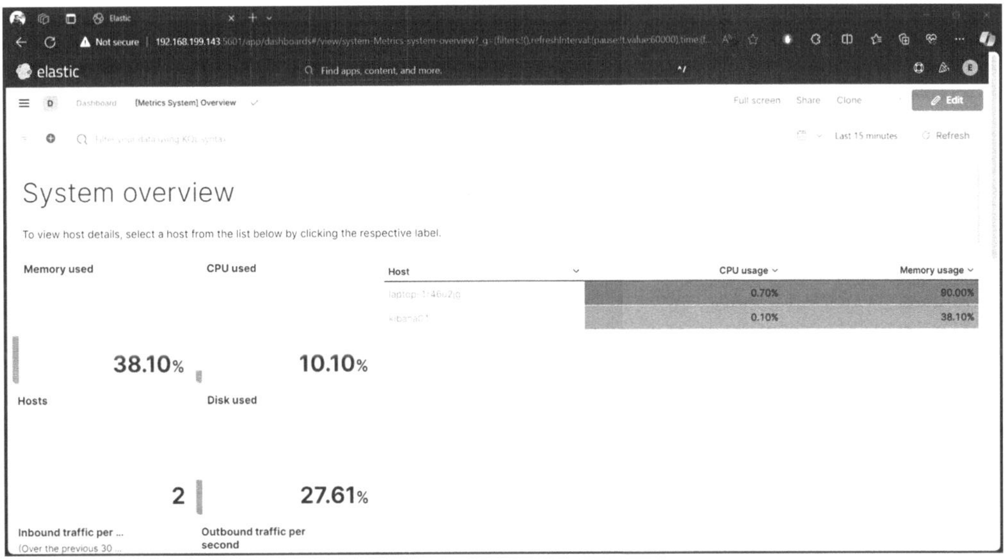

***Figure 3.15**: System Integration Dashboard*

g. Click your Windows hostname.

h. After that, you should see a dashboard from the Windows.

i. You also can explore other dashboards on **`Assets`** tab.

j. We can find all dashboards on **`Dashboards`** menu.

3. **Uninstall Elastic Agent**:

a. Open PowerShell as Administrator.

b. Navigate to **`C:\Program Files\Elastic\Agent\`**.

c. You can uninstall Elastic Agent using the following command:

```
.\elastic-agent.exe uninstall
```

If **`C:\Program Files\Elastic\Agent\`** folder was not deleted, you can delete it manually.

4. **Uninstall Integrations**:

a. After all Elastic Agents were uninstalled, we can uninstall integrations.

b. Open Kibana, and go to **`Management`** > **`Integrations`**.

c. On the Integrations page, click **`Installed integrations`** tab.

d. Click **`System`** integration.

e. Click **`Integration policies`** tab.

f. Click **Delete integration** button on the right side.

g. You also can delete all system assets. Click **Uninstall System** on **Settings** tab.

h. If you want to delete all dashboards, you can delete all dashboards on **Dashboards** menu.

Troubleshooting and Best Practices

This guide will provide insights into common issues and their solutions, along with the best practices to enhance the effectiveness of Elastic Agent.

Troubleshooting Elastic Agent

- **Connectivity Issues:**
  - **Symptom**: Elastic Agent is not communicating with Elasticsearch or Kibana.
  - **Solution**: Check network connectivity, validate Elasticsearch and Kibana URLs in the agent configuration, and ensure correct authentication credentials.
- **Data Ingestion Problems**:
  - **Symptom**: Elastic Agent is not sending data or data is missing.
  - **Solution**: Verify the configuration of data sources and integrations. Check the log files for any errors related to data collection or shipping.
- **Agent Not Responding:**
  - **Symptom**: The agent is unresponsive or not updating its status in Kibana.
  - **Solution**: Check the host system for resource constraints. Review the agent logs for any critical errors, and restart the agent, if necessary.
- **Integration-Specific Issues:**
  - **Symptom**: Problems with specific Beats integrations like Filebeat or Metricbeat.
  - **Solution**: Validate integration configurations, and ensure compatibility with the data source. Check for any known issues in the Elastic forums or documentation.
- **Upgrade Issues:**
  - **Symptom**: Problems after upgrading Elastic Agent or the Elastic Stack.
  - **Solution**: Ensure that all the components of the Elastic Stack are compatible. Review upgrade logs for any errors, and follow the official Elastic upgrade guides.

Best Practices for Elastic Agent

- **Regular Updates**: Keep Elastic Agent and the Elastic Stack components updated to the latest version for new features, performance improvements, and security patches.
- **Centralized Management**: Use Fleet for centralized management of agents. This approach simplifies deployment, configuration, and monitoring of agents across multiple hosts.
- **Policy Management**: Organize and manage policies effectively in Fleet. Ensure that policies are appropriately applied to the right group of agents for efficient data collection and security enforcement.
- **Resource Monitoring**: Monitor the resource usage of Elastic Agent on the host systems. Adjust resource allocation and agent configurations to prevent performance degradation.
- **Security Practices**: Secure communication channels between Elastic Agent, Elasticsearch, and Kibana. Use encryption and authentication methods to safeguard data.
- **Documentation and Community Support**: Leverage Elastic's extensive documentation and community forums for additional support and best practices.
- **Testing Configurations**: Before deploying configurations to production, test them in a controlled environment to ensure that they work as expected.
- **Backup and Recovery**: Regularly backup Elastic Agent configurations and policies. Have a recovery plan in place in case of system failures.
- **Scalability Considerations**: Plan for scalability as your data and monitoring needs grow. Ensure that Elastic Agent deployments can handle increased loads.
- **Custom Integration Development**: If developing custom integrations, follow Elastic's guidelines to ensure compatibility and performance.

By following these troubleshooting tips and best practices, you can effectively manage Elastic Agent in your environment, ensuring reliable data collection, enhanced security, and overall system health.

Web Crawler

In this section, we will learn about web crawling with Elastic. We will discuss the basics of web crawling, its key components, and how it can be implemented with Elastic. We will also explore the configuration and customization of web crawling with Elastic, along with its use cases and challenges.

Introduction to Web Crawling with Elastic

Web crawling is a vital technique in the realm of data collection and analysis, and Elastic, with its robust search and analysis capabilities, offers a powerful platform for implementing web crawlers. This introduction covers the basics of web crawling with Elastic, exploring its components, functionalities, as well as how it can be utilized effectively.

Web crawling involves systematically browsing the internet to collect data from websites. This data is then used for various purposes such as indexing for search engines, data analysis, and more. In the context of Elastic, web crawling can be a part of an extensive data ingestion and analysis pipeline.

Key Components of Elastic for Web Crawling

- **Elasticsearch**: At the heart of Elastic's capabilities is Elasticsearch, a search and analytics engine. It stores and indexes data collected by the web crawler.
- **Kibana**: Kibana serves as the visual interface for Elasticsearch. It allows users to manage their crawling projects, and visualize the collected data.
- **Beats**: Filebeat, one of the Elastic Beats, can be used for ingesting log files generated by web crawlers.
- **Logstash**: For more complex data processing needs, Logstash can transform and enrich the data, before it is indexed in Elasticsearch.

Setting Up a Web Crawler with Elastic

Elastic Web Crawler is a part of Elastic Enterprise Search. This feature is specifically designed to crawl, index, and search website content, making it more accessible and searchable through Elasticsearch.

However, the Elastic Web Crawler is not part of the open-source Elasticsearch package. It is included in the Elastic Enterprise Search solution which is a commercial offering from Elastic. While Elastic provides basic versions of some of their products under a free tier, the complete functionalities of Elastic Enterprise Search, including the Web Crawler, typically fall under their subscription or commercial license.

For open-source alternatives, or to implement web crawling with Elasticsearch, you might consider:

- **Building a Custom Crawler**: You can create a custom web crawler using open-source tools (like Scrapy for Python) and then ingest the data into Elasticsearch using Logstash, Filebeat, or a custom ingestion pipeline.
- **Third-Party Open-Source Crawlers**: There are several open-source web crawlers available that can be integrated with Elasticsearch. For instance,

Apache Nutch is a highly extensible and scalable open-source web crawler software project.

- **Community Plugins**: Some community-developed plugins or projects might offer web crawling capabilities compatible with open-source Elasticsearch.

In summary, while Elastic's Web Crawler itself is not available in the open-source version of Elasticsearch, there are various methods and tools that can be used to achieve similar functionality with the open-source Elasticsearch stack.

Use Cases of Web Crawling with Elastic

- **Search Engine Indexing**: Building a search index for a custom search engine.
- **Market Research**: Collecting data about products, prices, and reviews from e-commerce sites.
- **Content Aggregation**: Aggregating content from multiple sources for news, blogs, and so on.
- **SEO Analysis**: Analyzing websites for SEO optimization purposes.

Data Connectors

In this section, we will learn about pre-built data connectors in Elastic. We will discuss the key features of these connectors, their common types, and how they can be utilized effectively. We will also explore the process of setting up data connectors in Elastic.

Understanding Pre-built Connectors

Elastic, known for its powerful search and analytics capabilities, offers a range of pre-built data connectors that simplify the process of ingesting data from various sources into the Elastic Stack. Understanding these pre-built connectors is crucial for leveraging Elastic's full potential in data analysis, search, and observability. This content provides an overview of Elastic's pre-built connectors, their functionalities, and how they can be utilized effectively.

Pre-built connectors in Elastic are ready-to-use integrations that allow users to easily connect and ingest data from a variety of external data sources into Elasticsearch. These connectors are designed to simplify the data ingestion process, making it more efficient and less time-consuming.

Key Features of Pre-built Connectors

- **Diverse Data Source Support**: Elastic's connectors support a wide range of data sources, including cloud services, databases, applications, and much more. This versatility is crucial for organizations dealing with diverse data ecosystems.

- **Easy Configuration**: Connectors are designed for ease of use, with simple configuration steps that often involve just a few clicks in Kibana.
- **Real-Time Data Sync**: Many connectors offer real-time data synchronization, ensuring that the data in Elasticsearch is always up-to-date with the source.
- **Scalability and Efficiency**: Elastic's connectors are built to handle large volumes of data efficiently, and scale as your data needs grow.
- **Security and Compliance**: Data transferred via these connectors is handled securely, adhering to the best practices and compliance standards.

Common Types of Pre-built Connectors

- **Log and Metric Data Connectors**: For ingesting logs, metrics, and telemetry data from various monitoring tools and platforms.
- **Database Connectors**: To synchronize data from relational and NoSQL databases into Elasticsearch.
- **Cloud Service Connectors**: Designed for cloud-based services such as AWS, GCP, and Azure, enabling the ingestion of logs and metrics from cloud environments.
- **Application and Service Connectors**: Connectors for popular applications and services such as Salesforce, Slack, GitHub, and more, allowing for the integration of business and operational data.

Utilizing Pre-built Connectors

- **Data Integration and Analysis**: Use connectors to feed data into Elasticsearch for search, analysis, and visualization in Kibana.
- **Observability and Security**: Leverage connectors for observability solutions in Elastic, enabling comprehensive monitoring across your IT environment.
- **Building Search Experiences**: Use the ingested data to power search experiences in internal and external applications.
- **Streamlining Data Pipelines**: Simplify and streamline your data pipelines by using connectors to eliminate complex data integration processes.

Set Up Data Connectors

Elastic Data Connectors, especially the advanced integrations and connectors offered as part of Elastic's solutions like Elastic Enterprise Search, are typically not available for the open-source version of Elasticsearch. These connectors are often included in the commercial or subscription-based offerings provided by Elastic.

Elastic offers various tiers, including free and paid subscriptions. The advanced data connectors are usually part of their premium features which require a subscription. However, Elastic does provide a set of basic integrations and Beats (like Filebeat, Metricbeat, and so on.) that can be used with the open-source version of Elasticsearch to facilitate data ingestion from various sources.

For users of the open-source Elasticsearch, integrating with various data sources often involves:

- **Using Elastic Beats**: Elastic Beats are lightweight, single-purpose data shippers that are open source, and can be used with Elasticsearch. They include Filebeat for log files, Metricbeat for metrics, Packetbeat for network data, and many more.
- **Custom Integration Development**: Developing custom scripts or applications to send data to Elasticsearch. This can be done using Elasticsearch's RESTful API.
- **Third-Party Tools**: Leveraging other open-source tools or platforms that can integrate with Elasticsearch. For example, Logstash (also part of the Elastic Stack) is an open-source server-side data processing pipeline that ingests data from multiple sources simultaneously, transforms it, and then sends it to a "**`stash`**" like Elasticsearch.
- **Community Contributions**: Exploring plugins and integrations developed by the community that may offer connectivity to different data sources for open-source Elasticsearch.
- It is important to check the current Elastic licensing and product offerings for the latest information, as the availability and features of Elastic products can change over time.

API Integrations

In this section, we will learn about API integrations in Elastic. We will discuss the basics of Elastic Stack APIs, their common types, and how they can be utilized effectively. We will also explore the process of setting up API integrations in Elastic.

Basics of Elastic Stack APIs

The Elastic Stack, comprising Elasticsearch, Logstash, Kibana, and Beats, is known for its powerful search and analytics capabilities. A key component of its functionality is the extensive set of APIs it offers. These APIs allow for the interaction with the Elastic Stack in various ways, from data ingestion and querying to managing clusters and visualizing data. Understanding the basics of these APIs is crucial for anyone looking to harness the full potential of the Elastic Stack.

Working with Elasticsearch APIs

- **RESTful Interface**: Elasticsearch's APIs are exposed over a RESTful interface, where actions can be performed using standard HTTP methods (`GET`, `POST`, `PUT`, and `DELETE`).
- **JSON Over HTTP**: Interactions with the API generally involve sending JSON-formatted requests, and receiving JSON responses.
- **Common Operations**:
  - Indexing Documents: Adding data to Elasticsearch.
  - Searching: Retrieving data based on queries.
  - Aggregations: Summarizing or analyzing data.
  - Index Management: Creating or modifying indices.

Using Kibana APIs

- **Automating Kibana Tasks**: Use APIs to automate tasks like creating dashboards or migrating saved objects from one environment to another.
- **Integration with External Tools**: Integrate Kibana features with external applications or tools using these APIs.

Best Practices for API Integration

- **Security Considerations**: Secure your API usage, especially when exposing Elasticsearch to public networks. Use features such as API keys, role-based access control, and encryption.
- **Version Compatibility**: Ensure compatibility between the client's API version and the Elastic Stack version, you are using.
- **Performance and Scalability**: Be mindful of the performance implications of your API usage. Optimize query performance, and monitor the load on your Elasticsearch cluster.
- **Error Handling**: Implement robust error handling and logging for your API integrations.
- **API Rate Limiting and Throttling**: Be aware of the rate limits, and consider implementing throttling to maintain the stability of your Elastic Stack environment.

The APIs provided by the Elastic Stack are powerful tools for data manipulation, searching, visualization, and cluster management. A strong grasp of these APIs is essential for developers and administrators looking to fully utilize the capabilities of the Elastic Stack. Hence, whether it is for integrating Elasticsearch with your application, automating Kibana dashboard creations, or managing Logstash pipelines, understanding these APIs opens up a world of possibilities for efficient and effective data management.

Hands-On Lab: CRUD Operations with Elasticsearch API

Creating a hands-on lab for performing CRUD (Create, Read, Update, and Delete) operations using the Elasticsearch API is a great way to gain practical experience with Elasticsearch's fundamental capabilities.

This lab demonstrates the basic CRUD operations in Elasticsearch using its RESTful API with additional complexity of SSL self-signed certificates and basic authentication. Handling secure connections and authentication are essential skills for working with protected Elasticsearch instances in a real-world environment.

Objective

Learn to perform CRUD operations on documents within an Elasticsearch index, using its RESTful API with basic authentication and a self-signed SSL certificate.

Requirements

- Access to an Elasticsearch instance with SSL (HTTPS) enabled and using a self-signed certificate.
- Basic authentication credentials (username and password) for Elasticsearch.
- **`curl`** or a similar HTTP client capable of handling insecure requests and basic authentication.

Setup Steps

1. Verify Elasticsearch Setup:

    a. Ensure that your Elasticsearch instance is operational and accessible over HTTPS. The instance should be configured with basic authentication, and a self-signed SSL certificate.

    b. First, verify that Elasticsearch is running and accessible over HTTPS by sending a **`GET`** request to the root endpoint:

    ```
    curl --insecure -u username:password -X GET
    "https://localhost:9200/"
    ```

    c. Change **`username`** and **`password`** with your Elasticsearch username and password.

   d. You should receive a response with the Elasticsearch version, and other details.

2. **Create or Choose an Index**:

   a. Use an existing index or create a new one with a command like:

```
      curl --insecure -u username:password -X PUT "https://
localhost:9200/my_index" -H 'Content-Type: application/json'
-d'{}'
```

Lab Exercises

1. **Create (Index) a Document**:

   a. Add a document to your index, using the **PUT** or **POST** method.

   b. Example with **PUT**:

```
      curl --insecure -u username:password -X PUT
"https://localhost:9200/my_index/_doc/1" -H 'Content-Type:
application/json' -d'
      {
        "title": "Elasticsearch Basics",
        "description": "Introduction to CRUD operations",
        "tags": ["Elasticsearch", "CRUD", "API"]
      }'
```

2. **Read (Search for) a Document**:

   a. Retrieve the document using the **GET** method:

```
      curl --insecure -u username:password -X GET
"https://localhost:9200/my_index/_doc/1"
```

3. **Update a Document**:

   a. Modify an existing document using the **POST** method with the update endpoint.

   b. Example:

```
      curl --insecure -u username:password -X POST
"https://localhost:9200/my_index/_doc/1" -H 'Content-Type:
application/json' -d'
      {
        "doc": { "tags": ["Elasticsearch", "CRUD", "API",
"Updated"] }
      }'
```

4. **Delete a Document**:

   a. Remove a document using the **DELETE** method.

   b. Example:

```
curl --insecure -u username:password -X DELETE "https://localhost:9200/my_index/_doc/1"
```

Advanced Features and Bulk Operations

Elasticsearch offers a plethora of advanced features and capabilities through its API, allowing for efficient management and manipulation of large datasets. Among these, bulk operations are particularly powerful, enabling the processing of multiple create, read, update, and delete (CRUD) operations in a single API request. This efficient approach is crucial for handling large volumes of data quickly and effectively.

Understanding Bulk Operations

Bulk operations in Elasticsearch allow you to perform multiple indexing or deletion operations in a single API call. This is significantly faster than issuing individual requests for each operation, especially when dealing with large datasets.

Key Features of Bulk API

- **Efficiency and Speed**: Process large numbers of documents in a single request, reducing network overhead, and increasing throughput.
- **Flexibility**: Mix different types of operations (index, update, delete) within a single bulk request.
- **Error Handling**: The bulk API returns information about each operation, making it easy to identify and handle any errors.

Sample Bulk Operation Using curl

Here is an example of how to use the bulk API with curl to perform multiple operations:

1. **Prepare Your Data**: Create a file named **bulk_data.json** containing the data for the bulk operations. Each operation's metadata and source must be on separate lines. For example:

```
{ "index" : { "_index" : "test_index", "_id" : "1" } }
{ "title": "Document 1", "content": "Elasticsearch bulk API" }
{ "index" : { "_index" : "test_index", "_id" : "2" } }
{ "title": "Document 2", "content": "Bulk data import" }
{ "delete" : { "_index" : "test_index", "_id" : "3" } }
```

2. **Perform the Bulk Operation**:

    a. Use **curl** to send this data to the bulk API endpoint:

    ```
    curl --insecure -u username:password -X POST
    "localhost:9200/_bulk" -H 'Content-Type: application/json'
    --data-binary @bulk_data.json
    ```

    b. Change **username** and **password** with your Elasticsearch username and password.

    c. This request will index two documents and delete one (if it exists) in the **test_index** index.

    d. Retrieve the document using the **GET** method:

    ```
    curl --insecure -u username:password -X GET
    "https://localhost:9200/test_index"
    ```

Advanced API Features

- **Search API Enhancements**: Elasticsearch's search API supports advanced features such as aggregation for data summarization, highlighting for emphasizing search terms, and suggesters for auto-complete suggestions.
- **Query DSL**: The Elasticsearch Query DSL (Domain Specific Language) allows for the creation of complex and precise queries to retrieve and manipulate data.
- **Scripting**: Use scripting (example, Painless scripts) for advanced data processing like custom scoring, on-the-fly document transformations, and complex update operations.
- **Machine Learning Integration**: For Elastic Stack users with appropriate licenses, Elasticsearch offers machine learning features for anomaly detection, and forecasting directly accessible via API.
- **Snapshot and Restore**: The API also allows for taking snapshots of your indices and restoring them which is crucial for backup and disaster recovery strategies.

Notes

- **Error Checking**: Always check for errors in the response of a bulk request, and handle them appropriately.
- **Optimal Sizing**: Experiment with the size of your bulk requests to find the optimal balance between performance and resource usage.
- **Rate Limiting**: Be mindful of the impact of bulk requests on your Elasticsearch cluster, and implement rate limiting, if necessary to maintain cluster health.

The Elasticsearch API's advanced features and bulk operations are essential tools for managing and querying large datasets efficiently. Understanding and utilizing these capabilities can significantly enhance your ability to interact with, and leverage Elasticsearch in various complex data handling scenarios.

Securing and Monitoring Your API Calls

Effectively securing and monitoring API calls is crucial in managing an Elasticsearch cluster, especially when dealing with sensitive data, and ensuring the integrity and availability of your services. Implementing robust security measures, and monitoring strategies not only protects your data but also provides insights into API usage patterns, potential issues, and performance bottlenecks. Here is an overview of how to secure and monitor API calls in Elasticsearch.

Securing API Calls

Here are some key practices for securing API calls in Elasticsearch:

- **Authentication and Authorization:**
    - Use Elasticsearch's built-in security features to enforce authentication. Basic authentication, API keys, and Role-Based Access Control (RBAC) are the key methods.
    - Define roles and privileges to control what actions users and applications can perform.
- **Secure Communication:**
    - Encrypt data in transit using SSL/TLS. This is crucial to protect the sensitive data and credentials from being intercepted.
    - Configure Elasticsearch to use HTTPS for all communications.
- **Audit Logging:**
    - Enable audit logging in Elasticsearch to track security-related events such as successful and failed authentication attempts, and changes to the security configuration.
    - Regularly review audit logs for suspicious activities.
- **API Key Management:**
    - Use API keys for service-to-service authentication. They are more secure and flexible compared to basic authentication.
    - Regularly rotate and revoke API keys to minimize security risks.

Monitoring API Calls

- **Elasticsearch Monitoring Features:**
    - Utilize the monitoring features in Elasticsearch and Kibana to keep an eye on cluster health, performance, and API usage.
    - Monitor key metrics such as response times, error rates, and throughput.
- **Logging and Log Analysis**:
    - Log API requests and responses. Consider including details such as endpoint, query parameters, user identity, and response time.
    - Use tools like Logstash and Kibana for log aggregation and analysis to gain insights into API usage patterns, and identify anomalies.
- **Performance Monitoring:**
    - Use the Elasticsearch `_cat` and `_cluster` APIs to monitor the performance and health of the cluster.
    - Set up alerts for abnormal conditions such as high response time, resource saturation, or a spike in error rates.
- **Third-Party Monitoring Tools:**
    - Integrate with third-party monitoring solutions for advanced analytics, alerting, and visualization capabilities.

Notes

- **Regularly Update Security Settings**: Keep up with the latest security patches and updates for Elasticsearch.
- **Limit API Exposure**: Expose APIs only to necessary networks and users. Consider using a VPN or firewall to restrict access.
- **Backup and Disaster Recovery**: Regularly backup your Elasticsearch cluster, and have a disaster recovery plan in place.
- **Capacity Planning**: Monitor your usage and plan for capacity to ensure your Elasticsearch cluster can handle the load, without performance degradation.

Securing and monitoring API calls in Elasticsearch is a multi-faceted approach that involves implementing robust security practices, auditing, and comprehensive monitoring. By adhering to these practices, you can ensure that your Elasticsearch environment remains secure, performant, and reliable, enabling you to leverage its full capabilities with confidence.

Elastic Language Clients

In this section, we will learn about Elastic language clients. We will discuss the key features of these clients, their common types, and how they can be utilized effectively. We will also explore the process of setting up Elastic language clients.

Overview of Official Elastic Language Clients

Elasticsearch, as a part of the Elastic Stack, provides powerful search and analytics capabilities, and is widely used in various applications. To facilitate the integration of Elasticsearch into different development environments, Elastic offers several official language clients. These clients are designed to work seamlessly with Elasticsearch, providing developers with robust, native libraries in their preferred programming languages. Here is an overview of some of the official Elastic language clients available:

Key Official Elastic Language Clients

- **Elasticsearch-Py (Python Client):**
    - A Pythonic client for Elasticsearch, offering easy integration for Python applications.
    - Supports asynchronous operations, and is compatible with various Python frameworks.
- **Elasticsearch-JS (JavaScript Client):**
    - Designed for Node.js and browser environments, it provides an easy-to-use interface for interacting with Elasticsearch from JavaScript applications.
    - Supports both callbacks and promises, making it adaptable to different coding styles.
- **Elasticsearch-Ruby (Ruby Client):**
    - Offers Ruby developers an idiomatic way to integrate Elasticsearch into their applications.
    - Provides support for various Ruby frameworks, and integrates well with Ruby on Rails.
- **Elasticsearch-Java (Java Client):**
    - A Java client that offers seamless integration with Elasticsearch in Java applications.
    - Provides strong typing and comprehensive Elasticsearch API coverage.

- **Elasticsearch .NET (Nest) and Elasticsearch .Net (C# Clients):**
    - Two distinct clients for .NET framework: Elasticsearch .NET is a low-level client, while NEST is a high-level client that provides a more abstracted view of Elasticsearch.
    - Both are feature-rich and provide support for LINQ queries and object mapping.
- **Elasticsearch-Go (Go Client):**
    - Provides Go developers with an efficient way to interact with Elasticsearch.
    - Supports various Go routines, and is optimized for performance.

Features of Elastic Language Clients

- **Complete Elasticsearch API Coverage**: Clients typically cover the full range of Elasticsearch API capabilities, from basic CRUD operations to advanced features such as aggregations and machine learning.
- **Native Integration**: Designed to feel natural in the host language, offering idiomatic syntax and structures.
- **Asynchronous Support**: Many clients support asynchronous operations, enhancing performance and scalability in applications.
- **Robust and Well-Tested**: These clients are officially supported by Elastic, ensuring robustness and regular updates.
- **Easy Configuration**: Simplified setup and configuration processes to connect to Elasticsearch clusters.
- **Customizable and Extensible**: Allow for customization and extension to meet the specific use cases and integration requirements.

Best Practices for Using Elastic Language Clients

- **Keep Clients Updated**: Use the latest version of the client for new features and security patches.
- **Handle Errors Gracefully**: Implement comprehensive error handling to manage API exceptions and connection issues.
- **Optimize Performance**: Utilize the client's features like connection pooling and request retries for improved performance.
- **Security Practices**: Secure your client-to-cluster communication, using SSL/TLS and proper authentication methods.

- **Resource Management**: Be mindful of resource usage, especially in asynchronous programming environments.

Creating a hands-on lab for implementing CRUD operations in Elasticsearch using the Python client is an excellent way to learn how to interact with Elasticsearch programmatically. In this lab, we will develop a simple Python program that performs basic Create, Read, Update, and Delete operations on documents within an Elasticsearch index. We will use the latest version of the Elasticsearch Python client compatible with Elasticsearch 8.10.x.

Hands-On Lab: CRUD Operations in Elasticsearch Using Python Client

Objective

Develop a Python program to perform CRUD operations on documents within an Elasticsearch index using the Elasticsearch Python client.

Requirements

- Python 3.x installed.
- Elasticsearch 8.10.x running locally or accessible remotely.
- Access to a terminal or command line interface.
- A text editor or Python IDE.

Setup Steps

1. **Install Elasticsearch Python Client**:
    a. Open your terminal or command prompt.
    b. Install the Elasticsearch client for Python using **`pip`**:

    ```
    pip install elasticsearch
    ```

2. **Verify Elasticsearch Connection:**
    a. Make sure your Elasticsearch instance is up and running.
    b. You can check its availability by accessing **`http://localhost:9200`** or your Elasticsearch URL.

Lab Exercise

1. **Create a Python Script**:
   a. Open your text editor or Python IDE.
   b. Create a new Python file named **elasticsearch_crud.py**.
2. **Import Elasticsearch Client**:
   a. At the beginning of your script, import the Elasticsearch client:
   ```
   from elasticsearch import Elasticsearch
   ```
3. **Connect to Elasticsearch**:
   a. Establish a connection to your Elasticsearch cluster:
   ```
   es = Elasticsearch(
      ["https://192.168.199.142:9200"],
      basic_auth=('elastic', 'pass123'),
      ca_certs="http_ca.crt",
   )
   ```
   b. Change the URL, username, and password to match your Elasticsearch instance.
   c. You can obtain the CA certificate **http_ca.crt** from your Elasticsearch instance that located in the **/etc/elasticsearch/certs/http_ca.crt** directory.
4. **Create (Index) a Document**:
   a. Index a new document in an Elasticsearch index (example, **my_index**):
   ```
   doc = {
     "title": "Elasticsearch Basics",
     "description": "Introduction to CRUD operations with
   Elasticsearch",
     "tags": ["Elasticsearch", "CRUD", "Python"]
   }
   res = es.index(index="my_index", document=doc, id=1)
   print("Document indexed:", res)
   ```
5. **Read (Get) a Document**:
   a. Retrieve the document you just indexed:
   ```
   res = es.get(index="my_index", id=1)
   print("Document retrieved:", res['_source'])
   ```

6. **Update a Document**:

   a. Update the existing document:

```
update_script = {
  "doc": {
    "tags": ["Elasticsearch", "CRUD", "Python", "Updated"]
  }
}
res = es.update(index="my_index", id=1, body=update_
script)
print("Document updated:", res)
```

7. **Delete a Document**:

   a. Delete the document from the index:

```
res = es.delete(index="my_index", id=1)
print("Document deleted:", res)
```

8. **Run Your Script**:

   a. Execute the script in your terminal or command prompt:

```
python elasticsearch_crud.py
```

   b. Observe the output for each CRUD operation.

This lab provides hands-on experience in using the Elasticsearch Python client for basic CRUD operations. By completing this exercise, you gain practical knowledge in interacting with Elasticsearch programmatically which is vital for developing applications that leverage its powerful search and analytics capabilities.

Conclusion

Thus, Chapter 3 delved into the multifaceted world of integrations within the Elastic ecosystem, highlighting the extensive capabilities and versatility that Elastic Stack offers. From Logstash's advanced data processing and pipeline management to the streamlined efficiency of Elastic Agent, this chapter has illuminated how each component contributes to a robust and scalable data management strategy. The exploration of Elastic's Web Crawler and Data Connectors underlines Elastic's commitment to offering comprehensive, user-friendly solutions for diverse data collection and integration needs. These tools not only simplify the ingestion process, but also enhance the scope and quality of data analysis.

The discussions on API Integrations and Elastic Language Clients have provided a clear understanding of how Elastic Stack's functionality can be extended and customized through programmatic means. The practical insights into API usage, coupled with detailed overviews of official language clients, equip users with the knowledge to seamlessly incorporate Elastic functionalities into various programming environments. This integration flexibility ensures that Elastic Stack can adapt to a wide array of use cases, from simple data retrieval to complex, large-scale data analytics applications.

Looking ahead, *Chapter* 4 will embark on a "*Deep Dive: Kibana.*" This next chapter promises to unravel the intricacies of Kibana, Elastic's powerful visualization tool. We will explore how Kibana transforms raw data into insightful visualizations, dashboards, and analytics, allowing users to derive meaningful interpretations, and make informed decisions. This exploration will cover everything from basic dashboard creation to advanced features such as machine learning and custom plugin development, providing a comprehensive understanding of how Kibana stands as an integral component of the Elastic Stack.

Points to Remember

When working with Integrations and related technologies, here are some key points to remember:

- **Enable Persistent Queues**: Set **`queue.type`** to persisted in **`logstash.yml`** to enable persistent queues.
- **Configure Queue Location**: Use **`path.queue`** to specify the directory for storing queue data files.
- **Manage Queue Size**: Set **`queue.max_bytes`** to define the total capacity of the queue on disk, considering disk capacity and workload.
- **Checkpoint Frequency**: Adjust **`queue.checkpoint.writes`** to balance between performance and data safety. This setting determines how often checkpoints are created.
- **Page Size in Queue**: Configure **`queue.page_capacity`** to control the size of each page in the queue. Larger pages can improve performance, but might increase memory usage.
- **Disk Space Requirements**: Ensure adequate disk space for the queue directory to avoid Logstash stopping due to a full disk.
- **Performance vs. Data Safety Trade-off**: Frequent checkpointing increases data safety, but may impact Logstash's performance.
- **Increased Memory Usage**: Be aware that persistent queues can lead to higher memory consumption.
- **Recovery Considerations**: Larger queue sizes can lead to longer recovery times in the event of a system crash.
- **Regular Backups**: Consider regular backups of the queue directory for additional data protection.

- **Monitoring and Maintenance**: Regularly monitor the disk space and performance of Logstash, especially when using persistent queues.
- **Test Before Production**: Before implementing persistent queues in a production environment, test the configuration in a controlled setting to understand its impact on your specific use case.
- **Elastic Agent Overview and Configuration**: Discussed the benefits, architecture, deployment, and configuration of Elastic Agent, including its unified data collection approach and integration with other Elastic Stack components like Beats and Endpoints.
- **Web Crawling with Elastic**: Explored Elastic's capabilities in web crawling, including an introduction to Elastic's web crawler, its configuration and customization, handling dynamic websites, and ensuring optimal crawling efficiency as well as data relevance.
- **Elastic Data Connectors**: Covered the concept of pre-built connectors in Elastic, the development of custom connectors, and best practices for data ingestion and transformation.
- **Elasticsearch API Integration**: Delved into the basics of Elastic Stack APIs, CRUD operations with Elasticsearch API, advanced features and bulk operations, as well as securing and monitoring API calls.
- **Official Elastic Language Clients**: Discussed the overview of official Elastic language clients, focusing on Python, Java, JavaScript, and .NET clients, including best practices for client integrations and tips for building custom clients.
- **CRUD Operations in Elasticsearch Using Python Client**: Provided a hands-on lab guide for performing CRUD operations in Elasticsearch using the Python client, adapted for a secure Elasticsearch setup with SSL and basic authentication.
- **Logstash Fundamentals and Advanced Usage**: Addressed Logstash's core concepts, advanced data processing pipelines, plugins, filters, codecs, and handling large datasets for scalability.
- **Securing and Monitoring Elasticsearch API Calls**: Highlighted the importance of securing API interactions with Elasticsearch and best practices for monitoring these calls effectively.

Multiple Choice Questions

1. What is the primary function of Logstash in the Elastic Stack?

   a. Data storage

   b. Data visualization

   c. Data processing and ingestion
   d. Security analysis
2. Which Logstash feature ensures data protection by buffering events on disk?
   a. In-memory queues
   b. Persistent queues
   c. Logstash filters
   d. Codec plugins
3. In a Logstash configuration file, what is the purpose of the **`'grok'`** filter plugin?
   a. To encrypt sensitive data
   b. To parse unstructured log data into a structured format
   c. To duplicate events to multiple outputs
   d. To compress log data for storage
4. Which configuration setting in Logstash determines the maximum size of the persistent queue on disk?
   a. **`queue.type`**
   b. **`path.queue`**
   c. **`queue.max_bytes`**
   d. **`queue.checkpoint.writes`**
5. What does the **`'input'`** section of a Logstash configuration file specify?
   a. The data processing rules.
   b. The destination for processed data.
   c. The source of the incoming data.
   d. The error handling mechanism.

Answers

a. c

b. b

c. b

d. c

e. c

Questions

1. How do persistent queues enhance Logstash's data processing capabilities, and what are the potential challenges associated with their implementation?
2. Explain the role and impact of conditional logic in Logstash configurations, particularly in terms of enhancing data processing efficiency and pipeline complexity.
3. Discuss the significance of pipeline-to-pipeline communication in Logstash for managing complex data processing tasks, and provide examples of scenarios where this feature is particularly beneficial.
4. What are the key considerations and best practices for configuring and managing Logstash in large-scale deployments, especially with respect to handling large data volumes and high throughput?
5. Analyze the impact of queue and buffer settings, such as **`queue.max_bytes`**, **`queue.checkpoint.writes`**, and **`queue.page_capacity`**, on the performance and reliability of Logstash, particularly in high-availability environments.
6. **Discuss the Role and Benefits of Elastic Agent in the Elastic Stack**: Explain how Elastic Agent simplifies data integration and management. Describe its integration with Beats and Endpoints, and its significance in the architecture of the Elastic Stack.
7. **Explain the Functionality of Web Crawling in Elastic and its Challenges**: Describe how Elastic's Web Crawler operates, and discuss the strategies for handling the challenges associated with crawling dynamic websites. Include the aspects of optimizing web crawling for relevance and efficiency.
8. **Explore the Use and Importance of Elasticsearch APIs**: Discuss how CRUD operations are performed using Elasticsearch APIs. Elaborate on the advanced features and bulk operations available in these APIs, and the importance of securing and monitoring API calls.
9. **Analyze the Functionalities and Significance of Logstash in the Elastic Stack**: Describe the core concepts and capabilities of Logstash, its role in advanced data processing pipelines, and the use of plugins, filters, and codecs. Discuss how Logstash handles large datasets and scalability.
10. **Evaluate the Integration of Official Elastic Language Clients with Elasticsearch**: Discuss how the official Elastic language clients (Python, Java,

JavaScript, and .NET) facilitate interactions with Elasticsearch. Highlight the best practices for client integrations and considerations for building customized clients.

Key Terms

Here is a list of key terms that encapsulate the main concepts and tools discussed in this chapter:

- **Persistent Queues**: A Logstash feature that enables the buffering of incoming events on disk to prevent data loss in case of unexpected shutdowns or crashes.
- **Queue Type**: A setting in Logstash configuration (**`queue.type`**) that determines whether to use in-memory or persistent queues.
- **Path Queue**: The **`path.queue`** setting in Logstash configuration, specifying the filesystem path where the persistent queue data files are stored.
- **Queue Max Bytes (`queue.max_bytes`)**: A configuration option in Logstash that sets the maximum size the persistent queue can occupy on the disk.
- **Checkpoint Writes (`queue.checkpoint.writes`)**: This configuration controls the frequency of checkpoints in persistent queues, balancing between performance and data safety.
- **Queue Page Capacity (`queue.page_capacity`)**: Determines the size of each page file within the queue, affecting memory usage and performance.
- **Data Safety**: Refers to the protection of data from loss or corruption, a key consideration when configuring persistent queues.
- **Performance**: In the context of Logstash, it generally refers to the speed and efficiency of data processing and throughput.
- **Memory Usage**: The amount of RAM used by Logstash, particularly important when dealing with large queue sizes or page capacities.
- **Recovery Time**: The time taken by Logstash to become fully operational after a crash, especially relevant for large persistent queues.
- **Disk Space**: The storage capacity required on the disk for Logstash, particularly for storing persistent queue files.
- **Checkpointing**: The process of saving the current state of the queue to disk at regular intervals to ensure data safety.
- **Backups**: Copying and archiving the persistent queue data for additional safety and recovery purposes.
- **Monitoring**: Keeping track of Logstash's performance and resource usage, crucial when using features like persistent queues.

- **Logstash Configuration File (`logstash.yml`)**: The primary configuration file for Logstash where various settings, including those for persistent queues are defined.
- **Elastic Agent**: A unified data collection agent part of the Elastic Stack that simplifies data integration and management.
- **Web Crawler**: A tool used in the Elastic Stack for automated browsing and data collection from websites.
- **Data Connectors**: Pre-built integrations in Elastic that allow for easy data import from various sources.
- **Elasticsearch API**: The RESTful API provided by Elasticsearch for performing operations like search, indexing, and data manipulation.
- **Language Clients**: Official libraries provided by Elastic for interacting with Elasticsearch in various programming languages such as Python, Java, JavaScript, and .NET.
- **CRUD Operations**: Refers to Create, Read, Update, and Delete operations, fundamental to database and Elasticsearch interactions.
- **Secure Sockets Layer (SSL)**: A standard security technology for establishing an encrypted link between a server and a client.
- **Basic Authentication**: A simple authentication scheme built into the HTTP protocol.
- **Logstash**: A data processing pipeline in the Elastic Stack that ingests data from multiple sources, transforms it, and sends it to a "`stash`" like Elasticsearch.
- **Plugins, Filters, and Codecs in Logstash**: Extendable components in Logstash that allow for additional functionality in data processing.
- **Scalability**: The ability of a system, network, or process to handle a growing amount of work or its potential to be enlarged to accommodate that growth.
- **Python Elasticsearch Client**: A Python library for connecting and interacting with Elasticsearch.
- **Hypertext Transfer Protocol Secure (HTTPS)**: An extension of HTTP for secure communication over a computer network.
- **API Security**: Measures and protocols used to protect APIs from misuse and unauthorized access.
- **Bulk Operations**: Features in Elasticsearch that allow processing multiple indexing or deletion operations in a single API call.

CHAPTER 4
Deep Dive: Kibana

Introduction

Kibana, as a cornerstone in the domain of data visualization and analytics, offers a unique blend of features that empower users to transform the raw data into compelling stories. In *Chapter 4, Deep Dive: Kibana*, we immerse ourselves into the intricacies of this versatile tool, unraveling its potential to enhance data interpretation and decision-making processes.

Positioned as an integral component of the Elastic Stack, Kibana excels in real-time data visualization and analysis. This chapter is designed to provide a detailed exploration of Kibana's advanced capabilities, guiding you through its sophisticated features and practical applications.

Structure

In this chapter, we will discuss the following topics:

- Practical Use Cases and Scenarios for Kibana
- Introduction to Kibana Visualization
- Hands-on Lab: Basic Data Visualization Using Kibana
- Developing Custom Visualizations
- Introduction to Vega Visualizations in Kibana
- Hands-on Lab: Hello World in Kibana with Vega and Vega-Lite
- Hands-on Lab: Developing Custom Visualizations
- Overview of Kibana Dashboard
- Advanced Dashboard Design
- Hands-on Lab: Building a Kibana Dashboard
- Using Canvas and Machine Learning Features
- Hands-on Lab: Creating a Simple Canvas in Kibana

- Alerting and Reporting
- Hands-on Lab: Creating Basic Alerts

Practical Use Cases and Scenarios for Kibana

Kibana, as a versatile tool in the Elastic Stack, finds its applications across a broad spectrum of industries and scenarios. Its capability to handle large datasets, and present them through intuitive visualizations makes it invaluable for data-driven decision-making. This section highlights the key use cases and scenarios where Kibana's features are particularly beneficial.

- **Monitoring and Analytics in IT Operations**
  - **Scenario**: Real-time monitoring of network and system performance in a large IT infrastructure.
  - **How Kibana Helps**: Kibana enables IT professionals to create dashboards that provide real-time views of their network and system status. It helps in identifying performance bottlenecks, monitoring server health, and tracking system logs for security analysis.
- **Business Intelligence and Data Analysis**
  - **Scenario**: A retail company analyzing customer data to optimize sales strategies.
  - **How Kibana Helps**: Kibana can be used to visualize sales trends, customer demographics, and buying patterns. Retailers can track the Key Performance Indicators (KPIs), and adjust their strategies based on real-time data insights.
- **Financial Market Analysis**
  - **Scenario**: Tracking and analyzing stock market trends for informed investment decisions.
  - **How Kibana Helps**: Financial analysts can use Kibana to create dashboards that display live market data, historical trends, and predictive analytics. This helps in spotting investment opportunities and risk management.
- **Healthcare Data Visualization**
  - **Scenario**: Hospitals analyzing patient data to improve healthcare services.
  - **How Kibana Helps**: Kibana allows for thc aggregation and visualization of patient data, helping healthcare providers identify patterns, track treatment outcomes, and manage hospital resources effectively.

- **Security and Fraud Detection**
    - **Scenario**: A banking institution monitoring transactions for fraudulent activities.
    - **How Kibana Helps**: Kibana can be integrated with security tools to analyze transaction data in real-time. It helps in detecting unusual patterns indicative of fraud, and triggering alerts for further investigation.
- **Log Analysis and Event Management**
    - **Scenario**: A web service provider analyzing logs for troubleshooting and optimizing user experience.
    - **How Kibana Helps**: Kibana excels in parsing and visualizing large volumes of log data, making it easier to identify errors, user behavior patterns, and system inefficiencies.
- **Environmental Monitoring**
    - **Scenario**: Monitoring environmental data such as air quality or weather patterns.
    - **How Kibana Helps**: Environmental scientists can use Kibana to visualize data from sensors, track changes over time, and predict trends, aiding in environmental protection efforts.

The flexibility and power of Kibana make it an indispensable tool in a wide array of domains. By transforming the raw data into actionable insights through its advanced visualization capabilities, Kibana empowers organizations to make informed decisions, and optimize their operations across various scenarios.

Introduction to Kibana Visualization

Kibana, as a powerful data visualization and exploration tool in the Elastic Stack, offers a diverse range of components for visualizing and interpreting data. These components range from simple, intuitive tools like Kibana Lens, to more advanced options such as Time Series Visual Builder (TSVB), and Aggregation-Based Visualizations. This introduction provides an overview of these key components, including Kibana Maps and Custom Visualizations, highlighting their functionalities and use cases. The following *Figure 4.1* shows the visualization options available in Kibana.

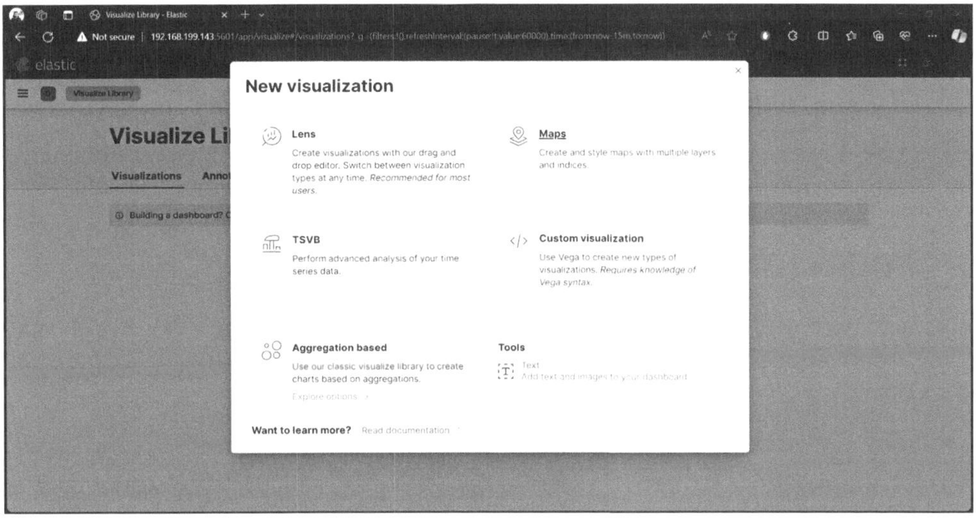

Figure 4.1*: Visualization Options on Kibana*

Kibana Lens

Kibana Lens is a user-friendly visualization tool designed to simplify the process of creating complex visualizations. It offers a drag-and-drop interface that allows users to quickly build visualizations from their data.

- **Key Features:**
  - **Intuitive Interface**: Easy-to-use for beginners and advanced users, alike.
  - **Smart Suggestions**: Provides visualization recommendations, based on the selected data.
  - **Flexibility**: Allows mixing of different types of visualizations in a single view.
- **Use Cases**: Ideal for quick data exploration, and creating visualizations without requiring in-depth knowledge of Kibana's query language.

Time Series Visual Builder (TSVB)

TSVB is a powerful tool for creating time-series data visualizations. It allows for detailed control over the display of time-based data, and includes additional features not found in traditional visualizations.

- **Key Features:**
  - **Advanced Time Series Analysis**: Capable of handling complex time-based data and calculations.

- **Multiple Chart Types**: Supports various chart types, including metrics, gauges, and top N charts.
- **Annotations**: Allows adding annotations for specific time points or events.

- **Use Cases**: Best suited for detailed analysis of time-series data such as monitoring system performance metrics or financial trends.

Aggregation-Based Visualizations

These are the traditional visualizations in Kibana that rely on Elasticsearch aggregations. They include a wide variety of chart types such as bar, line, pie charts, and so on.

- **Key Features:**
    - **Versatility**: Supports a wide range of visualizations.
    - **Aggregations**: Leverages Elasticsearch's powerful aggregation capabilities for summarizing data.
    - **Customizable**: Offers extensive options for customizing and refining visualizations.
- **Use Cases**: Useful for general data analysis tasks, where summarizing and grouping data is essential.

Kibana Maps

Kibana Maps provide geospatial data visualization capabilities, allowing users to visualize and analyze the location-based data.

- **Key Features:**
    - **Layered Approach**: Allows adding multiple layers to maps for rich, complex visualizations.
    - **Geo Data Enrichment**: Supports various forms of geographical data, including points, shapes, and tracks.
    - **Interactive**: Users can interact with the map to explore different aspects of the data.
- **Use Cases**: Ideal for scenarios, where location data is crucial such as tracking vehicle movements, analyzing geographic sales data, or environmental monitoring.

Custom Visualizations

Custom Visualizations in Kibana allow users to create unique visualizations that are not available by default.

- **Key Features**:
  - **Extensibility**: Users can develop their own visualizations using Kibana's plugin architecture.
  - **Integration**: Custom visualizations can be integrated into Kibana dashboards like any other visualization.
  - **Personalization**: Offers the ability to tailor visualizations to specific business or data needs.
- **Use Cases**: Suitable, when specific visualization needs cannot be met by the existing Kibana components, or when there is a requirement for branding or unique data representation.

Kibana's visualization components offer a wide range of functionalities to suit different data analysis needs. From the simplicity and intuitiveness of Kibana Lens to the detailed control offered by TSVB, and the geographical insights of Kibana Maps, each component plays a vital role in making Kibana a versatile tool for data visualization. Custom Visualizations further extend this capability, ensuring that Kibana can meet the specific visualization requirements of any use case.

Hands-On Lab: Basic Data Visualization Using Kibana

Creating a hands-on lab for basic data visualization using Kibana involves outlining a step-by-step tutorial that users can follow. This lab will guide users through the process of creating a basic visualization in Kibana. Before starting, ensure that you have Kibana and Elasticsearch installed and running.

Objective

Learn how to create a basic data visualization in Kibana using sample data.

Prerequisites

- Kibana and Elasticsearch are installed and running.
- Access to Kibana's web interface.

Step 1: Accessing Kibana

a. Open your web browser, and navigate to the Kibana interface (usually http://localhost:5601).

b. If your Kibana server is remote, replace localhost with the server's IP address.

Step 2: Loading Sample Data

a. In the Kibana Home page, click on "**`Try sample data`**" as shown in *Figure 4.2*.

b. Select a sample data set (for example, "**`Sample eCommerce orders`**") and load it.

c. Click **`Add data`** button.

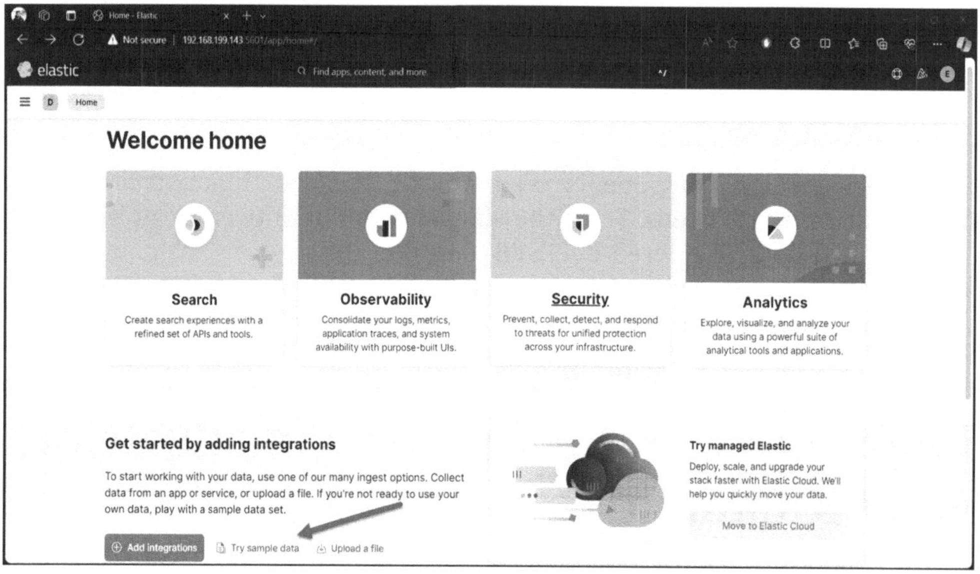

Figure 4.2: *Add Sample Data in Kibana*

Step 3: Creating Your First Visualization

a. Navigate to the **`Visualize Library`** tab in the side menu.

b. After clicking on the **`Visualize Library`** tab, you will be presented with a list of visualizations.

c. Click **`Create new visualization`**.

d. You will be presented with a list of visualization types. For this lab, select **`Aggregation based`**.

e. Then, you have a list of visualization types.

f. For this lab, select a visualization type (for example, **`Line Chart`**).

g. Choose the sample data index (for example, **`Kibana Sample Data eCommerce`**).

h. After selecting the data source, you will be presented with the visualization editor as shown in *Figure 4.3*.

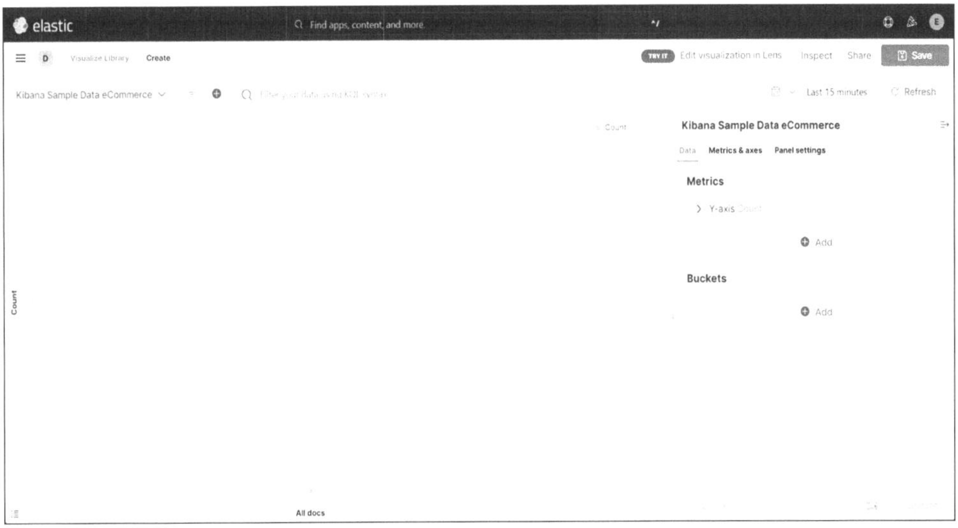

Figure 4.3: *Visualization Editor in Kibana*

i. Configure your visualization:
   - **Metrics**: Set an Aggregation type, like **Average**, and select a field to visualize (example, **`products.price`**).
   - **Buckets**: Choose select X-axis, and then select an Aggregation type (example, **Date Histogram**) as well as select a field (example, **`order_date`**).

j. Click **`Update`** to see the visualization.

k. If you do not see the data, set the time range to **`Last 7 days`**.

l. You should see a line chart similar to *Figure* 4.4.

Figure 4.4: *Line Chart in Kibana*

Step 4: Exploring and Saving the Visualization

a. Experiment with different metrics and buckets to see how they change the visualization.

b. Once satisfied, click **`Save`** at the top.

c. You will be presented with a dialog box.

d. Give your visualization a name, **`My First Visualization`**.

e. Select **`None`** on **`Add to dashboard`**.

f. Click **`Save, and add to library`** button.

g. Now, you can see your visualization in the **`Visualize Library`**.

Additional Exercises

- **Create Different Visualizations**: Try creating other types of visualizations such as Pie Charts, Bar Graphs, or Area Charts.
- **Combine Visualizations in a Dashboard**: Create a new dashboard, and add your visualizations to it.
- **Filter and Search**: Learn to apply filters, and use the search function to refine your visualizations.

Summary

This hands-on lab has introduced you to the basics of creating visualizations in Kibana. You have learned how to load sample data, create a simple line chart, and save your visualization. The skills acquired here form the foundation for more advanced data analysis and visualization techniques in Kibana.

Developing Custom Visualizations

Kibana, known for its robust data visualization capabilities, offers extensive features for developing custom visualizations. This section delves into the process of creating bespoke visualizations in Kibana, guiding users to harness the full potential of their data.

Understanding the Basics

Before diving into custom visualizations, it is crucial to understand Kibana's core components:

- **Data Sources**: Familiarize yourself with the data sources, Kibana can connect to, primarily Elasticsearch indices.

- **Visualization Types**: Explore the variety of built-in visualization types in Kibana, from simple line charts to complex heat maps.

Steps to Develop Custom Visualizations

1. **Identify the Data Source**: Begin by selecting the appropriate Elasticsearch index that contains the data you wish to visualize.
2. **Choose the Right Visualization Type**: Depending on your data and the insights you want to derive, choose a visualization type that best suits your needs.
3. **Customizing Visual Elements**:
   a. **Fields and Metrics**: Select the fields and metrics from your data source that you want to visualize.
   b. **Filters and Queries**: Apply filters and queries to narrow down the data for more specific insights.
   c. **Design and Layout**: Customize the design elements such as colors, labels, and axes to make your visualization intuitive and insightful.
4. **Aggregation and Calculation**: Use Kibana's aggregation capabilities to summarize data such as counting occurrences, calculating averages, or finding maximum values.
5. **Advanced Features**:
   a. **Scripted Fields**: Create scripted fields in Kibana to compute new data values on the fly.
   b. **Custom Queries**: Write custom queries in Elasticsearch's query DSL for more complex data retrieval.
6. **Integration and Interaction:**
   a. **Dashboard Integration**: Integrate your custom visualization into dashboards for a comprehensive view of multiple data points.
   b. **Interactive Elements**: Add interactive elements like filters and controls to allow users to explore data dynamically.

Best Practices for Developing Custom Visualizations

- **Keep It User-Friendly**: Ensure that your visualizations are easy to understand, avoiding overly complex representations.
- **Responsive Design**: Make sure your visualizations are responsive, and render well on different devices.
- **Performance Considerations**: Be mindful of the performance impact, especially when dealing with large datasets or complex queries.

- **Iterative Approach**: Start with a basic visualization, and iteratively add complexity as needed.

Developing custom visualizations in Kibana empowers users to tailor their data exploration and presentation to their specific needs. Thus, by understanding the tools and features available in Kibana, you can create powerful, insightful, and interactive visualizations that bring your data to life!

Introduction to Vega Visualizations in Kibana

Vega is a powerful visualization grammar that allows users to create complex, interactive visualizations. In Kibana, Vega integration offers a level of customization and control beyond the conventional visualization types. This introduction will explore the capabilities of Vega within Kibana, guiding users on how to leverage this tool for advanced data visualization.

Why Vega in Kibana?

- **Customization and Flexibility**: Vega provides a higher degree of customization compared to standard Kibana visualizations. Users can create virtually any graphical representation of their data.
- **Interactive Features**: With Vega, you can build interactive visualizations that respond to user inputs and changes in data, enhancing the user experience.
- **Integration with Elasticsearch**: Vega visualizations in Kibana are fully integrated with Elasticsearch, allowing users to query and visualize data in real-time.
- **Rich Visualization Grammar**: Vega uses a JSON syntax to describe visualizations, offering a rich set of visualization components, including marks, scales, axes, and data transforms.

Getting Started with Vega in Kibana

We will explore the steps involved in creating a Vega visualization in Kibana to understand the process of developing custom visualizations.

- **Access Vega Editor**: In Kibana, Vega visualizations can be created through the Visualize App. Users can start a new Vega visualization, and access the Vega editor.
- **Vega Syntax**: Familiarity with JSON is beneficial as Vega specifications are written in JSON format. Users define data sources, scales, axes, and marks (graphical representations of data), as well as much more.

- **Data Queries**: Vega visualizations in Kibana utilize Elasticsearch queries to fetch data. Understanding Elasticsearch's query language enhances the ability to manipulate data sources.
- **Visualization Design**: Users can design the visual aspects of their chart, including layout, colors, and interactivity. The Vega grammar offers extensive options for customization.

Examples and Use Cases

We will explore some examples of Vega visualizations in Kibana to understand the possibilities of this tool.

- **Complex Chart Types**: Create advanced chart types like heatmaps, tree maps, and custom geo maps that are not available in Kibana's standard visualization library.
- **Dynamic Data Exploration**: Build dashboards with Vega visualizations that include interactive filters, allowing users to explore data dynamically.
- **Combining Multiple Data Sources**: Use Vega to combine data from multiple Elasticsearch indices or external data sources in a single visualization.
- **Custom Interaction Logic**: Implement complex interaction logic such as tooltips, zoom controls, and dynamic data filtering.

Vega in Kibana opens up a realm of possibilities for data visualization, allowing for sophisticated and tailored visual representations of data. Its integration with Elasticsearch makes it a powerful tool for real-time data analysis and exploration. Whether you are a data analyst, a developer, or someone with a keen interest in data visualization, learning Vega can significantly enhance your ability to communicate data insights effectively.

In Kibana, you have the option to use either Vega or Vega-Lite for creating custom visualizations. Both are powerful, but they cater to different needs and skill levels. Understanding the differences between them can help you choose the right tool for your visualization tasks.

Vega in Kibana

- **Complexity and Control**: Vega is a more comprehensive visualization grammar compared to Vega-Lite. It offers greater control and customization over the visualization, allowing for more complex and intricate designs.
- **Interactivity**: Vega provides advanced interactivity features, making it suitable for creating highly interactive and dynamic visualizations.
- **Learning Curve**: Vega's complexity means it generally has a steeper learning curve. It requires a deeper understanding of its JSON syntax and visualization concepts.

- **Flexibility**: With Vega, you can create a wide range of visualizations, including those not possible with Vega-Lite. It is particularly useful for complex data transformations and custom interactions.

Vega-Lite in Kibana

- **Simplicity and Convenience**: Vega-Lite is a higher-level visualization grammar that provides a more concise and easier way to create common visualizations. It is designed to be more user-friendly.
- **Rapid Prototyping**: With its simpler syntax, Vega-Lite is ideal for quickly creating standard visualizations such as bar charts, line charts, and scatter plots.
- **Less Flexibility, But Easier to Use**: While not as flexible as Vega, Vega-Lite is more approachable, especially for those new to JSON-based visualization grammars.
- **Sufficient for Most Use Cases**: For many standard visualization needs in Kibana, Vega-Lite offers sufficient functionality, and is easier to get started with.

Choosing Between Vega and Vega-Lite

- **Complexity of Visualization**: If you need to create a highly complex and interactive visualization, or if you need to perform complex data operations, Vega is the better choice.
- **Ease of Use and Learning Curve**: If you prefer simplicity and quicker results, especially for standard visualizations, Vega-Lite is more suitable.
- **Use Case and Audience**: Consider your audience and the specific use case. For detailed, interactive data analysis, Vega might be necessary. For straightforward data presentation, Vega-Lite often suffices.

Both Vega and Vega-Lite in Kibana are powerful tools that serve different purposes. Your choice depends on the complexity of the visualization you intend to create, and your comfort level with JSON-based visualization grammars. Vega-Lite is generally recommended for those new to Kibana custom visualizations due to its simplicity, while Vega is more suited for advanced users, who need more control over their visualizations.

Hands-On Lab: Hello World in Kibana with Vega and Vega-Lite

This lab will guide you through creating simple, "`Hello World`" visualizations in Kibana using both Vega and Vega-Lite, using predefined data (no external dataset required).

Objective

- Learn the basics of creating Vega and Vega-Lite visualizations in Kibana.
- Understand the differences between Vega and Vega-Lite syntax.

Prerequisites

- Access to Kibana.

Part 1: Hello World with Vega in Kibana

1. **Creating a New Vega Visualization**
    a. Open Kibana.
    b. Navigate to Analytics menu, click "**`Visualize and Analyze`**" > "**`Create visualization`**".
    c. Select "**`Custom visualization`**".
2. **Entering the Vega Visualization Script**
    a. In the Vega editor, erase any existing content and paste the vega script from **`vega.json`** file in chapter 4 source code.
3. **Viewing the Visualization**
    a. Once the script is pasted, the visualization should render a simple bar chart with "**`Hello`**" and "**`World`**" as categories as shown in *Figure 4.5*.
    b. Save your Vega visualization as "**`Demo Vega Visualization`**", and select **None** on **`Add to dashboard`**.

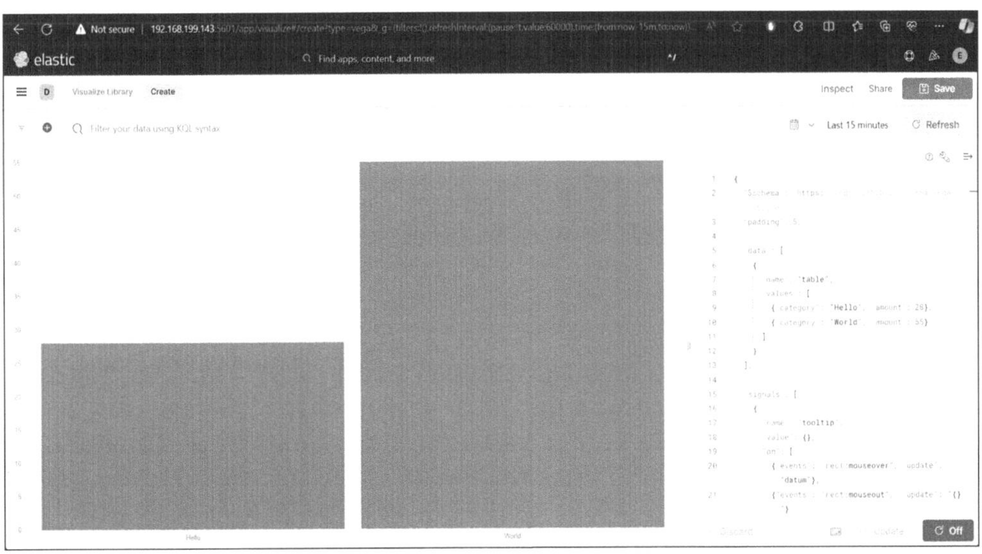

Figure 4.5: *Show Vega Visualization in Kibana*

Part 2: Hello World with Vega-Lite in Kibana

1. **Creating a New Vega-Lite Visualization**
    a. Repeat the same steps as above, but select "**`Vega-Lite`**" this time.
2. **Entering the Vega-Lite Visualization Script**
    a. In the Vega-Lite editor, paste the vega-lite script from **`vega-lite.json`** file in chapter 4 source code.
3. **Viewing the Visualization**
    a. The visualization should now render a bar chart similar to the one created with Vega, showcasing the simpler syntax of Vega-Lite.
    b. Save your Vega visualization as "**`Demo Vega Visualization`**", and select `None` on **`Add to dashboard`**.

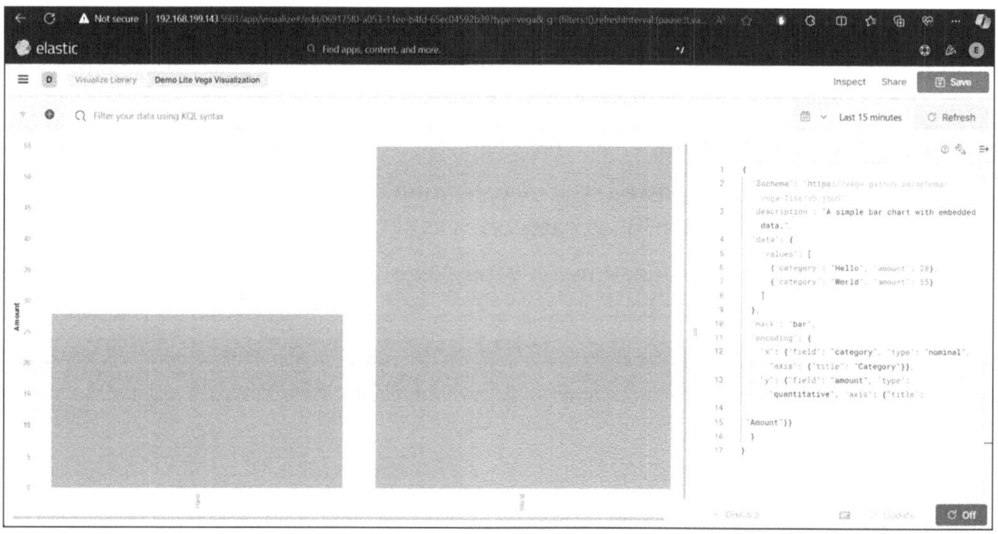

Figure 4.6: *Show Vega Lite Visualization in Kibana*

Summary

In this lab, you have created basic visualizations using both Vega and Vega-Lite in Kibana. This exercise demonstrates the differences in syntax and approach between Vega and Vega-Lite, providing a foundation for more complex visualizations. Vega offers more control and customization, while Vega-Lite allows for quicker and simpler visualization creation.

Hands-On Lab: Developing Custom Visualizations

In this hands-on lab, you will learn how to create custom visualizations in Kibana. You will explore the process of selecting data, applying aggregations, and customizing the appearance of your visualizations. Before starting, ensure that you have Kibana and Elasticsearch installed and running.

Objective

Create a Vega-Lite visualization in Kibana to show the total number of products per category from the **`kibana_sample_data_ecommerce`** dataset.

Prerequisites

- Access to Kibana with the **`kibana_sample_data_ecommerce`** dataset loaded.
- If you do not have the dataset, you can load it from the Kibana Home page. Select "**`Add sample data`**", and choose "**`Sample eCommerce orders`**".

1. **Creating a New Vega-Lite Visualization**
   a. Open Kibana.
   b. Navigate to Analytics menu, and click "**`Visualize and Analyze`**" > "**`Create visualization`**".
   c. Select "**`Custom visualization`**".
2. **Entering the Vega-Lite Visualization Script**

Paste the following Vega-Lite script from **`custom-vega-lite.json`** file in chapter 4 source code into the Kibana Vega editor.

Explanation

- **Data Source**: The script targets the **`kibana_sample_data_ecommerce`** index in Elasticsearch.
- **Aggregation**: It uses a terms aggregation on the **`category.keyword`** field to count the occurrences of each category.
- **Visualization**: It plots a bar chart with categories on the x-axis, and the count of products on the y-axis.

3. **Viewing and Analyzing the Visualization**
   a. After pasting the script, the visualization should render in Kibana, displaying the count of products in each category as a bar chart.

b. Save your visualization as "**`Product Count per Category`**", and select **`None`** on **`Add to dashboard`**.

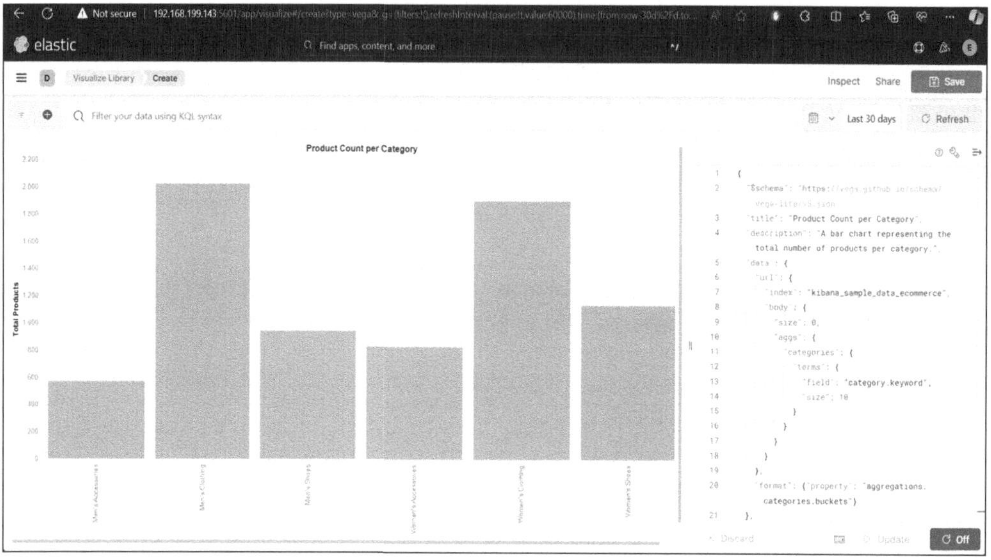

Figure 4.7*: Show Vega Lite Visualization in Kibana*

Summary

You have created a Vega-Lite visualization in Kibana that displays the total number of products per category using the **`kibana_sample_data_ecommerce`** dataset. This example demonstrates how you can leverage Vega-Lite's simplified syntax for effective and quick data visualizations in Kibana. As you become more comfortable with Vega-Lite, you can extend this basic chart with more interactivity, different visual styles, or additional data aggregations.

Overview of Kibana Dashboard

In Kibana 8.x, the "**`Dashboard`**" feature under the Analytics menu is a powerful and flexible tool for creating and organizing visual representations of your data. It allows you to aggregate various visualizations and searches into a single, interactive, and customizable interface. Here is a closer look at the Kibana Dashboard and its capabilities:

- **Unified View**: Dashboards provide a unified view of your data, combining different visualizations such as charts, maps, tables, and more onto a single, interactive canvas.
- **Interactivity**: Users can interact with the data in real-time, applying filters, changing time ranges, and drilling down into specific aspects of the data.

- **Customization**: Dashboards are highly customizable. Users can arrange, resize, and format the visual components to create a tailored view that matches specific analysis needs or presentation styles.
- **Real-time Data**: With the integration of Elasticsearch, the dashboards in Kibana are capable of reflecting real-time data, providing up-to-date insights.
- **Sharing and Collaboration**: Dashboards can be easily shared with team members or external stakeholders. They can be exported as PDFs, shared as links, or embedded in external sites.

Components of a Kibana Dashboard

Here are the key components of a Kibana dashboard:

- **Visualizations**: The core components of dashboards are the visualizations. These can range from simple line charts to complex geo maps, and everything in between.
- **Controls**: Interactive controls such as sliders, dropdowns, or date pickers can be added to dashboards, allowing users to dynamically filter or modify the data displayed.
- **Canvas Workpads**: For more stylized presentations, users can incorporate workpads from Kibana's Canvas feature into their dashboards, blending art with data.
- **Machine Learning**: Integrations with Kibana's machine learning features can provide predictive insights and anomaly detection directly within the dashboard.

Creating and Managing Dashboards

- **Creating**: Dashboards are created by adding and arranging visualizations as well as configuring settings. Users typically start by creating individual visualizations in the Visualize App, and then adding them to a dashboard.
- **Editing**: Dashboards can be edited at any time. Users can add new visualizations, remove the existing ones, or change layout as well as configuration settings.
- **Saving and Loading**: Once created or modified, dashboards can be saved for future access. Users can also load the pre-existing dashboards to continue their analysis, or update them with the new data.

Use Cases for Kibana Dashboards

- **Business Intelligence**: Creating comprehensive overviews of business metrics and KPIs.

- **Operational Monitoring**: Building operational dashboards to monitor IT, network, or infrastructure health.
- **Data Exploration**: Combining various data sources for exploratory analysis or investigative purposes.
- **Reporting**: Regular reporting on sales, marketing, finance, or other departmental data.

Hands-On Lab: Building a Kibana Dashboard

This hands-on lab will guide you through the process of creating a dashboard in Kibana, using the **`kibana_sample_data_ecommerce`** dataset. You will create four different visualizations: A bar chart, a pie chart, a line chart, and a data table. Then, you can add these visualizations to a new dashboard.

Objective

- Learn to create and customize various visualizations, using the **`kibana_sample_data_ecommerce`** dataset.
- Understand how to compile different visualizations into a comprehensive dashboard.

Prerequisites

- Access to Kibana with the **`kibana_sample_data_ecommerce`** dataset loaded.

Step 1: Creating the Visualizations

1. **Bar Chart - Average Product Price per Category**

    a. Navigate to "**`Analytics`**" menu, and click "**`Visualize & Analyze`**" > "**`Create visualization`**".

    b. Select "**`Aggregation based`**".

    c. Choose the type "**`Vertical Bar`**".

    d. Select the **`Kibana Sample Data eCommerce`** index.

    e. Set the Y-axis to the average of **`products.base_price`**.

    f. On Buckets, add the X-axis to the terms of **`category.keyword`**.

    g. Click **`Update`** button to see the visualization.

h. Save the visualization with a meaningful name, for example, "**`Avg Price per Category`**", and select **`None`** on **`Add to dashboard`**.

i. You can see the visualization in *Figure* 4.8.

j. If you do not see the data, set the time range to **`Last 30 days`**.

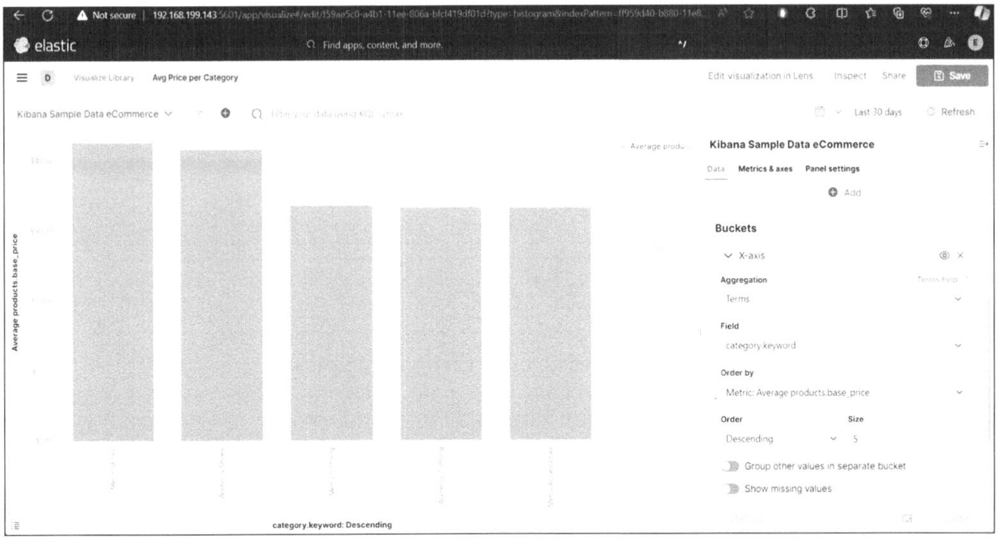

Figure 4.8: *Show Bar Chart in Kibana*

2. **Pie Chart - Order Count by Manufacturer**

   a. Repeat the process to create a new visualization, this time selecting "**`Pie Chart`**".

   b. For slices, click **`Split slices`** on Buckets.

   c. Use the terms aggregation on the **`manufacturer.keyword`** field.

   d. Set the metric to count.

   e. Click **`Update`** button to see the visualization.

   f. Save the visualization, for example, "**`Order Count by Manufacturer`**", and select **`None`** on **`Add to dashboard`**.

   g. You can see the visualization in *Figure* 4.9.

   h. If you do not see the data, set the time range to **`Last 30 days`**.

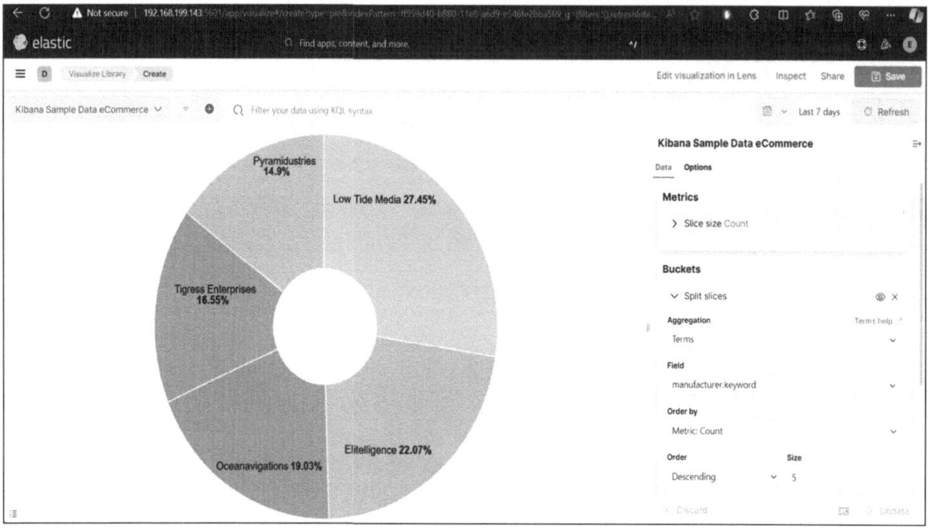

Figure 4.9: *Show Pie Chart in Kibana*

3. **Line Chart - Total Sales Over Time**
    a. Create a new visualization, choosing "`Line Chart`".
    b. Set the Y-axis to the sum of **`taxful_total_price`**.
    c. On buckets, add the X-axis to a date histogram on the **`order_date`** field.
    d. Click **`Update`** button to see the visualization.
    e. Save it as "**`Total Sales Over Time`**", and select **None** on **`Add to dashboard`**.
    f. You can see the visualization in *Figure* 4.10.
    g. If you do not see the data, set the time range to **`Last 30 days`**.

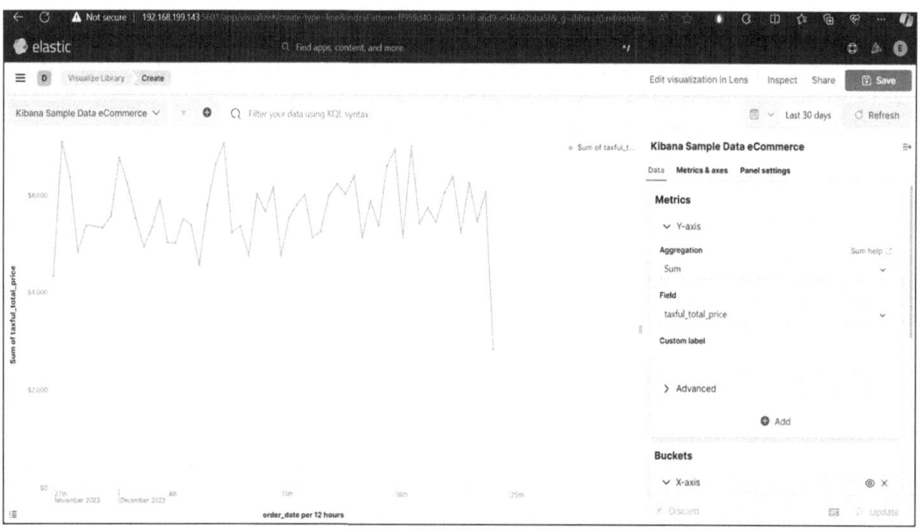

Figure 4.10: *Show Line Chart in Kibana*

4. **Data Table - Top Products by Sales**

   a. Create a new visualization, this time selecting "**`Data Table`**".

   b. For the Metrics, select the sum of **`taxful_total_price`**.

   c. For Buckets, click **`Split rows`**, and choose the terms aggregation on **`products.product_name.keyword`**.

   d. Click **`Update`** button to see the visualization.

   e. Save the visualization as "**`Top Products by Sales`**", and select **`None`** on `Add to dashboard`.

   f. If you do not see the data, set the time range to **`Last 30 days`**, as shown in *Figure 4.11*.

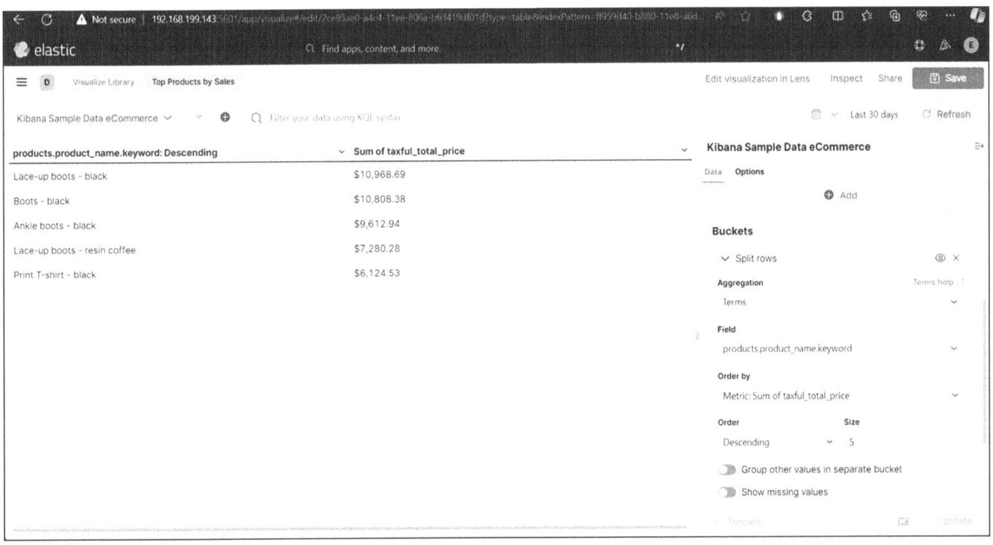

***Figure 4.11**: Show Data Table in Kibana*

Step 2: Creating the Dashboard

1. **Accessing Dashboards**

   a. Navigate to "**`Analytics`**" > "**`Dashboard`**".

2. **Creating a New Dashboard**

   a. Click "**`Create dashboard`**".

   b. Click "**`Add`**" or "**`Add from library`**" to open the list of available visualizations.

3. **Adding Visualizations**

   a. Add the four visualizations, you created earlier: "**`Avg Price per Category`**", "**`Order Count by Manufacturer`**", "**`Total Sales Over Time`**", and "**`Top Products by Sales`**".

4. **Arranging the Dashboard**

   a. Drag and resize the visualizations to arrange them in a way that makes sense for the data story you are telling. You might put "**`Total Sales Over Time`**" prominently at the top, followed by the bar, pie, and data table charts.

5. **Saving the Dashboard**

   a. Give your dashboard a descriptive title such as "**`Ecommerce Insights`**".

   b. Save your dashboard.

   c. You can see the dashboard in *Figure 4.12*.

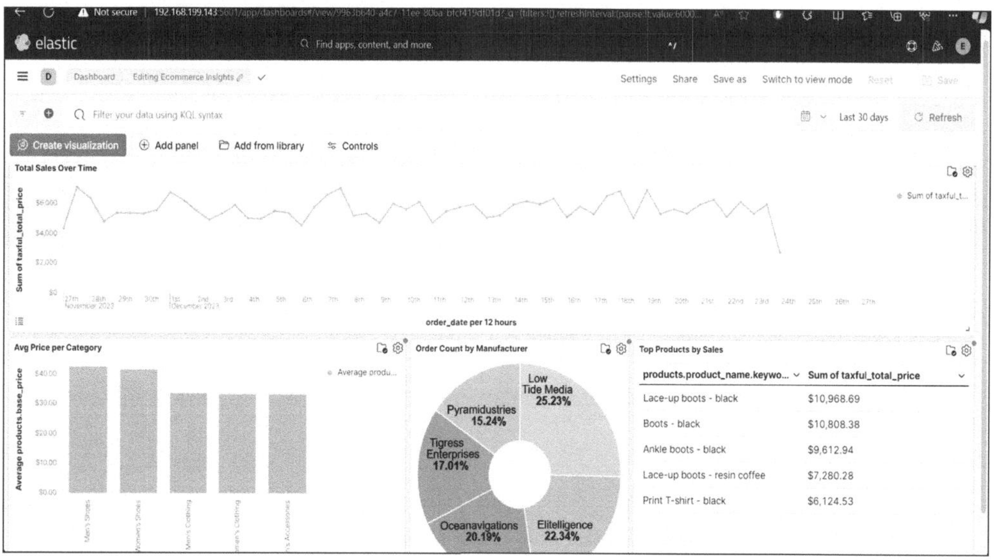

Figure 4.12: *Show Dashboard in Kibana*

Summary

You have now created a multi-faceted Kibana dashboard, using the **`kibana_sample_data_ecommerce`** dataset. It showcases various aspects of the ecommerce data, providing insights into average prices, order distributions, sales trends, and top-selling products. This hands-on lab demonstrates the power of Kibana for visual data exploration and dashboard creation. With these skills, you can continue to explore and visualize your own datasets in meaningful ways.

Using Canvas Features

In this section, we turn our focus to two of Kibana's most innovative features: Canvas and Machine Learning. These tools represent the cutting edge of data visualization and analysis within Kibana, offering users the ability to create visually stunning, live data presentations, and harness powerful machine learning capabilities for predictive insights.

Exploring Canvas in Kibana

Canvas is a feature in Kibana that allows users to create custom and dynamic presentations of their data. It combines live data with an artist's touch, enabling the creation of visually appealing reports and dashboards.

Key Features and Applications

- **Custom Layouts and Styling**: Offers a variety of design options, including custom CSS, for personalized layouts and themes.
- **Real-Time Data**: Integrates live data from Elasticsearch, ensuring presentations are always up-to-date.
- **Rich Media Support**: Allows the inclusion of images, videos, and other media types to enhance storytelling.
- **Expression Language**: Utilizes a powerful expression language for manipulating data, and customizing visualizations.

Use Cases

- Creating high-impact, dynamic business reports.
- Building visually-rich dashboards for presentations and storytelling.
- Displaying complex data sets in an easy-to-understand, engaging format.

Canvas vs. Visualize Library

In Kibana, both Canvas and the Visualize Library are powerful tools for creating data visualizations, but they serve different purposes, and offer unique features. Understanding the differences between Canvas and the Visualize Library is key to selecting the right tool for your specific needs.

Canvas in Kibana

Canvas is a feature in Kibana that allows for the creation of custom, dynamic data presentations. It offers a high degree of artistic freedom and customization.

Key Features

- **Custom Styling**: Canvas provides extensive options for custom styling, including the use of CSS for personalized layouts and themes.
- **Rich Media Integration**: Users can incorporate images, videos, and other media types, making it ideal for storytelling.
- **Real-Time Data**: It integrates live data from Elasticsearch, offering up-to-date presentations.
- **Expression Language**: Canvas uses a unique expression language that allows for advanced data manipulation and customization of visual elements.

Use Cases

- Best for creating highly customized, visually rich reports and presentations.
- Suitable for scenarios where storytelling and visual appeal are priorities.

Visualize Library in Kibana

The Visualize Library is a collection of various visualization types within Kibana, focused on displaying data through standard charts, maps, and diagrams.

Key Features

- **Variety of Visualizations**: Includes a wide range of pre-built visualization types such as bar charts, line charts, pie charts, maps, and so on.
- **Aggregation-Based**: Visualizations in the library are primarily based on Elasticsearch aggregations.
- **Interactive Elements**: Supports interactive elements like filters and controls for data exploration.
- **Integration with Dashboards**: Easily integrates with Kibana dashboards for a comprehensive view of data insights.

Use Cases

- Ideal for standard data analysis and reporting, where traditional visualization types are sufficient.
- Suitable for users, who need to quickly create and integrate various visualizations, without requiring extensive customization.

Comparison

- **Customization**: Canvas offers more customization and styling options, compared to the Visualize Library.
- **Complexity**: Canvas requires a steeper learning curve due to its expression

language and advanced styling options, while the Visualize Library is more straightforward and user-friendly.

- **Data Integration**: Both can integrate live data from Elasticsearch, but Canvas allows for more creative data presentations.
- **Purpose**: Canvas is geared towards creating individual, standalone presentations with a focus on design and storytelling. In contrast, the Visualize Library is designed for creating traditional data visualizations that can be combined into dashboards for analytical purposes.

Choosing between Canvas and the Visualize Library in Kibana depends on the specific requirements of your project. If you need to create highly customized, visually engaging presentations, Canvas is the way to go. However, for standard data visualization tasks, where ease of use and quick integration into dashboards are important, the Visualize Library is more suitable. Both tools offer unique capabilities, and understanding their strengths and limitations will help you make the most effective use of Kibana's visualization features.

Hands-On Lab: Creating a Simple Canvas in Kibana

In this hands-on lab, you will learn how to create a simple Canvas in Kibana. You will explore the process of adding elements, configuring data sources, and customizing the appearance of your Canvas. Before starting, ensure that you have Kibana and Elasticsearch installed and running.

Objective

Learn how to use Kibana's Canvas feature to create a visually appealing and dynamic presentation of live data. In this lab, we will create a simple Canvas that showcases the sales data from the **`kibana_sample_data_ecommerce`** dataset.

Prerequisites

- Access to Kibana with the **`kibana_sample_data_ecommerce`** dataset loaded.
- Basic familiarity with Kibana's interface.

1. **Accessing Canvas and Creating a New Workpad**

    a. Navigate to "**`Analytics`**" > "**`Canvas`**" in Kibana.

    b. Click on "**`Create workpad`**".

c. Give your workpad a name, for example, "`Ecommerce Sales Overview`", and set the desired dimensions for your canvas.

2. **Adding Elements to the Canvas**

    a. **Add a Text Element**: Click "`Add element`" > "`Text`". Add a title to your Canvas, for example, "`Ecommerce Sales Dashboard`". Customize the font size, type, and alignment as desired.

    b. **Add a Chart Element**: Click "`Add element`" > "`Chart`". Choose a chart type that you want to use to represent the data. For simplicity, you can start with a vertical bar chart or pie chart as shown in *Figure* 4.13.

    c. You can add the existing visualizations from the Visualize Library or create new ones directly within the Canvas environment.

3. **Configuring Data Sources and Expressions**

    a. **Connect to the Data Source**: With the chart element selected, link it to the **`kibana_sample_data_ecommerce`** index. Use the expression editor to write or modify the expression to fetch and display data. For instance, you might use an Elasticsearch SQL query to retrieve total sales by product category.

    b. **Customize the Expression**: Adjust the parameters such as aggregation methods or filters to reflect what you want to display, for example, total sales per category.

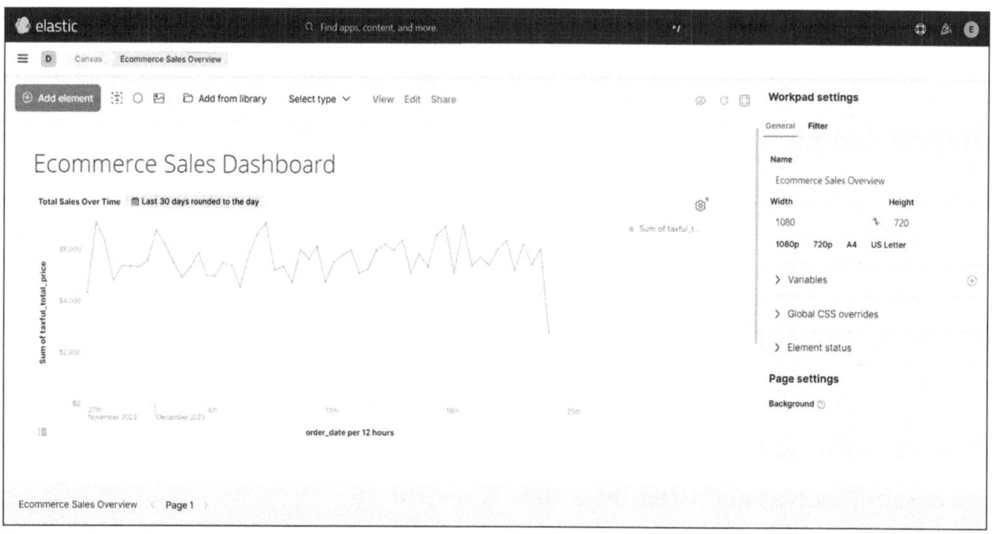

***Figure 4.13**: Add a Chart Element in Kibana*

4. **Styling and Finalizing the Canvas**

    a. **Style Your Elements**: Customize the look and feel of your text and chart elements. Adjust colors, borders, or backgrounds to make the visualizations more appealing.

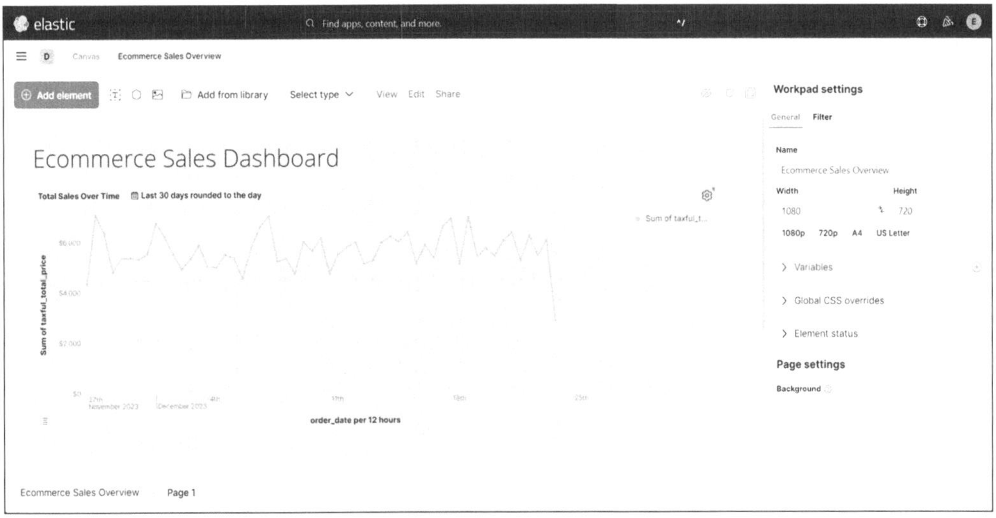

***Figure 4.14**: Style Your Elements in Kibana*

b. **Arrange Your Layout**: Position your elements on the canvas to create a visually coherent and attractive layout.

5. **Previewing and Sharing the Canvas**
   - **Preview**: Click the "`Preview`" button to see how your Canvas looks with live data.
   - **Share**: Once satisfied, you can share your Canvas as a PDF or as a live link. Look for the "`Share`" options within the Canvas environment.

Summary

You have now created a simple yet powerful Canvas in Kibana, showcasing live ecommerce sales data. This exercise demonstrates how Kibana's Canvas can be used to build visually compelling and data-driven presentations. As you become more comfortable with Canvas, you can explore more complex elements, add interactivity, and create even more sophisticated visual narratives. This lab serves as a foundation for endless creative and analytical possibilities.

Alerting and Reporting

This functionality in Kibana is pivotal for businesses and organizations to stay ahead of potential issues, and maintain an informed decision-making process. We will explore how Kibana's alerting and reporting features enable users to monitor their data proactively, and communicate insights effectively.

Understanding Alerting in Kibana

Alerting in Kibana is a feature that allows users to set up automated alerts, based on specific conditions in their data. It is a proactive measure to monitor data for anomalies, trends, or specific occurrences.

Key Features and Configurations

- **Real-Time Monitoring**: Set up alerts that monitor data in real-time, triggering notifications, when predefined conditions are met.
- **Customizable Conditions**: Create complex conditions using Kibana's query language and thresholds.
- **Notification Channels**: Alerts can be configured to send notifications through various channels such as email, Slack, or custom webhooks.
- **Use Cases**: Ideal for scenarios like detecting security breaches, monitoring performance metrics, or tracking business KPIs.

Exploring Reporting in Kibana

Reporting in Kibana refers to the generation of reports, based on visualizations or dashboards which can be shared or automated for regular distribution.

Key Features and Applications

- **Scheduled Reports**: Automate the generation and distribution of reports at regular intervals.
- **Format Flexibility**: Generate reports in various formats like PDF or CSV for easy sharing and analysis.
- **Snapshots and Live Reports**: Create static snapshots or live reports linked to real-time data.
- **Integration with Dashboards**: Directly generate reports from the existing dashboards and visualizations.

Use Cases

- Regularly scheduled business reports for stakeholders.
- Compliance reporting for regulatory requirements.
- Sharing insights across teams, or with clients.

Best Practices for Alerting and Reporting

- **Define Clear Objectives**: Understand the purpose of alerts and reports to set up relevant and meaningful conditions.
- **Balance Sensitivity and Relevance**: Configure alerts to be sensitive enough to catch anomalies but not so sensitive that they generate excessive false positives.
- **Iterative Refinement**: Continuously refine alert conditions and report contents, based on feedback and changing data.
- **Effective Communication**: Ensure that reports are clear, concise, and visually engaging to communicate the desired message effectively.

Alerting and Reporting in Kibana are essential tools for any data-driven organization. These features not only help in keeping a proactive check on data anomalies and trends, but also play a significant role in the effective communication of insights.

Hands-On Lab: Creating Basic Alerts

In Kibana 8.0 and later versions, the alerting framework has been updated to include more features, and a more integrated user experience. This lab will guide you through creating a basic alert, based on the **`kibana_sample_data_ecommerce`** dataset to monitor for large transactions.

Objective

- Learn to create and manage alerts, using the updated Kibana 8.0 or later interface.

Prerequisites

- Access to Kibana 8.0 or later with the **`kibana_sample_data_ecommerce`** dataset loaded.
- Basic understanding of Kibana and Elasticsearch.

Step 1: Accessing the Rules and Connectors UI

a. Click "**`Management`**" in the Kibana side navigation menu.

b. Click "**`Stack Management`**".

c. Navigate to "**`Alerts and Insights`**" > "**`Rules`**" from the Kibana side navigation menu. This is the new centralized location for managing alerts and actions in Kibana 8.0+.

Step 2: Creating a New Rule (Alert)

a. Click on "**`Create rule`**", and choose the appropriate rule type for your alert. For monitoring large transactions, you might use the "**`Threshold`**" rule type under the "**`Index threshold`**" category.

b. Name your rule something descriptive, like "**`High Value Transactions Alert`**".

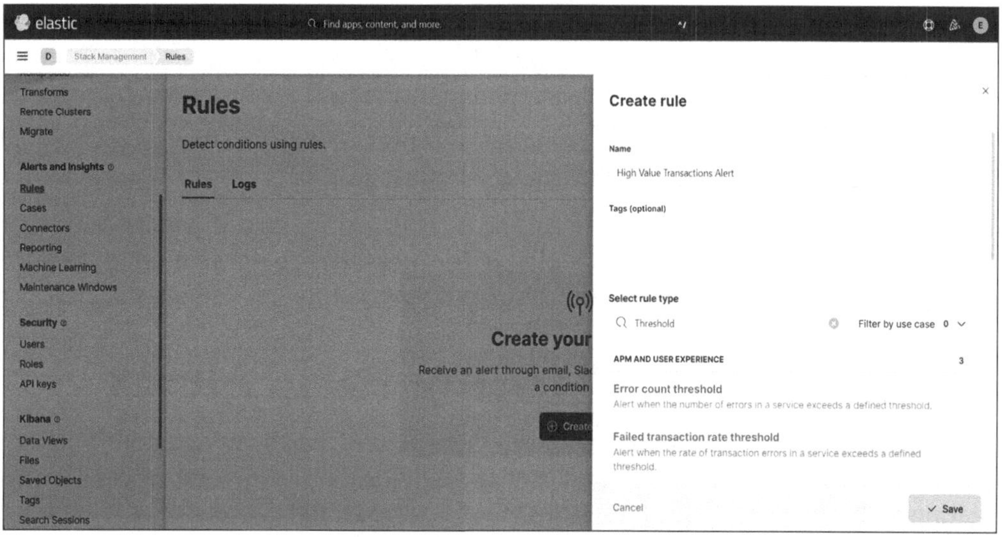

***Figure 4.15**: Create a New Rule in Kibana*

Step 3: Configuring Alert Details and Conditions

a. **Choose the Data Source**: Select the **`kibana_sample_data_ecommerce`** index as the data source for your alert.

b. **Define the Condition**: Set up the condition to trigger the alert. For instance, you might want to trigger the alert when the **`taxful_total_price`** of any transaction exceeds a certain value. Configure the threshold value, aggregation type, and field accordingly.

c. **Set the Time Range and Check Interval**: Define how often Kibana should check for this condition, and the time range of data, it should consider each time it checks.

d. You can see the configuration in *Figure* 4.16.

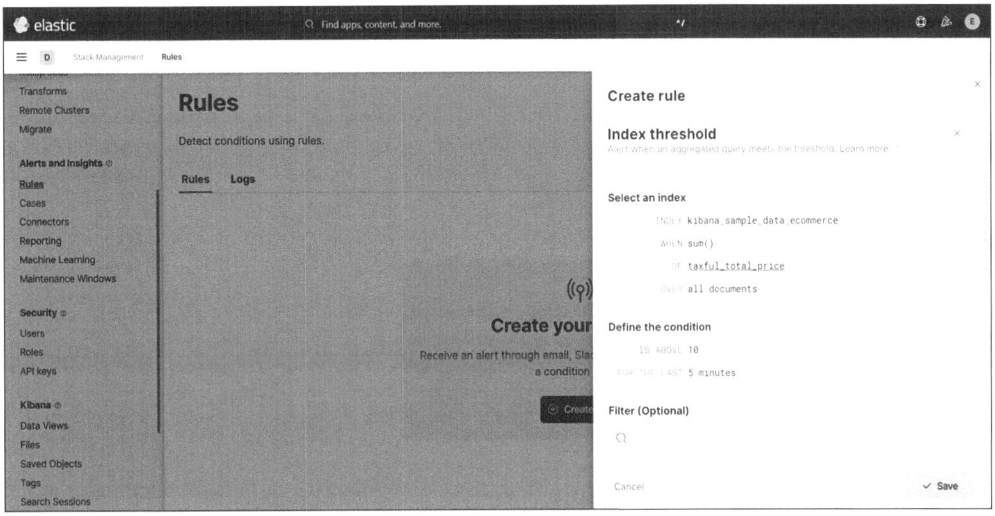

***Figure 4.16**: Configure Alert Details and Conditions in Kibana*

Step 4: Setting Up Actions for Notifications

a. **Choose Action Type**: Click on "**`Add action`**", and select an action type such as sending an email, logging a message, or creating an index. You might need to set up a connector first, if you have not already.

b. Some connectors need licenses to be activated. For example, the email connector requires a Gold license.

c. For instance, we can set up an index action to create a new index called **`my-connector-101`**, and add the transaction details to it.

d. You can create a new index by Dev Tools > Console, and run the following command:

```
PUT /my-connector-101
{
    "settings" : {
        "number_of_shards" : 1
    },
    "mappings" : {
        "properties" : {
            "rule_id" : { "type" : "text" },
            "rule_name" : { "type" : "text" },
            "alert_id" : { "type" : "text" },
            "context_message": { "type" : "text" }
        }
    }
}
```

e. You can see a response from the server.

f. **Configure Action Details**: Provide the necessary details for the action. For example, if sending an email, specify the sender, recipient, and message body. Utilize available context variables to include dynamic information from the alert condition.

g. If we use an index connector, we can add the following message to the index:

```
{
  "rule_id": "{{context.rule.id}}",
  "rule_name": "{{context.rule.name}}",
  "alert_id": "{{alert.id}}",
  "context_message": "{{context.message}}"
}
```

Step 5: Saving and Managing the Rule

a. Review all the details and configurations of your alert, then click "**`Save`**" to activate it.

b. Once saved, your rule will appear in the list under the "**`Rules`**" section, where you can manage it further – enabling, disabling, muting, or deleting as needed.

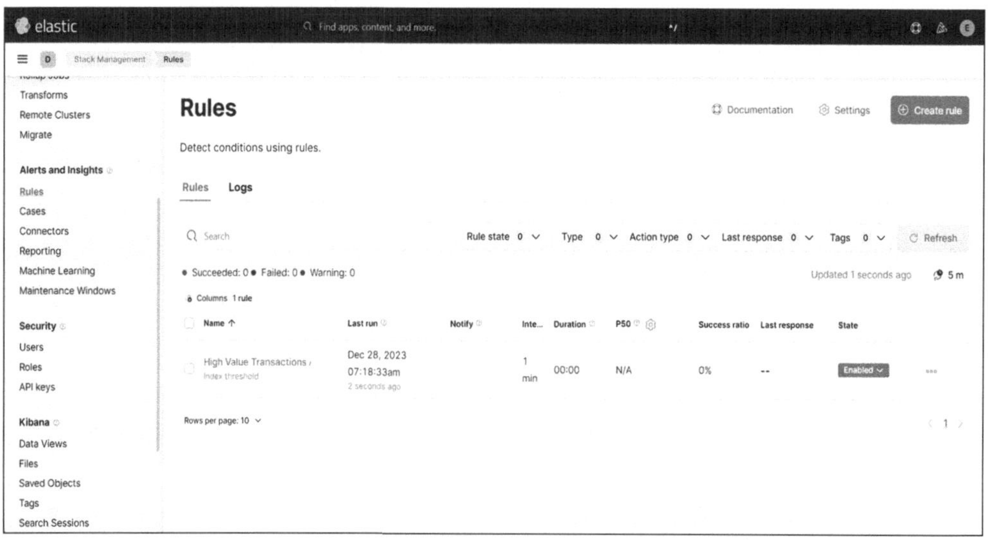

***Figure 4.17**: Manage the Rule in Kibana*

Summary

You have now created a basic alert in Kibana 8.0 or later, capable of monitoring and notifying you about large transactions in the ecommerce data. This lab demonstrates the fundamental concepts and steps involved in setting up and managing alerts in the newer versions of Kibana which are vital for proactive monitoring and response in data-driven operations. As you become more comfortable with the alerting features, you can explore more complex conditions, integrate additional actions, and fine-tune your alerts to suit a wide range of monitoring scenarios.

Conclusion

Throughout *Chapter 4, Deep Dive: Kibana*, we have embarked on a comprehensive journey exploring the multifaceted capabilities of Elasticsearch, and its integral role in data analysis and visualization, particularly within the Kibana ecosystem. We began by understanding the core functionalities of Elasticsearch, recognizing its powerful full-text search capabilities, distributed nature, and real-time data processing. We delved into creating and managing indices, documents, and explored the robust querying capabilities that allow for complex search operations and data retrieval.

As we moved further, we unraveled the intricacies of Kibana, a versatile tool in the Elastic Stack designed for visualizing Elasticsearch data. We learned about creating various visualizations and dashboards, providing insights into data through customizable and interactive means. From simple visualizations such as line charts and pie charts to more complex Canvas workpads and Vega or Vega-Lite visualizations, we explored how Kibana leverages Elasticsearch's powerful analytics to bring data to life. We also navigated through the practicalities of setting up alerts in Kibana, ensuring proactive monitoring and timely responses to data trends or anomalies.

Furthermore, our discussion highlighted the importance of Elasticsearch's architecture, scalability, and reliability for handling large volumes of data. We touched upon essential concepts such as sharding, replication, and cluster management, understanding how Elasticsearch achieves high availability and horizontal scalability. These features make it an indispensable tool for a wide range of applications, from logging and monitoring to business intelligence and advanced analytics.

As we conclude this chapter, it is evident that Elasticsearch and Kibana together form a potent combination for searching, analyzing, and visualizing data. The skills and knowledge acquired in this deep dive are foundational for anyone looking to leverage the Elastic Stack for powerful data insights. Yet, our journey does not end here.

In the next chapter, we will pivot from usage to development, exploring "*Developing for the Elastic Stack.*" We will dive into the development aspects, including working with Elasticsearch APIs, integrating with different applications, and extending the capabilities of the Elastic Stack. Get ready to elevate your understanding from user to creator, as we continue to unravel the extensive possibilities offered by the Elastic Stack.

Points to Remember

- **Elasticsearch Fundamentals**: Understand the basic concepts of Elasticsearch, including its role as a distributed, full-text search and analytics engine. It is designed for horizontal scalability, reliability, and real-time search.
- **Kibana Visualization and Dashboards**: Kibana is an open-source visualization interface for Elasticsearch that provides real-time summary and analysis of the data in the Elasticsearch cluster. It allows you to create and share visualizations and dashboards.
- **Data Ingestion and Management**: Learn how to ingest and manage data in Elasticsearch. This includes understanding how to create, update, and delete indices, and perform CRUD operations on documents.
- **Query DSL**: Familiarize yourself with Elasticsearch's Query DSL for performing and fine-tuning searches. It is powerful and flexible, allowing for a wide range of queries.
- **Kibana's Vega and Vega-Lite**: Understand the difference between Vega and Vega-Lite for creating custom visualizations in Kibana. Vega is more powerful and complex, while Vega-Lite provides a simpler, more concise syntax for creating a wide array of visualization types.
- **Alerting and Monitoring**: Know how to set up basic alerts in Kibana to monitor data and trigger notifications, based on certain conditions using Kibana's alerting features.
- **Machine Learning Features**: Acknowledge that Machine Learning features in Kibana are part of the commercial offerings of the Elastic Stack, and understand the basic steps to activate and utilize these features, if available.
- **Index and Connector Creation**: Be aware of how to create indices and connectors in Elasticsearch using Kibana's Dev Tools with HTTP requests for various purposes such as logging alerts or storing data.

Multiple Choice Questions

1. What is Elasticsearch primarily used for?
    a. Distributed database management
    b. Full-text search and analytics engine
    c. Network monitoring
    d. Content management system

2. Which Kibana feature allows you to create complex, interactive visualizations beyond the standard types?
    a. Lens
    b. Vega
    c. Canvas
    d. Maps
3. What type of data store is Elasticsearch?
    a. Relational database
    b. NoSQL database
    c. NewSQL database
    d. Graph database
4. In Kibana, what is the purpose of creating an index pattern?
    a. To define how data should be stored in Elasticsearch
    b. To set up visualizations and dashboards
    c. To format the data before ingestion
    d. To provide Kibana with a schema for accessing Elasticsearch data
5. How can you activate Machine Learning features in Kibana?
    a. By installing additional plugins
    b. By using the open-source version of Kibana
    c. By subscribing to at least the Platinum subscription or activating a trial
    d. Machine Learning features are automatically activated in all versions

Answers

1. b
2. b
3. b
4. d
5. c

Questions

1. Describe the architecture of Elasticsearch, and its role in the Elastic Stack. How does it ensure scalability and reliability in handling data?
2. Explain the different types of visualizations available in Kibana, and the purpose of each. How can these visualizations enhance data analysis?
3. Discuss the process of data ingestion in Elasticsearch. How does one go about indexing data, and what are the considerations for structuring an index?
4. Detail the Query DSL in Elasticsearch. Provide examples of how different types of queries can be used to retrieve and manipulate data.
5. Compare and contrast Vega and Vega-Lite in Kibana. What are the scenarios where one might be preferred over the other?
6. Describe a scenario where using Vega or Vega-Lite in Kibana would be more beneficial than using standard Kibana visualizations. What unique features do Vega and Vega-Lite offer?
7. Outline the steps to set up a basic alert in Kibana. What are the components of an alert, and how can it be used to monitor data effectively?
8. Discuss the commercial Machine Learning features in Kibana. How can these features be activated, and what are the potential applications?
9. Explain how to create and use an index in Elasticsearch as a connector for alerts or other purposes. What are the steps and considerations in this process?
10. Provide an overview of the "*Canvas*" feature in Kibana. How does it differ from other visualization tools in Kibana, and what are its unique use cases?

Key Terms

- **Elasticsearch**: A distributed, RESTful search and analytics engine capable of addressing a growing number of use cases.
- **Kibana**: A free and open user interface that lets you visualize your Elasticsearch data, and navigate the Elastic Stack.
- **Visualization**: The representation of data in a graphical format, made possible in Kibana through various types of charts, maps, and diagrams.
- **Dashboard**: A collection of visualizations or panels, arranged on a single page, and used to track the related data metrics.
- **Vega and Vega-Lite**: A visualization grammar that allows for building complex and custom visualizations in Kibana beyond the predefined types.

- **Canvas**: A feature in Kibana that allows users to create a custom, pixel-perfect report or infographic with live data.
- **Query DSL**: Elasticsearch's domain-specific language used to execute queries to retrieve or manage data.
- **Aggregations**: The process of collecting and summarizing data in Elasticsearch, often used in Kibana visualizations for metrics and bucketing.
- **Index**: The collection of documents in Elasticsearch with similar characteristics, serving as the primary storage unit.
- **Alerts**: Automated notifications in Kibana that monitor data and send alerts, based on specified conditions.
- **Machine Learning (ML)**: A suite of features in Elastic Stack offering anomaly detection and forecasting capabilities.
- **Data Ingestion**: The process of importing data into Elasticsearch from various sources.
- **Threshold Alert**: A type of alert in Kibana that triggers, when data crosses a defined threshold.
- **NoSQL Database**: A type of database that provides a mechanism for storage and retrieval of data which Elasticsearch is categorized under.
- **Elastic Stack**: The group of products comprising Elasticsearch, Kibana, Beats, and Logstash (often referred to as ELK Stack with Elastic Beats).

CHAPTER 5
Developing for the Elastic Stack

Introduction

Welcome to Chapter 5 of the "*Ultimate Elastic Stack Handbook*," where we delve into the fascinating world of Elastic Stack development. This chapter is dedicated to those looking to extend and customize the Elastic Stack's capabilities, covering three critical components: Elasticsearch, Logstash, and Kibana. Whether you are a developer, a data engineer, or an IT professional, this section provides the guidance needed to tailor the Elastic Stack to your unique needs and challenges.

The Elastic Stack is a powerful suite of tools, but every organization has unique requirements that off-the-shelf solutions cannot always meet. Understanding how to extend and customize these tools can significantly enhance their value, allowing for more precise and efficient data handling, analysis, and visualization tailored specifically to your operational context.

By the end of this chapter, you will have a solid foundation in developing for the Elastic Stack, equipped with the skills and insights to create custom solutions and enhancements. So, whether you are addressing specific business needs, optimizing performance, or innovating with data, the journey into Elastic Stack development opens up a world of possibilities. Prepare to unleash the full potential of Elasticsearch, Logstash, and Kibana, as we embark on this developmental adventure.

Structure

In this chapter, we will discuss the following topics:

- Building Custom Elasticsearch Plugins
- Hands-On Lab: Building Elasticsearch Plugins
- Extending Logstash with Ruby

- Hands-On Lab: Extending Logstash with Ruby
- Kibana Plugin Development

Building Custom Elasticsearch Plugins

Custom Elasticsearch plugins allow you to extend the capabilities of Elasticsearch to meet the unique needs of your organization. Whether you are looking to add new REST endpoints, extend the existing functionalities, or create new custom data types, a well-crafted plugin can significantly enhance your Elastic Stack's performance and capabilities. This section guides you through the process of building custom Elasticsearch plugins, from setup to deployment.

Introduction to Elasticsearch Plugins

- **What is a Plugin?** Understand the concept of plugins in the context of Elasticsearch and the various types of plugins you can create, including modules, script engines, and custom functionalities.
- **Why Custom Plugins?** Learn about the scenarios and benefits of developing custom plugins, including performance optimization, custom data processing, or introducing new features not available in the standard distribution.

Setting Up the Development Environment

- **Tools and Prerequisites**: List the tools, languages (primarily Java), and environment setups needed to start developing plugins.
- **Elasticsearch Plugin SDK**: Introduction to the SDK provided by Elasticsearch for plugin development, and how it simplifies the creation as well as testing of plugins.

Creating Your First Plugin

- **Plugin Structure**: Overview of the standard structure of an Elasticsearch plugin, including the main components like plugin descriptors, and the core Java classes.
- **Developmental Steps**: Step-by-step instructions to create a simple plugin, including:
    - Setting up the project structure.
    - Writing the core plugin code.
    - Integrating with Elasticsearch's lifecycle.
    - Adding custom settings and configuration options.

Testing and Deployment

- **Local Testing**: How to test your plugin locally in a development environment, ensuring that it works as expected with Elasticsearch.
- **Unit and Integration Testing**: Best practices for writing and running unit and integration tests to validate the functionality and performance of your plugin.
- **Packaging and Deployment**: Guide to packaging your plugin into a zip file, and deploying it to an Elasticsearch cluster, including version compatibility and security considerations.

Advanced Topics

- **Custom REST Endpoints**: Creating custom RESTful endpoints for your plugin to handle specific types of requests or introduce new APIs.
- **Handling Cluster and Node Events**: How to make your plugin aware of and reactive to cluster and node lifecycle events.
- **Performance Considerations**: Tips for ensuring that your plugin does not negatively impact the overall performance of Elasticsearch, including profiling and optimization techniques.

Best Practices and Common Pitfalls

- **Coding Standards**: Importance of following coding standards and conventions, specific to Elasticsearch plugin development.
- **Security Implications**: Understanding the security implications of running custom code within Elasticsearch, and how to develop secure plugins.
- **Troubleshooting and Support**: Common issues faced during plugin development, and how to troubleshoot them, as well as where to find community and official support.

Hands-On Lab: Building Elasticsearch Plugins

Welcome to the hands-on lab on building Elasticsearch plugins. In this exercise, you will create a simple Elasticsearch plugin that adds a new REST endpoint to Elasticsearch. This endpoint will return a customized greeting message with the current server time. This lab will guide you through setting up your development environment, coding the plugin, testing it, and finally deploying it to an Elasticsearch cluster.

Objective

Create a custom Elasticsearch plugin that adds a new REST endpoint **`/greet`** which returns a JSON response with a custom greeting, and the current server time.

Prerequisites

- Basic knowledge of Java (as Elasticsearch plugins are typically written in Java).
- Elasticsearch source code for reference (optional but helpful).
- Java Development Kit (JDK) installed.
- An IDE for Java development (for example, IntelliJ IDEA, Eclipse, and Visual Studio Code).
- Elasticsearch environment set up for testing the plugin.

In this lab, we use Visual Studio Code with Java extensions for development and testing. We can install **Extension Pack for Java** and **Gradle for Java** from Microsoft. However, you can use any IDE of your choice, as long as it supports Java development. We also assume that you have a local Elasticsearch instance running on your machine.

Figure 5.1: *Extensions from Visual Studio Code*

Lab Steps

The following steps will guide you through the process of creating a custom Elasticsearch plugin. You will start by setting up your development environment, then create the plugin, test it locally, and finally deploy it to your Elasticsearch instance.

Step 1: Setting Up the Development Environment

a. **Install Elasticsearch**: Ensure that you have Elasticsearch installed and running on your machine. Use the official documentation to install, if not already done.

b. **Setup IDE**: Open your Java IDE, and set up a new Gradle project for the Elasticsearch plugin.

c. For Visual Studio Code, click "**`View`**" -> **`Command Palette`** -> "**`Java: Create Java Project`**" -> "**`Gradle`**" with Kotlin DSL.

d. Select the folder where you want to create the project, and give it a name. For instance, we use **`myplugin`** as folder name, and **`myplugin`** as project name.

Step 2: Creating the Plugin Structure

a. **Generate Plugin Skeleton**: Use Gradle to generate the skeleton of your plugin. This will create the necessary files and folders for your plugin.

b. You can see project structure as shown in *Figure 5.2*.

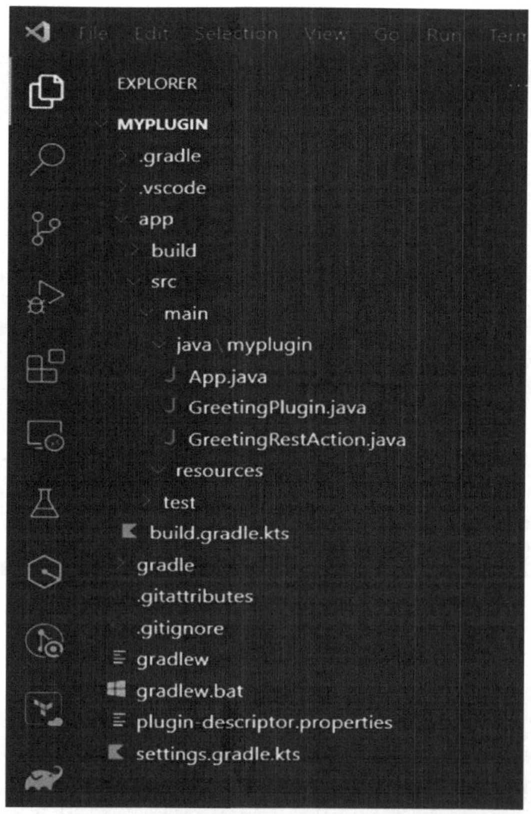

***Figure 5.2**: Generate Plugin Skeleton*

c. **Understand the Structure**: Familiarize yourself with the main components of the plugin: The plugin descriptor file, the main plugin class, and so on.

d. You can find the plugin descriptor file information in official documentation. For instance, the plugin descriptor file for Elasticsearch 8.x https://www.elastic.co/guide/en/elasticsearch/plugins/current/plugin-descriptor-file-classic.html .

Step 3: Developing the Plugin

a. **Implementing the Main Plugin Class**: Create a Java class extending from Plugin class. Implement the necessary methods to define your plugin.

b. We create **`GreetPlugin.java`** file in **`src/main/java/myplugin`** folder. You can see the code in *Figure* 5.3.

c. Write the code to implement the plugin on the following codes:

```
package myplugin;

import org.elasticsearch.plugins.Plugin;
import org.elasticsearch.cluster.metadata.IndexNameExpression
Resolver;
import org.elasticsearch.common.settings.ClusterSettings;
import org.elasticsearch.common.settings.IndexScopedSettings;
import org.elasticsearch.common.settings.Settings;
import org.elasticsearch.common.settings.SettingsFilter;
import org.elasticsearch.plugins.ActionPlugin;
import java.util.List;

import org.elasticsearch.rest.RestController;
import org.elasticsearch.rest.RestHandler;
import org.elasticsearch.cluster.node.DiscoveryNodes;
import java.util.function.Supplier;

import static java.util.Collections.singletonList;
public class GreetingPlugin extends Plugin implements Action-
Plugin {

    @Override
    public List<RestHandler> getRestHandlers(final Settings
settings,
                                              final RestController
restController,
                                              final ClusterSettings
clusterSettings,
                                              final IndexScopedSet-
```

```
tings indexScopedSettings,
                                                final SettingsFilter
settingsFilter,
                                                final IndexName
ExpressionResolver indexNameExpressionResolver,
                                                final Supplier
<DiscoveryNodes> nodesInCluster) {

        return singletonList(new GreetingRestAction());
    }
}
```

Code Explanation

The provided Java code defines a class **GreetingPlugin** which extends the Plugin class, and implements the **ActionPlugin** interface from the Elasticsearch framework. The class is intended to be used as an Elasticsearch plugin that registers a custom REST action, in this case, a greeting action.

This method **getRestHandlers()** is overridden from the **ActionPlugin** interface and is used to return the list of **RestHandler** instances that the plugin wants to register. These handlers will manage REST actions added by the plugin.

- **Parameters**: It receives several parameters, including various settings and controllers needed for the handlers to interact with the rest of the Elasticsearch system.
- **Functionality**: In this method, it returns a singleton list containing a new instance of **GreetingRestAction**, which is presumably the class defined earlier to handle the greeting action. This means the plugin will manage one REST endpoint, as defined by the **GreetingRestAction** class.

When the **GreetingPlugin** is loaded into Elasticsearch, it registers the custom REST handlers defined in it. Specifically, it registers the **GreetingRestAction** handler, which listens for requests on the **/greet** endpoint and responds accordingly. The registration is done by overriding the **getRestHandlers** method from the **ActionPlugin** interface, which is a common pattern for adding new REST actions to Elasticsearch through plugins.

In essence, the **GreetingPlugin** serves as a container and registrar for custom actions (in this case, just one) that augment the functionality of an Elasticsearch instance with new REST endpoints.

The **GreetingPlugin** class represents a straightforward example of an Elasticsearch plugin designed to extend the platform's REST interface. By implementing the ActionPlugin interface, and providing a custom implementation of **getRestHandlers**, it directs Elasticsearch to handle certain types of requests with the **GreetingRestAction**. This pattern is central to developing plugins that introduce new behaviors or integrate external services into the Elasticsearch ecosystem.

a. **Adding a REST Action**: Create a new REST action class that extends **`BaseRestHandler`**. Implement your logic to return a greeting and the current server time in JSON format.

b. On **`GreetingPlugin`** class, we return **`singletonList`** of **`GreetingRestAction`** class. We create **`GreetingRestAction`** class in **`src/main/java/myplugin`** folder. You can see the code in *Figure* 5.3.

```
package myplugin;
// libraries
public class GreetingRestAction extends BaseRestHandler {

    @Override
    public String getName() {
        return "greeting_rest_action";
    }
    @Override
    public List<Route> routes() {
        return List.of(
            new Route(GET, "/greet"));
    }
    @Override
    protected Set<String> responseParams() {
        return Set.of("name");
    }
    @Override
    protected RestChannelConsumer prepareRequest(RestRequest
request, NodeClient client) throws IOException {
        return channel -> {
            String who = request.param("name", "world");
            XContentBuilder builder = channel.newBuilder();
            builder.startObject();
            builder.field("greeting", "Hello, " + who + "!");
            builder.field("time", System.currentTimeMillis());
            builder.endObject();
            try {
                channel.sendResponse(new RestResponse(RestStatus.
OK, builder));
            } catch (final Exception e) {
                channel.sendResponse(new RestResponse(channel, e));
            }
        };
    }
}
```

Code Explanation

This Java code defines a class **GreetingRestAction** that extends **BaseRestHandler** which is part of the Elasticsearch framework. The class is intended to create a custom REST action for an Elasticsearch plugin. Here is an explanation of its components and functionality:

```
package myplugin;
```

This line declares the package name for the class, which is **myplugin**. It is a convention in Java to organize classes into packages.

The import statements bring in various classes and methods needed for the **GreetingRestAction** class to function, such as components from the Elasticsearch framework (**NodeClient**, **BaseRestHandler**, etc.) and standard Java libraries (IOException, List, Set).

```
public class GreetingRestAction extends BaseRestHandler {
    //...
}
```

This line defines the **GreetingRestAction** as a public class extending **BaseRestHandler**, which is an abstract base class for handling REST requests in Elasticsearch.

```
getName():

@Override
public String getName() {
    return "greeting_rest_action";
}
```

This method is overridden from **BaseRestHandler** and provides a unique name for the handler. It's used in logging and other purposes to identify the handler.

```
routes():
java
@Override
public List<Route> routes() {
    return List.of(new Route(GET, "/greet"));
}
```

This method returns the routes that this handler will manage. It defines that this handler responds to HTTP GET requests at the path /greet.

```
responseParams():
java
@Override
protected Set<String> responseParams() {
```

```
        return Set.of("name");
    }
```

This method returns the names of parameters used in the response. In this case, it's declaring that the name parameter is expected in the request. It helps Elasticsearch understand what parameters are valid for this handler, preventing unrecognized parameter exceptions.

```
prepareRequest():
@Override
protected RestChannelConsumer prepareRequest(RestRequest request,
NodeClient client) throws IOException {
    // Implementation
}
```

This is the most critical method, where the actual handling of the **REST** request happens. It's invoked with every request that matches the defined routes. Inside this method:

- It defines a **RestChannelConsumer** that takes a **RestChannel**, and writes a response to it.
- It extracts the name parameter from the request, defaulting to "world" if not provided.
- It builds a JSON response using **XContentBuilder** including a greeting message and the current server time.
- Finally, it sends the response back to the client. In case of any exception, it sends an error response.

In summary, the **GreetingRestAction** class creates a simple Elasticsearch REST endpoint at **/greet**. When a GET request is sent to this endpoint, the server responds with a greeting message. The message can be personalized by including a **name** parameter in the query string (for example, **/greet?name=John**), otherwise, it defaults to "**Hello**, **world!**". It also includes the current server time in the response.

This kind of plugin extension allows for customized behavior in an Elasticsearch instance, which can be particularly useful for adding new functionalities or integrating with other systems and processes.

a. **Registering the REST Action**: Modify the plugin class to register your custom REST action.

b. We create descriptor file, **plugin-descriptor.properties**.

```
description=My first plugin
version=1.0
name=my-first-plugin
classname=myplugin.GreetingPlugin
```

```
java.version=19
elasticsearch.version=8.10.4
```

c. Modify **elasticsearch.version** based on your Elasticsearch version. For instance, we use Elasticsearch 8.10.4.

d. We modify **build.gradle.kts** file as follows:

```
...
dependencies {
    ...
    implementation("org.elasticsearch:elasticsearch:8.10.4")
}
...
```

Step 4: Building the Plugin

a. **Compile the Plugin**: Use Gradle to build your plugin, and generate a ZIP file.

b. **Understand the Output**: Ensure that your build includes the plugin descriptor and JAR files.

c. ZIP your JAR file and plugin descriptor file. For instance, we use **myplugin.zip** as the name of the ZIP file.

d. Copy the ZIP file to your Elasticsearch instance.

Step 5: Testing the Plugin Locally

a. **Install the Plugin**: Install your plugin to a local Elasticsearch instance, using the **elasticsearch**-plugin install command, along with the path to your plugin ZIP file.

b. Navigate to Elasticsearch home directory (default: **/usr/share/elasticsearch** folder) and run the following command:

```
./bin/elasticsearch-plugin install file:///path/to/myplugin.zip
```

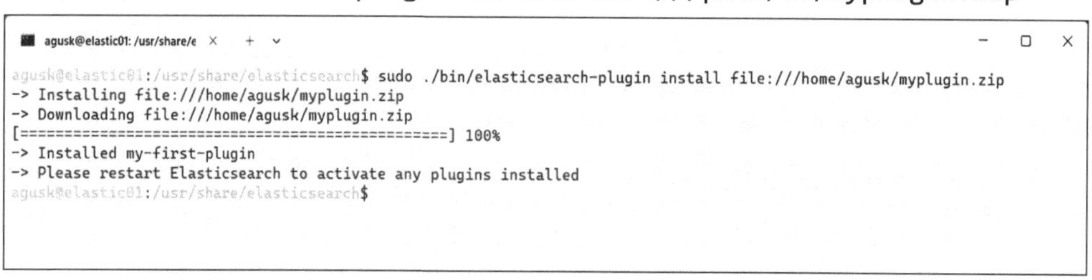

***Figure 5.3**: Install Plugin*

c. You may need to run the command with **sudo**, if you do not have the necessary permissions.

d. **Restart Elasticsearch**: Restart the Elasticsearch instance to pick up the new plugin.

```
sudo systemctl restart elasticsearch
```

e. You can check the plugin is installed by running the following command:

```
./bin/elasticsearch-plugin list
```

f. You should see the plugin listed in the output.

g. You can also check the plugin is installed by running the following command:

```
curl -XGET http://localhost:9200/_cat/plugins?v
```

if you DevTools in Kibana, you can run the following command:

```
GET /_cat/plugins?v
```

h. **Test the Endpoint**: Use a tool like cURL or Postman to send a request to your new **`/greet`** endpoint, and verify that it returns the expected response.

```
GET /greet?name=mr.abc
GET /greet
```

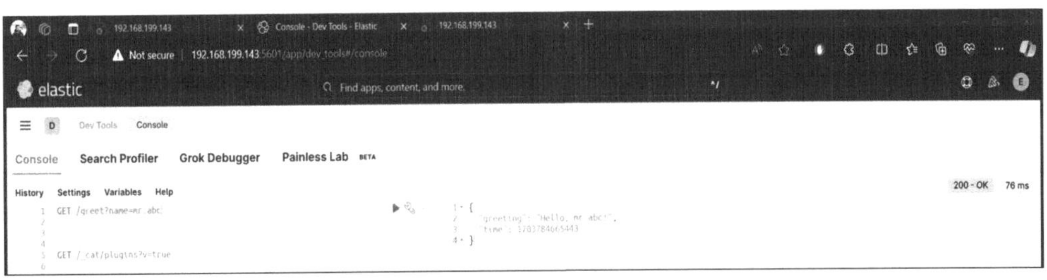

Figure 5.4: *Test Plugin*

Step 6: Debugging and Troubleshooting

a. Understand common issues that might occur during plugin development such as classpath issues, dependency conflicts, or permission problems.

b. Learn how to read logs to troubleshoot any errors that occur, while running your plugin.

Step 7: Documentation and Cleanup

a. **Document Your Plugin**: Write documentation for your plugin, describing its purpose, how to install it, and how to use it.

b. **Clean Up**: Ensure that your code is clean, well-commented, and follows the best practices for Elasticsearch plugin development.

c. You can remove the plugin by running the following command:

```
./bin/elasticsearch-plugin remove my-first-plugin
```

Summary

By completing this lab, you will have gained practical experience in building and deploying a simple Elasticsearch plugin. This exercise serves as a foundation for you to start developing more complex plugins tailored to your specific needs.

Extending Logstash with Ruby

Extending Logstash with Ruby allows developers to add custom functionalities, optimize data processing, and integrate with various systems and APIs. This section of the handbook focuses on guiding you through the process of creating custom extensions for Logstash using the Ruby programming language. It covers everything from understanding the basics of Ruby in the context of Logstash, to developing, testing, and deploying your custom filters, inputs, codecs, and outputs.

Why Extend Logstash?

- **Introduction to Extensibility**: Understand the flexible architecture of Logstash, and the reasons why you might need to extend it, including unique data transformation needs, performance optimizations, or proprietary integrations.
- **Types of Extensions**: Overview of the different types of extensions, you can create for Logstash such as filters, inputs, outputs, and codecs.

Ruby Primer for Logstash

- **Getting to Know Ruby**: A brief introduction to Ruby, focusing on the aspects most relevant to Logstash development, such as syntax, object-oriented principles, and the Ruby ecosystem.
- **Logstash and Ruby**: How Ruby is used within Logstash, including the Event API and the plugin API that you will use to interact with Logstash's core.

Creating Custom Filters and Outputs

- **Setting Up the Development Environment**: Guide to setting up your Ruby and Logstash development environment, including the installation of necessary tools and libraries.
- **Developing Custom Filters**: Step-by-step instructions on how to create custom filters, including parsing, mutating data, and applying conditional logic.
- **Developing Custom Outputs**: How to create outputs to send data to various destinations or services not supported out-of-the-box by Logstash.

Testing and Performance Considerations

- **Writing Tests for Plugins**: Importance of testing in the development process, and how to write unit and integration tests for your custom plugins.
- **Debugging and Performance Tuning**: Strategies for debugging your plugins, and tips for improving the performance of your custom Logstash extensions.

Deployment and Management

- **Packaging Your Plugin**: Instructions on how to package your custom plugin for distribution and deployment.
- **Deploying Custom Extensions**: How to deploy and manage your custom Logstash plugins in various environments, including security considerations and the best practices for maintenance.

Advanced Topics

- **Interacting with External APIs and Services**: Guidance on enhancing your Logstash pipeline by integrating with external APIs and services through custom plugins.
- **Plugin Lifecycle and Management**: Understanding the lifecycle of a plugin within Logstash's execution, and how to manage state and resources effectively.

Best Practices and Common Pitfalls

- **Coding Standards and Conventions**: Best practices for writing clean, maintainable, and efficient Ruby code in the context of Logstash plugins.
- **Common Pitfalls**: Common mistakes and pitfalls to avoid when developing for Logstash, and how to solve typical problems you might encounter.

By the end of this section, readers should be well-equipped to extend Logstash's capabilities using Ruby, allowing for customized and optimized data processing pipelines. The skills and knowledge gained here will enable you to meet your specific data transformation, enrichment, and shipping needs, making your Logstash implementation more powerful and tailored to your organization's requirements.

Hands-On Lab: Extending Logstash with Ruby

In this lab, you will create a simple Logstash filter plugin using Ruby. This filter will be designed to add a tag "**`example`**" to events that contain a specific field. This exercise will guide you through setting up your development environment, writing the Ruby filter plugin, and testing it within Logstash using Visual Studio Code as the editor.

Objective

To develop a simple Logstash filter plugin that adds a tag to events with a specific field.

Prerequisites

- Ruby development environment set up.
- Logstash installed on your machine.
- Visual Studio Code (VS Code) installed with Ruby extensions.
- Basic understanding of Ruby and Logstash.

Lab Steps

The following steps will guide you through the process of creating a custom Logstash filter plugin using Ruby. You will start by setting up your development environment, then create the plugin, test it locally, and finally deploy it to your Logstash instance.

For demo, we use a sample project from https://github.com/logstash-plugins/logstash-filter-example.

Step 1: Setting Up Visual Studio Code

a. **Install Visual Studio Code**: If not already installed, download and install it from the official website.

b. **Install Ruby Extension**: Open VS Code, go to the Extensions view (icon on the side menu or *Ctrl+Shift+X*), and search for "`Ruby`". Install it for enhanced Ruby language support.

c. If you are working in Ubuntu, you may opt for additional libraries to support Elastic plugin development. You can install them by running the following command:

```
sudo apt-get install ruby-bundler
```

Step 2: Cloning the Project

a. You can clone the project from **https://github.com/logstash-plugins/logstash-filter-example,** or download the project.

b. **Clone the Project**: Clone the project from GitHub, using the following command:

```
git clone https://github.com/logstash-plugins/logstash-filter-example
```

c. This project has a structure folder as shown in *Figure* 5.5.

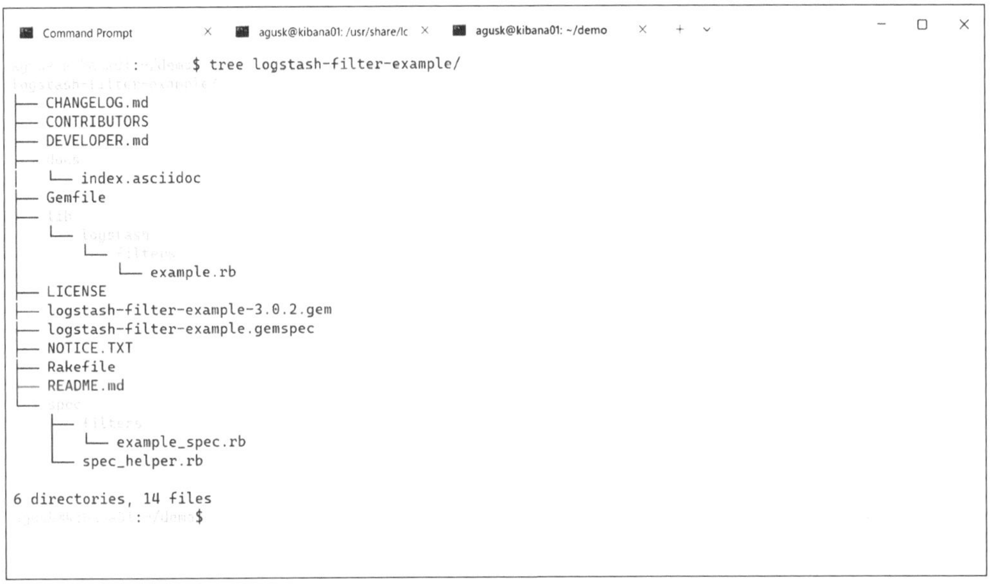

***Figure 5.5**: Project Structure*

Step 3: Compiling the Plugin

a. Navigate to the project directory, and run the following command to compile the plugin:

```
gem build logstash-filter-example.gemspec
```

b. You should see a file named **`logstash-filter-example-x.y.z.gem`** in the project directory.

Step 4: Installing the Plugin

1. **Install the Plugin**: Install the plugin to your local Logstash instance, using the **logstash-plugin install** command along with the path to your plugin GEM file.

```
bin/logstash-plugin install /path/to/logstash-filter-
example-x.y.z.gem
```

2. **Verify Installation**: Verify that the plugin is installed by running the following command:

```
bin/logstash-plugin list
```

3. You should see the plugin listed in the output.

Figure 5.6: *Install and List Plugin*

Step 5: Testing the Plugin with Logstash

a. **Configure Logstash**: Create a Logstash configuration file (for example, **`logstash.conf`**) in your project directory with the following content. This configuration sets up Logstash to use the standard input as the source and standard output as the sink, and includes your filter in the processing pipeline.

```
input { stdin { } }
filter {
  example { }
}
output { stdout { codec => rubydebug } }
```

b. **Run Logstash with Your Plugin**: Use the following command in the terminal to run Logstash with your configuration file and plugin path:

```
bin/logstash -f /you-path/logstash.conf --config.reload.automatic
```

c. **Test the Filter**: Once Logstash is running, type a test message into the console. If your filter is working, you should see the message event in the output.

d. You can see the result as shown in the following *Figure* 5.7.

***Figure 5.7**: Test Plugin*

Step 6: Debugging and Expanding

a. **Debugging**: Use VS Code's Ruby debugging tools to set breakpoints, and step through your code, if necessary.

b. **Expanding Functionality**: Try enhancing the filter by adding more conditions or manipulating the event data in different ways.

Summary

Congratulations! You have just created a simple Logstash filter plugin using Ruby, and tested it within your Logstash pipeline. This lab provides foundational skills to start creating more complex and functional plugins, allowing you to extend Logstash to meet your specific needs. Continue exploring the Logstash plugin ecosystem and Ruby language to enhance your data processing pipelines.

Kibana Plugin Development

Developing plugins for Kibana enables you to add new features, customize visualizations, and integrate third-party applications directly into the Kibana interface. This section aims to equip you with the knowledge and skills necessary to design, build, and maintain effective plugins for Kibana, enhancing the visualization and management capabilities of your Elastic Stack.

Understanding Kibana's Extensibility

- **Introduction to Kibana Plugins**: Discover what makes Kibana plugins powerful tools for customization and integration, including the ability to add new features, change application behavior, and embed external data sources.
- **Plugin Types and Uses**: Overview of the different types of plugins you can develop for Kibana such as new UI components, applications, or even modifications to the existing features.

Setting Up Your Development Environment

- **Tools and Prerequisites**: List the necessary tools, languages, and frameworks required for Kibana plugin development, focusing primarily on JavaScript and Node.js.
- **Kibana Development Environment**: Guide to setting up a development environment tailored for Kibana plugin creation, including cloning the Kibana repository, and understanding its directory structure.

Building Your First Kibana Plugin

- **Plugin Anatomy**: Dive into the anatomy of a Kibana plugin, understanding the fundamental components such as server-side modules, client-side components, and plugin manifest files.
- **Step-by-Step Plugin Creation**: Detailed walkthrough of creating a basic plugin, from generating the plugin skeleton to adding custom logic and user interfaces.
- **Interacting with Elasticsearch**: Learn how to fetch, manipulate, and display data from Elasticsearch within your plugin, utilizing Kibana's extensive APIs and services.

Best Practices and Advanced Topics

- **Design and Usability Considerations**: Importance of user experience and design in your plugin's interface, adhering to Kibana's design principles and guidelines.
- **Advanced Features and APIs**: Explore advanced development topics such as adding configuration options, internationalization, and leveraging Kibana's core APIs for more sophisticated plugin functionality.
- **Security and Authentication**: Implement security best practices, ensuring that your plugin adheres to the necessary authentication and authorization mechanisms used by Kibana.

Testing and Deployment

- **Testing Your Plugin**: Strategies for effectively testing your plugin, including unit tests, integration tests, and end-to-end tests using the tools and frameworks supported by Kibana.

- **Packaging and Deployment**: Guide to packaging your plugin for distribution and instructions for deploying it to a Kibana instance, including version compatibility and upgrade considerations.

Troubleshooting and Community Engagement

- **Common Developmental Challenges**: Discussion of common issues and challenges you may encounter, when developing Kibana plugins, and how to overcome them.
- **Engaging with the Community**: Resources for getting help, contributing to the Kibana community, and staying updated with the latest development practices and features.

Thus, by the end of this section, readers will have a thorough understanding of the Kibana plugin architecture and developmental process. You will be capable of designing and implementing custom plugins that meet the specific needs, whether for enhancing data visualization, integrating new data sources, or adding entirely new features to the Kibana interface. With these skills, you will be able to significantly increase the value and functionality of your Elastic Stack deployments.

Conclusion

In this chapter, we delved deep into the world of Elastic Stack development, exploring how to extend and enhance Elasticsearch, Logstash, and Kibana using custom plugins and scripts. We started by examining how to create custom Elasticsearch plugins, enabling personalized search and analytics capabilities tailored to specific needs. Through detailed examples and explanations, we have seen how plugins can intercept and process data, introduce new REST endpoints, or add novel functionalities to Elasticsearch clusters, thereby elevating its utility and performance.

We then navigated through the process of extending Logstash with Ruby, illustrating the powerful ways you can manipulate and transform data streams. By creating a custom filter plugin, you learned how to intercept, analyze, and modify event data as it flows through the Logstash pipeline. This ability to customize data processing logic is crucial for adapting Logstash to various data formats and sources, ensuring that the data is primed and ready for analysis in Elasticsearch, or other destinations.

Moving on to Kibana, we explored the intricate process of developing Kibana plugins. This journey uncovered how Kibana's flexible architecture allows for the creation of dynamic visualizations, custom applications, and enhanced features, all within its user interface. By integrating new visual components or functionalities into Kibana, developers can provide the end-users with powerful tools for data exploration and insight discovery, making data analytics more accessible and impactful.

Throughout these sections, we have emphasized the importance of understanding the core principles of the Elastic Stack, mastering the development environment, and adhering to the best practices in coding and plugin management. Thus, the journey through Elastic Stack development is filled with opportunities for innovation and optimization, allowing developers to build robust, efficient, and customized solutions.

As we move forward, the next chapter will focus on "*Troubleshooting and Best Practices*." Here, we will consolidate our learning, and ensure that our development endeavors are not only innovative, but also robust and maintainable. We will explore the common pitfalls, performance considerations, security implications, and maintenance strategies. This knowledge will equip you with the skills needed to troubleshoot issues effectively, optimize performance, and ensure that your custom Elastic Stack implementations are secure, reliable, and aligned with the best practices in the field.

Points to Remember

- **Understanding Elastic Stack Components**: Know the roles and capabilities of Elasticsearch, Logstash, and Kibana in the Elastic Stack. Each serves a unique purpose in data collection, storage, and visualization.
- **Custom Elasticsearch Plugins**:
    - Plugins can significantly extend Elasticsearch's capabilities. They can add new features, custom search strategies, or integrate with other systems.
    - Understand the plugin architecture, including the plugin descriptor and main class.
    - Ensure compatibility with the version of Elasticsearch, you are targeting.
- **Extending Logstash with Ruby**:
    - Ruby is used for writing filter, input, output, and codec plugins for Logstash.
    - Familiarize yourself with the Logstash API and Ruby scripting.
    - Testing and performance tuning are critical to ensure that your plugins do not degrade the performance of Logstash.
- **Kibana Plugin Development**:
    - Kibana plugins can range from new visualizations to complete applications.
    - Understand Kibana's plugin architecture and how to interact with its API.
    - User experience is paramount in Kibana plugin development; ensure that your plugins are intuitive, and enhance Kibana's functionality.
- **Plugin Development Environment**:
    - Set up a development environment specific to Elastic Stack development, including necessary tools and SDKs.

  - Use version control for your plugin source code, and maintain documentation.
- **Testing and Quality Assurance**:
  - Rigorously test your plugins in a controlled environment before deployment.
  - Use unit tests, integration tests, and performance tests to ensure reliability and efficiency.
- **Version Compatibility**:
  - Be aware of the Elastic Stack version you are developing against the above. Compatibility issues can arise if the plugin is not aligned with the version of Elasticsearch, Logstash, or Kibana, you are targeting.
- **Security and Performance Considerations**:
  - Always consider the security implications of your custom plugins. Ensure that you are not introducing vulnerabilities.
  - Be mindful of the performance impact of your plugins, especially in high-load environments.
- **Documentation and Community Engagement**:
  - Keep thorough documentation for your custom developments for future reference, and for others, who may use your plugins.
  - Engage with the Elastic community for support, updates, and sharing your contributions.

Multiple Choice Questions

1. What is the primary purpose of building custom Elasticsearch plugins?
   a. To change the underlying architecture of Elasticsearch
   b. To extend the capabilities of Elasticsearch by adding new features or modifying the existing functionality
   c. To replace Elasticsearch with another search engine
   d. To create visualizations for data stored in Elasticsearch
2. Which programming language is primarily used for writing Logstash plugins?
   a. Python
   b. Ruby
   c. Java
   d. JavaScript

3. What should you include in a `.gemspec` file for a Logstash plugin?
   a. The version of Logstash, the plugin is compatible with.
   b. A list of other plugins that are dependencies.
   c. Metadata about the plugin, including name, version, and dependencies.
   d. Command-line options for the Logstash service.
4. Which of the following is NOT a typical component of a Kibana plugin?
   a. Custom visualizations
   b. A new REST endpoint
   c. Data storage mechanisms
   d. User interface elements
5. What is a common practice when developing plugins for the Elastic Stack to ensure compatibility, and prevent future issues?
   a. Always use open-ended dependencies in your `plugin's.gemspec` file.
   b. Test your plugin with only the latest version of the Elastic Stack.
   c. Specify the exact version numbers for dependencies in your `plugin's.gemspec` file.
   d. Avoid documenting the plugin as Elastic Stack versions are self-explanatory.

Answers

1. b
2. b
3. c
4. c
5. c

Questions

1. Describe the process and key considerations for setting up a development environment for Elasticsearch plugin development.
2. Explain the architecture of a custom Elasticsearch plugin. What are the main components, and how do they interact with the Elasticsearch ecosystem?
3. Discuss the importance of version compatibility in Elasticsearch plugin development. How can developers ensure that their plugins remain compatible with different Elasticsearch versions?
4. Illustrate with examples how custom Logstash filters can transform data. What are some common use cases for these filters in data processing pipelines?
5. Describe the steps and necessary components for creating a simple Logstash filter plugin using Ruby. What are the specific roles of each component in the plugin?
6. Explain the concept of Kibana plugin development. What types of customizations and extensions can developers introduce to Kibana through plugins?
7. Discuss how to effectively test and validate a Kibana plugin. What are some best practices for ensuring that the plugin works as expected, and does not negatively impact Kibana's performance or usability?
8. Explain the role and structure of the **`plugin-descriptor.properties`** file in Elasticsearch plugin development. What critical information does it contain, and why is it important?
9. Describe how Elasticsearch handles custom REST endpoints through plugins. What are some potential use cases for adding custom endpoints to an Elasticsearch cluster?
10. Consider the security implications of developing plugins for the Elastic Stack. What are some best practices developers should follow to ensure their plugins do not introduce vulnerabilities?

Key Terms

- **Elasticsearch Plugins**: Custom additions or extensions to Elasticsearch that can enhance or modify its capabilities by adding new features, custom search strategies, or integrating with other systems.
- **Logstash Filters**: Components in Logstash that process the incoming data, typically used to transform or enrich data as it moves through the pipeline.

- **Kibana Plugins**: Extensions or customizations to Kibana which can range from new visualizations and UI elements to complete applications integrated within the Kibana interface.
- **Ruby**: The programming language predominantly used for writing Logstash plugins, particularly for filters, inputs, outputs, and codecs.
- **Plugin Descriptor (`plugin-descriptor.properties`)**: A file required in every Elasticsearch plugin that contains metadata about the plugin, such as its name, version, description, and the main class.
- **Gemspec (`.gemspec` file)**: A specification file used by RubyGems to package Ruby applications or libraries; it contains metadata about the gem, including name, version, authors, and dependencies.
- **Application Programming Interface (API)**: A set of rules and specifications that software programs can follow to communicate with each other, used extensively in developing plugins to interact with Elastic Stack components.
- **Gradle**: An open-source build automation system that is used to build, test, and deploy software, commonly used in the development of Elasticsearch plugins.
- **Maven**: A build automation tool used primarily for Java projects, similar to Gradle, and sometimes used in the context of Elasticsearch plugin development.
- **Rspec**: A 'Domain Specific Language' (DSL) testing tool written in Ruby to test Ruby code, often used for writing tests for Logstash Ruby plugins.
- **Logstash Pipeline**: A sequence of events processed by Logstash, typically consisting of inputs, filters, and outputs.
- **XContentBuilder**: A builder utility from Elasticsearch used to build JSON structures, often used in creating responses for custom REST endpoints in Elasticsearch plugins.
- **Version Compatibility**: Ensuring that plugins or software are compatible with the specific versions of other software they interact with, crucial in plugin development to ensure smooth functionality.
- **Logstash Core Plugin API**: An API provided by Logstash that defines how plugins should be written, and interact with the Logstash core.

Chapter 6
Troubleshooting and Best Practices

Introduction

Welcome to *Chapter 6* of the "*Ultimate Elastic Stack Handbook*," where we delve into the critical areas of troubleshooting and best practices for maintaining a robust, efficient, and secure Elastic Stack deployment. This chapter is designed as a comprehensive guide to help you navigate the complexities of managing large-scale data environments, ensuring that your infrastructure not only performs optimally, but is also resilient against common pitfalls and evolving challenges.

Troubleshooting is an inevitable requirement for any technology stack, more so for a versatile and complex one like the Elastic Stack. No matter the level of expertise, users encounter issues that can range from minor inconveniences to major system outages. Understanding how to systematically approach these problems, diagnose their roots, and apply effective solutions which is the key to maintaining continuous operation and performance. In this section, we will provide you with the strategies, tools, and methodologies that are most effective for troubleshooting common and complex issues, within the Elastic Stack.

Best Practices are distilled from the collective experience of thousands of users, and the insights of Elastic's developers. They encompass a broad range of topics, including system design, performance tuning, security, maintenance, and upgrades. Adhering to these best practices is critical for ensuring that your deployment is not only stable and performant, but also secure and scalable. We will explore the most important best practices you should follow, offering practical advice and actionable tips to help you get the most out of your Elastic Stack implementation.

By the end of this chapter, you will have a deeper understanding of how to approach troubleshooting systematically, and how to implement the best practices that will lead to a successful Elastic Stack deployment. Thus, whether you are a novice user getting to grips with Elastic Stack, or a seasoned professional looking to refine your skills, this chapter will provide valuable insights to enhance your operational efficiency and problem-solving strategies.

Let us begin by exploring the rich landscape of troubleshooting, followed by the essential best practices that will serve as the cornerstone of your Elastic Stack journey.

Structure

In this chapter, we will discuss the following topics:

- Common Pitfalls and Their Solutions
- Optimizing for Large Scale Deployments
- ELK Stack Security Best Practices
- Maintenance and Upgrades
- Hands-On Lab: Maintenance and Upgrades for Elasticsearch and Kibana

Common Pitfalls and Their Solutions

When discussing **Common Pitfalls and Their Solutions** in the context of **Troubleshooting and Best Practices** for something like the Elastic Stack, you might be looking at addressing frequent challenges that users face, and how best to overcome them. Here is a general approach based on common issues in similar technology stacks:

Inadequate Planning and Configuration

- **Pitfall**: Jumping into deployment, without understanding the needs and scale of your Elastic Stack can lead to performance issues, higher costs, and inadequate resource allocation.
- **Solution**: Plan capacity, understand your data flow and structure, and configure your stack accordingly. Use Elastic Stack's planning and monitoring tools to make informed decisions.

Ignoring Security Best Practices

- **Pitfall**: Leaving clusters unsecured can lead to significant vulnerabilities, including unauthorized access and data breaches.
- **Solution**: Implement security features such as encryption, role-based access control, and auditing. Regularly update and patch your systems to protect against the known vulnerabilities.

Poor Data Modeling

- **Pitfall**: Inefficient data models or inappropriate index strategies can lead to slow search performance and increased resource consumption.
- **Solution**: Understand the nature of your data, and how you will query it. Optimize your data model for the Elastic Stack, considering factors like indexing strategies and sharding.

Neglecting Log and Error Monitoring

- **Pitfall**: Not monitoring or poorly monitoring logs and errors can lead to missed insights and unresolved issues.
- **Solution**: Use Elastic Stack's extensive logging and monitoring capabilities to keep an eye on system performance and errors. Set up alerts and dashboards to stay informed about the health of your system.

Overlooking Hardware and Infrastructure Needs

- **Pitfall**: Underestimating the hardware requirements can result in poor performance and system instability.
- **Solution**: Regularly review and adjust your hardware and infrastructure setup to meet the demands of your data volume and complexity. Consider factors such as memory, CPU, and storage.

Complex Scaling without Strategy

- **Pitfall**: Scaling up your Elastic Stack without a clear strategy can lead to unmanageable complexity and cost.
- **Solution**: Develop a scaling strategy that aligns with your growth. Understand when to scale up or out, and consider using Elastic's cloud offerings for flexibility.

Inefficient Query Design

- **Pitfall**: Poorly designed queries can be resource-intensive and slow, affecting user experience and system performance.
- **Solution**: Optimize your queries for efficiency and speed. Leverage query DSL features, and understand how different queries impact performance.

Lack of Regular Maintenance and Optimization

- **Pitfall**: Failing to regularly maintain and optimize your stack can lead to degraded performance over time.

- **Solution**: Establish routine maintenance practices, including index optimization, archiving old data, and updating to the latest Elastic Stack versions.

These points are derived from common issues across various database and search engine platforms, tailored to what you might find in Elastic Stack environments. It is important to understand the context of your deployment and the specific challenges you face to develop the most effective solutions. For the most accurate and effective strategies, it is crucial to continually refer to Elastic's official documentation, and stay updated with the latest best practices and features provided by Elastic Stack.

Optimizing for Large-Scale Deployments

When discussing optimizing for large-scale deployments in the context of Elastic Stack, it is important to focus on strategies that ensure scalability, performance, and stability. Here is a general approach based on common issues in similar technology stacks:

Hardware Optimization

- **Strategy**: Tailor hardware to the needs of your deployment. For large-scale operations, invest in high-quality, scalable infrastructure focusing on fast I/O, ample memory, and robust networking.
- **Best Practices**: Use SSDs for faster data retrieval, ensure adequate RAM for caching, and select CPUs based on the workload.

Cluster and Index Design

- **Strategy**: Design clusters and indexes to distribute the load efficiently, and maintain performance.
- **Best Practices**: Use multiple smaller indices, rather than a few large ones, implement index sharding and replicas for high availability, and consider index rollover strategies for time-based data.

Data Modeling and Management

- **Strategy**: Optimize data structures and types for the nature of your queries and storage efficiency.
- **Best Practices**: Normalize data only as needed, use appropriate field types, and compress data to reduce storage needs, without compromising retrieval speed.

Caching and Memory Management

- **Strategy**: Leverage caching to improve performance for frequently accessed data.
- **Best Practices**: Allocate adequate heap size for Elasticsearch nodes, but avoid excessive memory allocation to prevent long garbage collection pauses. Understand and utilize Elasticsearch's cache settings.

Query Optimization

- **Strategy**: Design and optimize queries for efficiency and speed.
- **Best Practices**: Use filters for frequent and fast queries, avoid heavy aggregations on large data sets, and pre-compute results, when possible.

Monitoring and Alerting

- **Strategy**: Implement a robust monitoring and alerting system to detect and address issues early.
- **Best Practices**: Use Elastic Stack's built-in monitoring tools, set up alerts for anomalies or performance issues, and monitor both system and application-level metrics.

Scalability Planning

- **Strategy**: Plan and implement a scalability strategy that allows your deployment to grow with demand.
- **Best Practices**: Understand the difference between vertical and horizontal scaling, and when to apply each. Pre-plan for capacity increases, and automate the scaling process as much as possible.

Security Considerations

- **Strategy**: Ensure that the system is secure, and able to handle the sensitive data, especially at scale.
- **Best Practices**: Implement encryption, access controls, and auditing. Regularly update systems to patch vulnerabilities, and use secure communication protocols.

Maintenance and Continuous Improvement

- **Strategy**: Regularly update and maintain the Elastic Stack deployment to ensure optimal performance.
- **Best Practices**: Schedule regular downtime for maintenance, keep abreast

of updates and improvements in the Elastic Stack, and periodically review architecture for potential improvements.

Each of these strategies should be adapted to the specific context and needs of your deployment. Large scale brings its own set of challenges, and as such, it requires meticulous planning, execution, and ongoing management. It is also beneficial to look at case studies or examples of large-scale Elastic Stack deployments to understand real-world challenges and solutions. For the most accurate and effective strategies, it is crucial to continually refer to Elastic's official documentation, and stay updated with the latest best practices and features provided by Elastic Stack.

ELK Stack Security Best Practices

When discussing ELK Stack Security Best Practices in the context of Elastic Stack, you are addressing the critical aspect of securing data and access at every layer of the stack. Here is a general approach, based on common issues in similar technology stacks:

Use Built-in Security Features

- **Best Practice**: Enable and configure the security features provided by Elastic Stack such as encryption, role-based access control, and auditing.
- **Details**: Utilize X-Pack security features for encryption, file-based user authentication, and role-based access control. Ensure that communication between nodes and clients is encrypted using SSL/TLS.

Data Encryption

- **Best Practice**: Encrypt data at rest and in transit to protect the sensitive information from unauthorized access.
- **Details**: Use disk-level encryption for data at rest, and SSL/TLS for data in transit. Ensure that all the nodes, Kibana, and client applications use encrypted connections.

Access Control

- **Best Practice**: Implement strict access control policies.
- **Details**: Define roles and permissions carefully, ensuring that users and applications only have the minimum necessary privileges. Regularly review and update permissions.

Audit Logging

- **Best Practice**: Enable and configure audit logging to keep a record of all activities.
- **Details**: Use Elasticsearch's audit logs to track who accessed what and when. Monitor and analyze logs to detect unusual activities, or potential security breaches.

Regularly Update and Patch

- **Best Practice**: Keep all the components of the ELK Stack updated to the latest version.
- **Details**: Regularly update Elastic Stack components and dependencies to patch known vulnerabilities. Keep abreast of security advisories from Elastic.

Network Security

- **Best Practice**: Secure network access to the ELK Stack.
- **Details**: Use firewalls, VPNs, or network access control lists to restrict access to Elastic Stack services. Limit exposure of the stack to the internet, and segregate internal networks.

Secure Kibana

- **Best Practice**: Implement security measures for Kibana, the Elastic Stack's visualization tool.
- **Details**: Use Kibana's built-in security features for access control. Place Kibana behind a VPN, or access control gateway and disable unnecessary features.

Backup and Recovery

- **Best Practice**: Regularly back up ELK Stack data and configurations.
- **Details**: Implement a robust backup strategy covering all critical data and configuration files. Regularly test recovery procedures to ensure data integrity and availability.

Incident Response Plan

- **Best Practice**: Prepare for security incidents with a response plan.
- **Details**: Develop and document an incident response plan. Train the staff on procedures for identifying, reporting, and responding to security incidents.

Security Monitoring and Anomaly Detection

- **Best Practice**: Use Elastic Stack's monitoring and anomaly detection features to identify potential security threats.
- **Details**: Leverage machine learning features in X-Pack for anomaly detection. Monitor security logs and metrics to detect and respond to threats promptly.

Secure Integration and API Use

- **Best Practice**: Securely integrate ELK Stack with other systems, and manage API usage.
- **Details**: Ensure that any API keys or integration points are secured and monitored. Use API gateways and service meshes to manage and secure communications.

By following these best practices, you can significantly enhance the security posture of your ELK Stack deployment, protecting against unauthorized access, data breaches, and other cyber threats. It is also vital to continually educate and train the team managing the ELK Stack on security awareness and best practices. Security is a continually evolving field, and staying informed about the latest threats and protective measures is crucial for maintaining a robust defense.

Maintenance and Upgrades

In the context of Elastic Stack, discussing "*Maintenance and Upgrades*" in your "*Ultimate Elastic Stack Handbook*" would revolve around strategies for keeping the stack stable, efficient, and up-to-date. Here is how you might structure such content in the chapter, "*Troubleshooting and Best Practices*":

Routine Maintenance

- **Best Practice**: Establish regular maintenance schedules to ensure optimal performance.
- **Details**: Regularly check the health of nodes, monitor disk usage, and clean up unneeded data or indices. Use Elastic Stack monitoring tools to track performance metrics and logs.

Version Upgrades

- **Best Practice**: Plan and execute version upgrades to benefit from the latest features, improvements, and security patches.
- **Details**: Follow Elastic's upgrade guidelines, test upgrades in a staging environment first, and back up all data and configurations before proceeding.

Understand the compatibility between different versions, especially for major upgrades.

Plugin Management

- **Best Practice**: Keep plugins up-to-date, and audit regularly.
- **Details**: Regularly review and update the plugins used within your Elastic Stack to maintain compatibility and security. Remove unnecessary plugins to reduce complexity and potential vulnerabilities.

Index Management and Optimization

- **Best Practice**: Implement index lifecycle management, and optimize indices regularly.
- **Details**: Use Elasticsearch's Index Lifecycle Management (ILM) to automate index rollover, optimize, and deletion. Regularly review index settings and mappings for performance and relevance.

Backup and Recovery Planning

- **Best Practice**: Implement a robust backup and recovery strategy.
- **Details**: Regularly back up Elasticsearch data and cluster configuration settings. Ensure that your backup strategy allows for quick and reliable recovery in case of data loss.

Hardware and Infrastructure Monitoring

- **Best Practice**: Monitor and maintain the underlying hardware and infrastructure.
- **Details**: Keep the operating system and hardware drivers up to date. Monitor hardware health, including disk I/O, memory usage, and CPU load to prevent hardware failures.

Performance Tuning

- **Best Practice**: Continuously tune the performance of the Elastic Stack.
- **Details**: Regularly review query performance, index and search speeds, as well as system latency. Adjust configurations such as JVM settings, shard sizes, and cache settings, for optimal performance.

Security Audits and Updates

- **Best Practice**: Conduct regular security reviews and updates.

- **Details**: Regularly update to the latest security patches for Elastic Stack and its components. Conduct security audits to identify and mitigate vulnerabilities, ensuring that security configurations and policies are up to date.

Documentation and Change Management

- **Best Practice**: Maintain thorough documentation, and adhere to change management protocols.
- **Details**: Document all changes, configurations, and setups in your Elastic Stack environment. Use a change management process to track modifications, and ensure that they are tested and approved before implementation.

Community and Support Engagement

- **Best Practice**: Engage with the Elastic Stack community and support resources.
- **Details**: Stay informed about the latest developments, tips, and tricks from the Elastic community. Utilize support forums, documentation, and professional support services for troubleshooting and advice.

Maintenance and upgrades are critical for the long-term health and performance of the Elastic Stack. By following these best practices, you ensure that your deployment remains efficient, secure, and aligned with the evolving needs of your organization. Regularly reviewing and adjusting your maintenance and upgrade strategies in response to changes in your operating environment, and the Elastic Stack itself is key to a successful, resilient deployment.

Hands-On Lab: Maintenance and Upgrades for Elasticsearch and Kibana

For a hands-on lab focusing on maintenance and upgrades of Elasticsearch and Kibana, you will want to guide the user through the key steps and provide examples, they can follow. This lab will assume a basic level of familiarity with Elastic Stack, and administrative access to the Elasticsearch and Kibana instances.

Objectives

- Learn how to perform routine maintenance tasks for Elasticsearch and Kibana.
- Understand and execute an upgrade process for Elasticsearch and Kibana.

Prerequisites

- An existing Elasticsearch and Kibana setup.
- Administrative access to the Elasticsearch cluster, and the server running Kibana.

- A backup of current Elasticsearch data and Kibana configurations (always create a backup before making significant changes).

Part 1: Maintenance of Elasticsearch

1. **Check Cluster Health:**
   - **Task**: Use the `_cluster/health` endpoint to review the status of your cluster.
   - **Command**: `GET /_cluster/health`

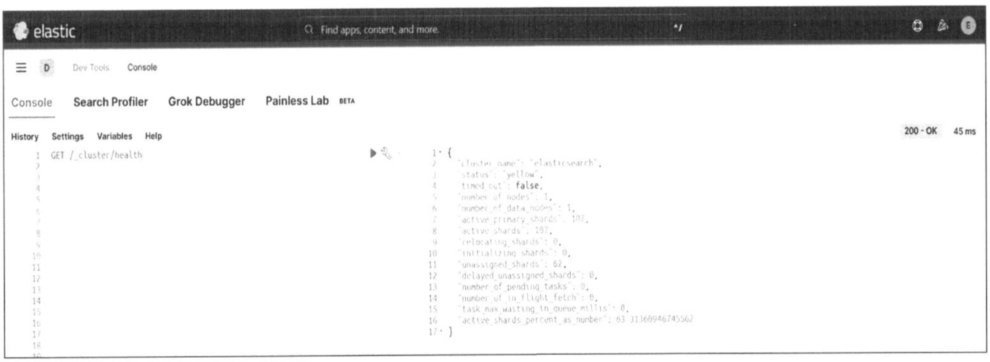

Figure 6.1: *Check Cluster Health*

2. **Review and Clean Up Indices:**
   - **Task**: Identify unused or old indices that can be deleted or archived.
   - **Command**: List the indices with `GET /_cat/indices?v` and delete with `DELETE /index_name`
3. **Optimize Indices:**
   - **Task**: Use the Force Merge API for optimizing indices.
   - **Command**: `POST /index_name/_forcemerge`
4. **Snapshot and Backup:**
   - **Task**: Create a snapshot repository, and take a backup of your current indices.
   - **Command**: Follow the detailed steps from Elasticsearch documentation to set up a snapshot repository, and take a snapshot.

Part 2: Upgrading Elasticsearch

1. **Preparation:**
   - **Task**: Read the release notes, and understand the changes and requirements of the new version.

- **Note**: Ensure that no indices are using deprecated features that will be removed in the new version.

2. Full Cluster Restart Upgrade (for major upgrades):

- **Task**: Follow the documented process for a full cluster restart which generally involves:
  - Disable shard allocation.
  - Stop non-essential indexing, and perform a synced flush.
  - Stop and upgrade each node.
  - Re-enable shard allocation, and wait for the cluster to recover.

3. Rolling Upgrade (for minor upgrades):

- **Task**: Upgrade nodes one at a time while the cluster remains operational.
- **Steps**: Detailed in the Elasticsearch documentation, typically involves:
  - Disable shard reallocation.
  - Upgrade one node.
  - Start the node and confirm it joins the cluster.
  - Re-enable shard reallocation.
  - Wait for the cluster to rebalance.
  - Repeat for each node.

Part 3: Maintenance of Kibana

1. **Review Logs and Metrics:**
   - **Task**: Check Kibana logs for any errors or warnings that need attention.
   - **Note**: Look into the status of Kibana by visiting the status page.
2. **Upgrade Plugins:**
   - **Task**: Ensure that all the plugins are compatible with the current Kibana version, and upgrade, if necessary.

Part 4: Upgrading Kibana

1. **Preparation:**
   - **Task**: Similar to Elasticsearch, read the release notes, and understand the changes.

2. **Execution:**
   - **Task**: Perform the upgrade. For Kibana, this is usually simpler than Elasticsearch, and often involves:
     - Stopping Kibana.
     - Upgrading the Kibana package.
     - Adjusting any configuration changes, if necessary.
     - Starting Kibana back up.
3. **Post-Upgrade Tasks:**
   - **Task**: Verify that the Kibana is operating correctly, and that all visualizations and dashboards are functioning.

Part 5: Upgrade Assistant

Elastic stack provides an upgrade assistant to help you upgrade your cluster. The upgrade assistant is a Kibana plugin that helps you identify and resolve issues that may prevent you from upgrading your cluster. The upgrade assistant is available in Kibana 6.5, and later.

You can find the upgrade assistant in the Management section of Kibana. The upgrade assistant is available only when you have a cluster running Elasticsearch 6.5 or later. The upgrade assistant is not available, when you have a cluster running Elasticsearch 7.0 or later.

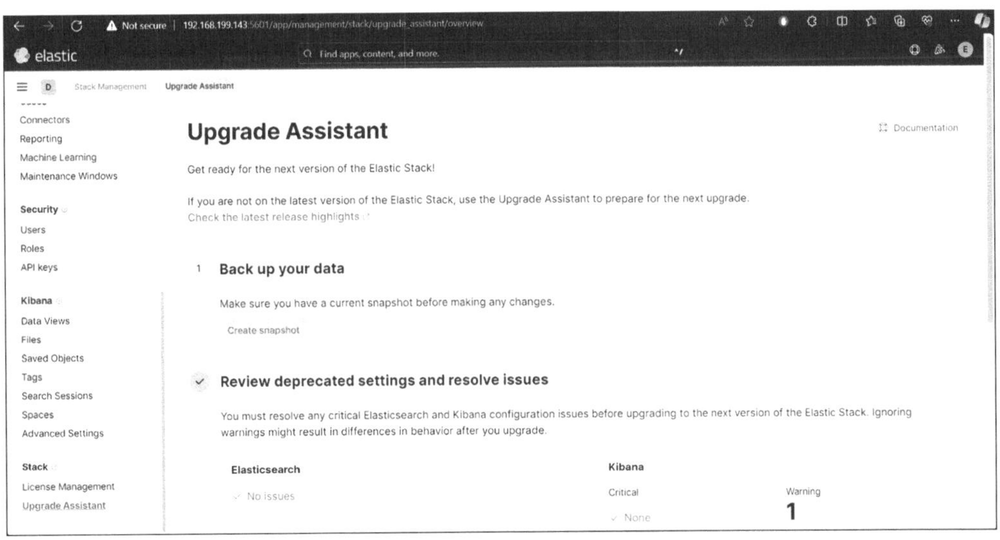

Figure 6.2: *Upgrade Assistant*

Summary

In this lab, you have learned the key maintenance and upgrade tasks for both Elasticsearch and Kibana. It is critical to plan, backup, and test in a staging environment, before performing any operations in production. Always refer to the official Elasticsearch documentation for the most up-to-date and detailed instructions, especially since procedures can vary between different versions.

Conclusion

Throughout our discussion, we have delved deeply into the "*Ultimate Elastic Stack Handbook*," particularly focusing on *Chapter 6, Troubleshooting and Best Practices*. We began by exploring common pitfalls and their solutions, where understanding the typical mistakes made in Elastic Stack deployments helps preemptively mitigate issues, and streamline performance. This chapter aims to empower users with the knowledge and strategies needed to navigate the complexities associated with managing a robust, scalable, and efficient Elastic Stack deployment.

In the realm of optimizing for large-scale deployments, we discussed how planning, monitoring, and adapting are necessary for handling the demands of the growing data and user bases. The Elastic Stack's ability to scale and perform under pressure is one of its most valuable traits, and harnessing that requires a deep dive into topics such as cluster design, data modeling, and performance tuning. Security, being paramount, was addressed with a comprehensive look at best practices, emphasizing the importance of a proactive approach to protecting data integrity and access. We covered everything from encryption and access control to audit logging and incident response, providing a blueprint for securing Elastic Stack deployments.

Maintenance and upgrades were identified as crucial ongoing processes, with detailed strategies for routine checks, version upgrades, and performance optimizations. The hands-on lab provided practical steps and commands to guide users through essential maintenance and upgrade tasks, ensuring that both newcomers and seasoned professionals can confidently apply these practices to their Elastic Stack environments.

Finally, as we look beyond the traditional boundaries of Elasticsearch, Logstash, and Kibana, we anticipate diving into the broader ecosystem of Elastic products. In the chapter, "*Beyond ELK: Integrating Other Elastic Products*," we will explore how tools like Beats, Elastic Cloud, Elastic APM, and Elastic SIEM extend the capabilities of the Elastic Stack. These integrations not only enhance data ingestion, visualization, and analysis, but also open up new avenues for observability, security, and enterprise search. This exploration will provide insights into building a more comprehensive, integrated, and efficient data platform tailored to the evolving needs of businesses and organizations.

As we conclude, it is clear that the journey through Elastic Stack is one of continuous learning and adaptation. The best practices and troubleshooting tips discussed serve as a guide, but the real strength lies in the community and the ongoing evolution of the Elastic products. By staying engaged, experimenting, and integrating new tools and features, users can ensure their Elastic Stack deployments remain powerful, insightful, and ahead of the curve.

Points to Remember

- **Understand Common Pitfalls**: Familiarize yourself with the common mistakes and challenges associated with Elastic Stack deployments to avoid them effectively.
- **Plan Capacity and Scalability**: Adequately plan for your data volume and query load, considering both current needs and future growth to ensure scalability and performance.
- **Implement Security Measures**: Prioritize security by implementing features such as encryption, role-based access control, and audit logging to protect your data and infrastructure.
- **Regular Maintenance is Crucial**: Perform routine checks and maintenance on your Elastic Stack deployment, including monitoring hardware resources, cleaning up indices, and optimizing performance.
- **Stay on Top of Updates**: Regularly update and upgrade your Elastic Stack components to benefit from the latest features, improvements, and security patches.
- **Optimize for Performance**: Continuously monitor and tune your system for optimal performance, focusing on aspects like query optimization, index management, and resource allocation.
- **Backup and Disaster Recovery**: Always maintain a robust backup and recovery strategy to protect against data loss, and ensure quick recovery in case of failures.
- **Monitor System Health**: Use Elastic Stack's monitoring tools to keep an eye on system performance, and set up alerts for any anomalies or issues.
- **Understand Upgrade Paths**: Know the difference between full cluster restarts and rolling upgrades, and choose the appropriate path based on your version and requirements.
- **Engage with the Community**: Stay connected with the Elastic community for support, insights, and to keep up with the best practices and emerging trends.
- **Explore Elastic Ecosystem**: Look beyond ELK by integrating other Elastic products to enhance capabilities in observability, security, and enterprise search.

Multiple Choice Questions

1. What is a critical first step in preventing common pitfalls in Elastic Stack deployments?
   a. Ignoring minor errors
   b. Understanding common mistakes
   c. Expanding the team
   d. Upgrading hardware
2. Which feature is essential for securing your Elastic Stack deployment?
   a. Disabling all plugins
   b. Using only default settings
   c. Implementing encryption and access control
   d. Limiting documentation
3. When planning for large-scale deployments, what is crucial for maintaining performance?
   a. Decreasing security measures
   b. Planning for capacity and scalability
   c. Avoiding updates
   d. Reducing the number of users
4. What type of maintenance task is important for ensuring data integrity and system recovery in Elastic Stack?
   a. Reducing feature usage
   b. Decreasing team size
   c. Backup and disaster recovery planning
   d. Ignoring logs
5. Which strategy is important, when looking beyond ELK to enhance the Elastic Stack's capabilities?
   a. Decreasing monitoring
   b. Reducing security
   c. Integrating other Elastic products
   d. Limiting user access

Answers

1. b.
2. c.
3. b.
4. c.
5. c.

Questions

1. Discuss the importance of understanding common pitfalls in Elastic Stack deployments, and describe some strategies to avoid them.
2. Explain how capacity planning impacts the scalability and performance of Elastic Stack deployments. What factors should be considered during this planning?
3. Detail the key security measures that should be implemented in any Elastic Stack deployment. How do these measures protect the data and infrastructure?
4. Describe the routine maintenance tasks that are crucial for the long-term health and performance of an Elastic Stack. Why is each task important?
5. Explain the process and significance of regularly updating and upgrading Elastic Stack components. What are the risks of neglecting this process?
6. Discuss how performance tuning is conducted in an Elastic Stack environment. What are some common adjustments that might be made?
7. Outline a comprehensive backup and disaster recovery strategy for an Elastic Stack deployment. Why is this strategy critical for data integrity?
8. What role does system health monitoring play in the maintenance of an Elastic Stack deployment? Describe how you would set up and use monitoring tools.
9. Describe the differences between full cluster restarts and rolling upgrades in the Elastic Stack. When would you choose one method over the other?
10. Explore the benefits of integrating other Elastic products into an ELK deployment. How do these integrations enhance the capabilities of the Elastic Stack?

Key Terms

- **Elastic Stack**: A group of open-source products designed to help users take data from any type of source, and in any format and search, analyze, and visualize that data in real time.
- **Troubleshooting**: The process of diagnosing the source of a problem in the Elastic Stack, and resolving it effectively.
- **Best Practices**: Recommended strategies and techniques that are considered ideal for achieving efficient and secure Elastic Stack deployments.
- **Scalability**: The ability of the Elastic Stack to handle the growing amounts of data or an increasing number of queries, without compromising performance.
- **Capacity Planning**: The process of determining the necessary resources such as hardware and configurations needed to handle future data and workload volumes in Elastic Stack.
- **Security Measures**: Protocols and features implemented to protect Elastic Stack deployments from unauthorized access and cyber threats, including encryption, role-based access control, and auditing.
- **Routine Maintenance**: Regularly performed tasks to ensure the Elastic Stack is running efficiently, including monitoring, updating, and optimizing systems.
- **Upgrades**: The process of moving Elastic Stack components to a newer version to take advantage of improved features, bug fixes, and security patches.
- **Backup and Recovery**: Strategies and processes involved in copying and archiving data as well as configurations to protect against data loss, and ensure quick restoration after a failure.
- **Performance Tuning**: The practice of adjusting settings and configurations in Elastic Stack to improve its efficiency and speed.
- **Index Management**: The process of handling and organizing indexes in Elasticsearch to ensure that the data is accessible and queries are efficient.
- **Cluster Health**: A measure of the status of an Elastic Stack cluster, indicating its performance, stability, and any issues that need to be addressed.
- **Integration**: The process of combining Elastic Stack with other products and tools to enhance its capabilities and performance.

CHAPTER 7
High Availability, Fault Tolerance, and Security

Introduction

In today's digital age, ensuring the continuous availability and reliability of data systems is paramount. As organizations increasingly rely on real-time data for critical decision-making, the need for robust architectures that can withstand failures, and prevent data loss becomes ever more pressing. Elasticsearch, a powerful distributed search and analytics engine, offers various features and configurations designed to achieve high availability, fault tolerance, and security. This chapter delves into these crucial aspects, providing insights and practical guidance on how to build resilient and secure Elasticsearch clusters.

High availability ensures that an Elasticsearch cluster remains operational and accessible, even in the face of node failures or maintenance activities. This involves strategic planning around node roles, data distribution, and network configurations to minimize downtime, and maintain service continuity. Fault tolerance, on the other hand, focuses on the system's ability to handle and recover from unexpected disruptions. By implementing replication, sharding, and automated failover mechanisms, Elasticsearch can continue to function seamlessly, providing uninterrupted access to data.

Security is another critical component for maintaining a reliable Elasticsearch deployment. Protecting the sensitive data from unauthorized access and breaches is essential in preserving data integrity, and complying with the regulatory requirements. Elasticsearch offers several security features, including Role-Based Access Control (RBAC), Transport Layer Security (TLS), encryption at rest, comprehensive monitoring, and alerting capabilities. These measures help safeguard the cluster against potential threats, and ensure that the data is only accessible to authorized users.

In the following subchapters, we will explore these concepts in greater detail. We will start with hands-on labs to set up an Elasticsearch Cluster using Docker Compose, demonstrating practical steps to achieve high availability and fault tolerance. We will then move on to advanced security configurations, ensuring that your Elasticsearch cluster is both resilient and secure. By the end of this chapter, you will have a thorough understanding of how to design, implement, and maintain that a robust Elasticsearch deployment is capable of meeting the demands of modern data-driven applications.

Structure

In this chapter, we will discuss the following topics:

- Strategies for High Availability and Fault Tolerance
- Elasticsearch Cluster Management for HA
- Hands-On Lab: Building an Elasticsearch Cluster with Docker Compose
- Security and Access Control
- Backup and Restore for Disaster Recovery

Strategies for High Availability and Fault Tolerance

High Availability (HA) and fault tolerance are critical considerations for any system that needs to provide consistent and reliable access to data and services. In the context of the Elastic Stack, ensuring that your Elasticsearch clusters are resilient to failures, and can handle increased loads is paramount. This chapter outlines various strategies and best practices to achieve high availability and fault tolerance in your Elastic Stack deployment.

Cluster Architecture Design

Designing your Elasticsearch cluster with high availability in mind starts with the architecture. A well-architected cluster can withstand node failures, and continue to serve requests without interruption.

- **Node Roles and Responsibilities**: Distribute node roles across multiple machines to avoid single points of failure. Common roles include master nodes, data nodes, ingest nodes, and coordinating nodes.
- **Dedicated Master Nodes**: Configure dedicated master nodes to manage cluster state and elections. Use an odd number of master-eligible nodes (typically three or five) to ensure quorum.

- **Data Node Redundancy**: Ensure that the data nodes are distributed across different physical or virtual machines to mitigate the risk of data loss due to hardware failures.

Replication and Sharding

Replication and sharding are fundamental to Elasticsearch's ability to provide fault tolerance and scalability.

- **Index Sharding**: Divide your indices into multiple shards to distribute data and query load across nodes. This improves performance, and allows the cluster to scale horizontally.
- **Replication**: Configure replica shards to provide redundancy. Each primary shard should have at least one replica shard stored on a different node. This ensures that the data is not lost, if a node fails.

Cross-Cluster Replication (CCR)

Cross-Cluster Replication (CCR) allows you to replicate indices across multiple Elasticsearch clusters. This provides an additional layer of redundancy, and can be used for disaster recovery.

- **Active-Passive Replication**: Use CCR to maintain a passive backup cluster that can take over in case the primary cluster fails.
- **Geo-Redundancy**: Deploy clusters in different geographic regions to protect against regional failures.

Snapshots and Restore

Regular snapshots provide a way to back up your data, and restore it in case of catastrophic failures.

- **Automated Snapshots**: Schedule automated snapshots of your indices to an external repository, such as AWS S3 or HDFS.
- **Snapshot Management**: Use Elasticsearch's Snapshot Lifecycle Management (SLM) to automate the creation, retention, and deletion of snapshots.

Monitoring and Alerting

Proactive monitoring and alerting help detect and respond to issues, before they impact the availability of your Elastic Stack.

- **Cluster Health Monitoring**: Use tools like Kibana, Elastic Stack's own monitoring features, or external solutions such as Prometheus to keep an eye on cluster health.

- **Alerting**: Set up alerts for critical metrics such as node availability, disk usage, CPU, and memory usage. Use ElastAlert or Elastic's alerting features to notify your team of potential issues.

Load Balancing

Load balancing distributes traffic across multiple nodes, preventing any single node from becoming a bottleneck or point of failure.

- **Elastic Load Balancer (ELB)**: Use an ELB or other load balancer to distribute requests to the coordinating nodes in your Elasticsearch cluster.
- **Round-Robin DNS**: Configure DNS to distribute client requests across multiple endpoints.

Failure Testing and Chaos Engineering

Regular testing of your system's resilience can uncover weaknesses, and help improve overall fault tolerance.

- **Failure Injection**: Use tools such as "*Chaos Monkey*" to simulate node failures, and validate your cluster's ability to recover.
- **Disaster Recovery Drills**: Regularly conduct disaster recovery drills to ensure that your backup and restoration processes are effective.

Security Measures

Security is an essential aspect for maintaining high availability and fault tolerance.

- **Access Controls**: Implement Role-Based Access Control (RBAC) to restrict access to your Elastic Stack resources.
- **Encryption**: Use encryption in transit (TLS) and at rest to protect your data.
- **Audit Logging**: Enable audit logging to monitor access and changes to your Elasticsearch cluster.

By implementing these strategies, you can build an Elastic Stack deployment that is resilient, reliable, and capable of handling various failure scenarios. High availability and fault tolerance not only ensure continuous operation, but also protect the integrity and accessibility of your data.

Elasticsearch Cluster Management for HA

Managing an Elasticsearch cluster for high availability involves a combination of strategic node configuration, effective resource allocation, and robust monitoring. This section provides a comprehensive guide to configuring and managing an Elasticsearch cluster to ensure continuous operation and minimal downtime.

Node Configuration

We can optimize Elasticsearch node configuration to enhance cluster resilience and performance:

Dedicated Node Roles

Elasticsearch nodes can take on specific roles to distribute responsibilities, and enhance the cluster's resilience:

- **Master Nodes**: Handle cluster-wide operations, including cluster state updates, index creation/deletion, and node management. It is crucial to have an odd number of dedicated master nodes (at least three) to maintain a quorum, and prevent split-brain scenarios.
- **Data Nodes**: Store and manage the indexed data, performing search and aggregation operations. To achieve fault tolerance, distribute the data across multiple data nodes, and use shard replication.
- **Ingest Nodes**: Process and transform the incoming data before it is indexed. This offloads processing tasks from data nodes, and ensures a smooth data ingestion pipeline.
- **Coordinating Nodes**: Act as load balancers, routing client requests to the appropriate data nodes. They do not store data or participate in master node duties which helps optimize resource usage.

Shard Allocation and Replication

Sharding and replication are core features of Elasticsearch that contribute to high availability:

- **Shards**: An index in Elasticsearch is divided into smaller units called shards. Each shard is a self-contained index that can be distributed across multiple nodes, enhancing search and indexing performance.
- **Replication**: Replicas are copies of primary shards. They provide redundancy, and improve fault tolerance. Configuring multiple replicas ensures that data remains accessible, even if some nodes fail.

Cluster Configuration

We can optimize cluster-wide settings to improve availability and performance:

Discovery and Coordination

Configuring cluster discovery and coordination is necessary for maintaining high availability:

- **Zen Discovery**: Elasticsearch uses Zen Discovery to manage the joining and leaving of nodes in a cluster. Ensure that the `discovery.zen.minimum_master_nodes` setting is configured to a majority of the master-eligible nodes to prevent split-brain scenarios.
- **Unicast Discovery**: For larger clusters or when using dedicated master nodes, configure unicast discovery to specify the addresses of the master nodes explicitly.

Cluster State Management

Efficient management of cluster state is critical for high availability:

- **Cluster State Updates**: Cluster state updates should be minimized and optimized to reduce overhead. Avoid frequent index creation/deletion operations, and batch updates where possible.
- **Persistent Cluster State Storage**: Use persistent storage for cluster state to ensure that it can be quickly recovered in case of failures.

Resource Management

We can optimize resource allocation and management to ensure optimal performance and availability:

Hardware and Infrastructure

Proper hardware and infrastructure planning are key to maintaining high availability:

- **Node Sizing**: Ensure that the nodes have sufficient CPU, memory, and disk resources to handle the expected load. Over-provisioning can provide a buffer during peak times.
- **Network Configuration**: Use high-speed, low-latency network connections to reduce communication delays between nodes.

Load Balancing

Distribute client requests evenly across the cluster to prevent overloading individual nodes:

- **Coordinating Nodes**: Use dedicated coordinating nodes to handle incoming requests, and distribute them to the appropriate data nodes.

- **External Load Balancers**: Implement external load balancers (for example, NGINX, and HAProxy) to manage traffic distribution, and improve fault tolerance.

Monitoring and Maintenance

We can implement monitoring tools and maintenance practices to ensure cluster health and availability:

Monitoring Tools

Continuous monitoring is vital for detecting and responding to issues, before they impact availability:

- **Elasticsearch Monitoring**: Use built-in monitoring features such as Elasticsearch's X-Pack Monitoring or open-source alternatives such as Prometheus and Grafana to track cluster health, performance, and resource utilization.
- **Alerting**: Set up alerts for critical events such as node failures, high CPU/memory usage, and disk space issues. Automated alerting enables timely intervention.

Backup and Recovery

Regular backups and a well-defined recovery strategy are essential for data protection:

- **Snapshot and Restore**: Use Elasticsearch's snapshot, and restore functionality to create regular backups of your indices. Store snapshots in a reliable, off-site location.
- **Disaster Recovery Plan**: Develop and test a disaster recovery plan to ensure that you can quickly restore cluster operations in the event of a failure.

Hands-On Lab: Building an Elasticsearch Cluster with Docker Compose

In this hands-on lab, we will create a highly available Elasticsearch cluster using Docker and Docker Compose. Our setup will include three Elasticsearch nodes and one Kibana instance, as illustrated in the following diagram:

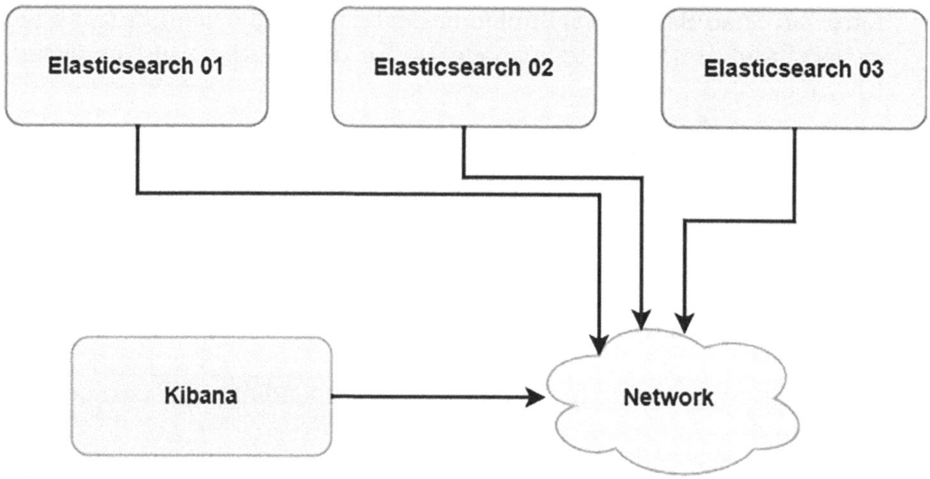

***Figure 7.1**: Elasticsearch and Kibana Network*

This setup is designed to simulate a real-world Elasticsearch deployment, where multiple nodes work together to provide redundancy, high availability, and distributed search capabilities. Kibana will serve as the web-based interface for visualizing and interacting with the data stored in the Elasticsearch cluster.

Thus, by the end of this lab, you will have a functional Elasticsearch cluster running locally on your machine, allowing you to explore the features and capabilities of Elasticsearch and Kibana in a controlled environment.

Let us get started!

Prerequisites

1. Docker installed on your machine.
2. Docker Compose installed on your machine.
3. Basic understanding of Docker and Docker Compose.

Step 1: Setup Docker Compose File

Create a directory for your Elasticsearch cluster setup, and navigate into it:

```
mkdir elasticsearch-cluster
cd elasticsearch-cluster
```

For demo, we use Elasticsearch version 8.14.0. We download **docker-compose.yml** file from Elasticsearch sample repository, https://github.com/elastic/elasticsearch/blob/8.14/docs/reference/setup/install/docker/docker-compose.yml .

This Docker Compose file defines a three-node Elasticsearch cluster.

Step 2: Launch the Cluster

Run the following command to start your Elasticsearch cluster:

```
docker-compose up
```

Docker Compose will download the Elasticsearch image (if not already downloaded), create the containers, and start the services.

Step 3: Verify the Cluster

Once the cluster is up and running, you can verify its status by opening a new terminal window, and running the following commands:

```
curl -X GET "localhost:9200/_cluster/health?pretty"
```

You should see a response indicating that the cluster is healthy.

To see the list of nodes in the cluster, run:

```
curl -X GET "localhost:9200/_cat/nodes?v"
```

This will show you the information about the nodes in your cluster.

Step 4: Access Elasticsearch

Elasticsearch should now be accessible on your local machine at the following URLs:

- **Node 1**: http://localhost:9200
- **Node 2**: http://localhost:9201
- **Node 3**: http://localhost:9202

You can now interact with Elasticsearch, using these URLs, for example:

```
curl -X GET "http://localhost:9200/_cat/indices?v"
```

This will list all the indices in your Elasticsearch cluster.

Step 5: Scaling the Cluster

You can scale your Elasticsearch cluster by adding more nodes. To add another node, you can extend your **`docker-compose.yml`** file with a new service definition, and follow the same environment configurations as the other nodes.

For example, to add a fourth node:

```
es04:
  image: docker.elastic.co/elasticsearch/elasticsearch:8.14.0
  container_name: es04
  environment:
```

```
          - node.name=es04
          - cluster.name=es-docker-cluster
          - discovery.seed_hosts=es01,es02,es03
          - cluster.initial_master_nodes=es01,es02,es03
          - bootstrap.memory_lock=true
          - ES_JAVA_OPTS=-Xms512m -Xmx512m
          - xpack.security.enabled=false
        ulimits:
          memlock:
            soft: -1
            hard: -1
        volumes:
          - esdata04:/usr/share/elasticsearch/data
        ports:
          - 9203:9200
          - 9303:9300

    volumes:
      esdata04:
        driver: local
```

Step 6: Cleanup

To stop and remove the containers and associated resources, run:

```
docker-compose down
```

This command will stop the containers, and remove the network and volumes created by Docker Compose.

Summary

By following these steps, you have successfully set up a multi-node Elasticsearch cluster using Docker Compose. This setup allows you to experiment with Elasticsearch in a local, simulated environment, giving you a deeper understanding of how to configure and manage Elasticsearch clusters.

Security and Access Control

Securing an Elasticsearch cluster is paramount to ensure that the sensitive data is protected, and that only authorized users have access to the system. This subchapter explores the vital security mechanisms, including Role-Based Access Control (RBAC), Transport Layer Security (TLS), encryption at rest, security monitoring and alerts. Implementing these measures helps safeguard your Elasticsearch deployment from unauthorized access as well as potential breaches.

Role-Based Access Control (RBAC)

Role-Based Access Control (RBAC) is a method of regulating access to computer or network resources, based on the roles of individual users within an organization. RBAC allows you to assign permissions to roles, rather than to individual users, simplifying the management of user permissions.

To implement RBAC in Elasticsearch, follow these steps:

- **Roles**: Define roles that specify a set of permissions for accessing Elasticsearch resources. For example, you can create roles for administrators, data analysts, and read-only users.
- **Users**: Create user accounts, and assign them to appropriate roles. This ensures that users only have the permissions necessary for their job functions.
- **Permissions**: Permissions can be fine-grained, allowing control over specific actions such as read, write, and manage indices. Use the Elasticsearch REST API or Kibana to manage roles and permissions.

The following example demonstrates how to create a role for a data analyst, and assign it to a user in Elasticsearch:

```
PUT /_security/role/data_analyst
{
  "cluster": ["monitor"],
  "indices": [
    {
      "names": ["logs-*"],
      "privileges": ["read"]
    }
  ]
}

PUT /_security/user/jane_doe
{
  "password": "password123",
  "roles": ["data_analyst"],
  "full_name": "Jane Doe",
  "email": "jane.doe@example.com"
}
```

This example creates a role **`data_analyst`** with read permissions on indices that match logs-* and assigns this role to the user **`jane_doe`**.

Transport Layer Security (TLS)

Transport Layer Security (TLS) is essential for encrypting data transmitted between

Elasticsearch nodes and between clients as well as the cluster. TLS ensures that the data remains confidential, and is not tampered with during transmission.

To enable TLS in Elasticsearch, follow these steps:

- **Generate Certificates**: Use the Elasticsearch **elasticsearch-certutil** tool to generate SSL/TLS certificates for your nodes.
- **Configure Elasticsearch**: Update the Elasticsearch configuration to enable TLS for both HTTP and transport layers.

Here is an example of how to configure TLS in Elasticsearch:

```
# In elasticsearch.yml
xpack.security.transport.ssl.enabled: true
xpack.security.transport.ssl.verification_mode: certificate
xpack.security.transport.ssl.key: /path/to/your/key.pem
xpack.security.transport.ssl.certificate: /path/to/your/cert.pem
xpack.security.transport.ssl.certificate_authorities: ["/path/to/
your/ca.pem"]

xpack.security.http.ssl.enabled: true
xpack.security.http.ssl.key: /path/to/your/key.pem
xpack.security.http.ssl.certificate: /path/to/your/cert.pem
xpack.security.http.ssl.certificate_authorities: ["/path/to/your/
ca.pem"]
```

This configuration enables TLS for both inter-node communication (transport layer) and HTTP clients.

Encryption at Rest

Encryption at rest protects the data stored on disk from unauthorized access. This is crucial for safeguarding sensitive information, even if physical access to storage devices is compromised.

To enable encryption at rest in Elasticsearch, consider the following options:

- **File System Encryption**: Use operating system-level encryption tools like dm-crypt (Linux) or BitLocker (Windows) to encrypt the disks where Elasticsearch data is stored.
- **Elasticsearch Configuration**: Enable Elasticsearch-native encryption for index data, using the Elasticsearch Security features.

Here is an example of how to enable encryption at rest in Elasticsearch:

```
# In elasticsearch.yml
xpack.security.enabled: true
xpack.security.encrypt_sensitive_data: true
```

Ensure that the Elasticsearch security features are enabled to use native encryption for the sensitive data.

Security Monitoring and Alerts

Continuous monitoring and timely alerts are crucial for detecting and responding to security incidents. By keeping an eye on security-related events, you can quickly identify and mitigate the potential threats.

Here are some tools and features, you can use to monitor security events in Elasticsearch:

- **Elasticsearch Audit Logging**: Enable audit logging to track security-related events such as authentication attempts, role changes, and access denials.
- **Kibana**: Use Kibana's Security App to monitor and visualize security events in your Elasticsearch cluster.

To configure alerts for security events in Elasticsearch, consider the following options:

- **Watchers**: Use Elasticsearch Watcher to create alerts based on specific conditions. For example, set up alerts for failed login attempts, changes in user roles, or access to sensitive indices.
- **Third-Party Integrations**: Integrate Elasticsearch with third-party monitoring tools such as Prometheus, Grafana, or SIEM systems for comprehensive security monitoring.

Here is an example of how to configure a watcher in Elasticsearch to send an email alert for failed login attempts:

```
PUT _watcher/watch/failed_login_attempts
{
  "trigger": {
    "schedule": {
      "interval": "10m"
    }
  },
  "input": {
    "search": {
      "request": {
        "indices": ["audit-*"],
        "body": {
          "query": {
            "bool": {
              "must": [
                { "term": { "event.action": "authentication_
failed" } },
```

```
                { "range": { "@timestamp": { "gte": "now-10m" } }
}
              ]
            }
          }
        }
      }
    }
  },
  "actions": {
    "notify_admin": {
      "email": {
        "to": "admin@example.com",
        "subject": "Failed Login Attempts Detected",
        "body": "Multiple failed login attempts detected in the
last 10 minutes."
      }
    }
  }
}
```

This example configures a watcher that checks for failed login attempts every 10 minutes, and sends an email notification, if any are found.

Implementing robust security measures such as RBAC, TLS, encryption at rest, and continuous monitoring, is crucial for protecting your Elasticsearch cluster. By following these practices, you can ensure that your data remains secure and accessible only to the authorized users, mitigating the risk of unauthorized access and data breaches.

Backup and Restore for Disaster Recovery

In the context of disaster recovery for Elasticsearch, ensuring reliable backup and restore processes is critical to maintaining data integrity and availability. This section provides an in-depth look at the best practices and strategies for managing Elasticsearch backups as well as restores using a systematic approach.

Understanding Snapshots in Elasticsearch

Snapshots in Elasticsearch are a built-in mechanism to capture the state of your indices and cluster metadata at a specific point in time. They provide an efficient way to back up your data incrementally, meaning that only the changes since the last snapshot are stored.

Snapshots are stored in repositories which can reside on various storage backends such as local filesystems, shared filesystems, Amazon S3, Azure Blob Storage, and Google Cloud Storage.

Configuring Snapshot Repositories

In Elasticsearch, you need to configure snapshot repositories to store your snapshots. Here is how you can set up different types of repositories:

To set up a snapshot repository on a local filesystem:

```
PUT /_snapshot/local_backup
{
  "type": "fs",
  "settings": {
    "location": "/mount/backups/local_backup"
  }
}
```

Ensure that the specified location is accessible by all nodes in the cluster.

For an Amazon S3 repository:

```
PUT /_snapshot/s3_backup
{
  "type": "s3",
  "settings": {
    "bucket": "my-elasticsearch-backups",
    "region": "us-west-2"
  }
}
```

Ensure that all the necessary permissions and configurations are set up in your AWS account.

Creating Snapshots

In Elasticsearch, you can create snapshots to back up your data and cluster state. Here is how you can create snapshots:

To create a snapshot of all indices:

```
PUT /_snapshot/local_backup/snapshot_1
{
  "indices": "*",
  "ignore_unavailable": true,
  "include_global_state": true
}
```

This command creates a snapshot named **`snapshot_1`** in the **`local_backup`** repository, including all indices and the global state.

To automate the snapshot creation process, use the Elasticsearch Curator tool, or create a scheduled job:

- **Using Curator**: Install and configure Curator to run snapshot tasks at regular intervals.
- **Scheduled Job Example**: Use a cron job or a similar scheduler to trigger snapshot creation via a script that calls the Elasticsearch API.

Restoring Snapshots

We can restore snapshots to recover data in case of data loss or cluster failures. Here is how you can restore snapshots in Elasticsearch:

To restore a snapshot:

```
POST /_snapshot/local_backup/snapshot_1/_restore
{
  "indices": "index_1,index_2",
  "ignore_unavailable": true,
  "include_global_state": true,
  "rename_pattern": "index_(.+)",
  "rename_replacement": "restored_index_$1"
}
```

This command restores **`index_1`** and **`index_2`** from **`snapshot_1`** in the **`local_backup`** repository, renaming them to **`restored_index_1`** and **`restored_index_2`**.

To restore the entire cluster, including the global state:

```
POST /_snapshot/local_backup/snapshot_1/_restore
{
  "include_global_state": true
}
```

This command restores all indices and the cluster state from the snapshot.

Best Practices for Backup and Restore

Here are some best practices to ensure an effective backup, and restore processes for disaster recovery:

- **Regular Backups**
  - **Frequency**: Schedule regular snapshots to minimize data loss in the event of a failure. The frequency depends on your data change rate, and business requirements.

    - **Retention Policy**: Implement a retention policy to manage the lifecycle of snapshots, ensuring that old and unnecessary snapshots are deleted to free up the storage space.
- **Verify Backup Integrity**
    - **Test Restores**: Regularly perform test restores to ensure that your snapshots are valid, and that the restore process works as expected.
    - **Checksum Validation**: Use checksum validation to verify the integrity of your snapshots.
- **Secure Backup Storage**
    - **Access Control**: Implement strict access controls on your snapshot repositories to prevent unauthorized access or tampering.
    - **Encryption**: Use encryption to protect your backup data, both in transit and at rest.

Disaster Recovery Plan

Here are some key steps to include in your disaster recovery plan for Elasticsearch:

- **Define Recovery Objectives**
    - **Recovery Point Objective (RPO)**: Determine the maximum acceptable amount of data loss measured in time. This will guide the frequency of your snapshots.
    - **Recovery Time Objective (RTO)**: Determine the maximum acceptable downtime. This will guide the complexity and speed of your restore procedures.
- **Document Recovery Procedures**
    - **Step-by-Step Instructions**: Document detailed, step-by-step instructions for restoring data from snapshots. Ensure that the procedures are clear and accessible to all relevant personnel.
    - **Role Assignments**: Assign specific roles and responsibilities for executing the disaster recovery plan, ensuring that all the team members understand their duties.
- **Regular Drills**
    - **Simulated Failures**: Conduct regular disaster recovery drills to simulate various failure scenarios, and practice the restore process.
    - **Review and Improve**: After each drill, review the outcomes, and identify areas for improvement in your disaster recovery plan and procedures.

By implementing these robust backup and restore strategies, you can ensure that your Elasticsearch cluster remains resilient, and that your data can be quickly recovered in the event of a disaster. Regular backups, thorough testing, and a well-documented disaster recovery plan are essential components of a comprehensive data protection strategy.

Conclusion

In this chapter, we have explored the critical components of achieving high availability, fault tolerance, and security in Elasticsearch deployments. These aspects are fundamental to ensuring that your Elasticsearch cluster remains robust, reliable, and secure, capable of handling real-time data processing needs, without interruption.

We began by examining the importance of cluster design, focusing on node roles, shard allocation, and replication strategies. By configuring dedicated master nodes, and appropriately distributing data across multiple data nodes, we can enhance the cluster's resilience against failures. The use of snapshots for regular backups and a well-documented disaster recovery plan further ensures that the data can be quickly restored in case of unexpected disruptions.

Our hands-on lab provided a practical demonstration of setting up a multi-node Elasticsearch cluster with Kibana using Docker Compose. This exercise highlighted the ease of deploying and managing a distributed Elasticsearch environment, emphasizing the benefits of containerization for scalability and flexibility. We also delved into advanced security configurations, including Role-Based Access Control (RBAC), Transport Layer Security (TLS), and encryption at rest, to protect the sensitive data, and maintain compliance with the security standards.

The comprehensive approach to security monitoring and alerts ensures that any potential threats are detected and addressed promptly, safeguarding the integrity and availability of your data. By following the strategies and best practices outlined in this chapter, you can build and maintain an Elasticsearch cluster that meets the high standards required for modern data-driven applications.

As we conclude our discussion on high availability, fault tolerance, and security, the next chapter will delve into advanced deployment strategies. We will cover pre-deployment planning, including sizing, capacity, and topology considerations, as well as various cloud deployment options such as Elastic Cloud, AWS, GCP, and Azure. Additionally, we will explore Docker and Kubernetes deployments, hybrid deployment models, and effective scaling strategies. Finally, we will provide insights into performance tuning and optimization to ensure that your Elasticsearch deployment runs efficiently and effectively.

Points to Remember

- **High Availability and Fault Tolerance:**
  - **Node Roles**: Properly configure and assign roles (master, data, ingest, coordinating) to nodes to ensure balanced workload distribution, and fault tolerance.
  - **Sharding and Replication**: Use sharding and replication to distribute data across nodes, enhancing redundancy and performance.
  - **Cluster State Management**: Efficient management of cluster state updates and persistence is crucial for stability.
- **Security:**
  - **Role-Based Access Control (RBAC)**: Implement RBAC to manage user permissions effectively, and ensure that only authorized access to data and cluster management functions.
  - **Transport Layer Security (TLS)**: Enable TLS for both HTTP and transport layers to encrypt data in transit, and protect it from unauthorized interception.
  - **Encryption at Rest**: Use filesystem-level or Elasticsearch-native encryption to secure the data stored on disk.
  - **Security Monitoring and Alerts**: Set up monitoring and alerting to detect and respond to security incidents promptly.
- **Backup and Restore for Disaster Recovery:**
  - **Snapshots**: Regularly create and verify snapshots to ensure that you can restore data accurately in case of failures.
  - **Snapshot Repositories**: Use appropriate storage backends for snapshot repositories such as local filesystems, shared filesystems, or cloud storage services.
  - **Disaster Recovery Plan**: Develop and document a comprehensive disaster recovery plan, including Recovery Point Objectives (RPO) and Recovery Time Objectives (RTO).
- **Hands-On Lab with Docker Compose:**
  - **Setup**: Create a `docker-compose.yml` file to define a multi-node Elasticsearch cluster and Kibana setup.
  - **Deployment**: Use Docker Compose to deploy and start the cluster, ensuring that the nodes are properly configured to form a resilient cluster.
  - **Verification**: Verify the health and status of the cluster and nodes, using Elasticsearch APIs.

- **Access and Management**: Access Elasticsearch and Kibana through defined ports, using appropriate credentials and secure configurations.

Multiple Choice Questions

1. What is the primary purpose of sharding and replication in Elasticsearch?
    a. To reduce the number of nodes required
    b. To enhance redundancy and performance
    c. To increase the size of the data stored
    d. To decrease the data access speed
2. Which role in Elasticsearch is responsible for managing cluster-wide operations such as creating or deleting indices?
    a. Data Node
    b. Ingest Node
    c. Coordinating Node
    d. Master Node
3. Which of the following security features in Elasticsearch ensures encrypted communication between nodes and clients?
    a. Role-Based Access Control (RBAC)
    b. Transport Layer Security (TLS)
    c. Encryption at Rest
    d. Security Monitoring and Alerts
4. What command is used to start the Elasticsearch **C**luster using Docker Compose in the hands-on lab?
    a. `docker-compose run`
    b. `docker-compose start`
    c. `docker-compose up`
    d. `docker-compose deploy`

5. In the context of disaster recovery, what is the purpose of regularly creating snapshots in Elasticsearch?
    a. To minimize data redundancy
    b. To decrease storage costs
    c. To ensure that the data can be quickly restored in case of failures
    d. To optimize the performance of the cluster

Answers

1. b.
2. d.
3. b.
4. c.
5. c.

Questions

1. Explain the importance of high availability in Elasticsearch deployments, and describe the strategies used to achieve it.
2. Discuss the role of dedicated master nodes in an Elasticsearch cluster, and explain how they contribute to the overall stability and performance of the cluster.
3. Describe the process of sharding and replication in Elasticsearch. How do these mechanisms improve fault tolerance and data redundancy?
4. Detail the steps involved in setting up a multi-node Elasticsearch cluster using Docker Compose. What configurations are necessary to ensure high availability and security?
5. How does Role-Based Access Control (RBAC) enhance security in an Elasticsearch deployment? Provide examples of how to configure roles and permissions.
6. Explain the significance of Transport Layer Security (TLS) in securing Elasticsearch communications. What configurations are required to enable TLS for both HTTP and transport layers?

7. Discuss the importance of encryption at rest in protecting data stored in Elasticsearch. What are the methods available for enabling encryption at rest, and how do they differ?

8. Outline the best practices for creating and managing snapshots in Elasticsearch for disaster recovery purposes. How do regular backups, and a well-documented recovery plan ensure data integrity?

9. Describe the purpose and process of security monitoring and alerts in Elasticsearch. How do these features help in maintaining the security and integrity of the cluster?

10. Looking ahead to advanced deployment strategies, what considerations should be taken into account for pre-deployment planning, and how do different cloud deployment options (Elastic Cloud, AWS, GCP, and Azure) affect these plans?

Key Terms

- **High Availability (HA)**: The capability of a system to remain operational and accessible, even in the event of component failures. In Elasticsearch, this involves configuring multiple nodes, and ensuring data redundancy through sharding and replication.
- **Fault Tolerance**: The ability of a system to continue operating properly in the event of the failure of some of its components. Fault tolerance in Elasticsearch is achieved through mechanisms like shard replication and automated failover.
- **Node**: An instance of Elasticsearch running on a physical or virtual machine. Nodes can have different roles, including master, data, ingest, and coordinating nodes, each with specific responsibilities within the cluster.
- **Master Node**: A node responsible for cluster-wide actions such as creating or deleting indices and managing the cluster state. It plays a critical role in maintaining the overall health and stability of the cluster.
- **Data Node**: A node that stores data and handles data-related operations such as search and indexing. Data nodes are essential for managing and processing the bulk of Elasticsearch data.
- **Ingest Node**: A node used to preprocess and transform documents, before they are indexed into Elasticsearch. Ingest nodes help offload processing tasks from data nodes.
- **Coordinating Node**: A node that does not hold data or participate in master node duties. It acts as a load balancer, routing client requests to the appropriate data nodes, and distributing the workload.

- **Sharding**: The process of splitting an index into smaller pieces called shards. Each shard is an independent index that can be distributed across multiple nodes, enhancing performance and scalability.
- **Replication**: The process of creating copies of shards (replica shards) to ensure data redundancy and fault tolerance. Replica shards can be used for reading operations, and improving search performance.
- **Role-Based Access Control (RBAC)**: A security mechanism that restricts access to resources, based on the roles of individual users within an organization. RBAC simplifies permission management, and ensures that users only have an access to the data as well as functions necessary for their roles.
- **Transport Layer Security (TLS)**: A protocol that provides encryption for data in transit, ensuring secure communication between Elasticsearch nodes, and between clients as well as the cluster. TLS helps protect data from unauthorized interception and tampering.
- **Encryption at Rest**: The practice of encrypting data stored on disk to protect it from unauthorized access. This is crucial for safeguarding sensitive information, even if physical access to storage devices is compromised.
- **Snapshots**: Incremental backups of Elasticsearch indices and cluster metadata, capturing the state of data at a specific point in time. Snapshots are necessary for disaster recovery, and can be stored in various types of repositories.
- **Snapshot Repository**: A storage location for Elasticsearch snapshots. Repositories can be configured on local filesystems, shared filesystems, or cloud storage services such as Amazon S3, Azure Blob Storage, and Google Cloud Storage.
- **Disaster Recovery**: Strategies and processes for recovering data, and restoring system functionality after a catastrophic failure. In Elasticsearch, this involves regular backups, well-documented recovery procedures, and testing restore processes.
- **Docker Compose**: A tool for defining and running multi-container Docker applications. In the context of Elasticsearch, Docker Compose is used to set up, and manage multi-node clusters for development and testing.
- **Kibana**: A visualization and management tool for Elasticsearch. Kibana provides a web-based interface for exploring data stored in Elasticsearch, creating dashboards, and managing cluster operations.

CHAPTER 8
Advanced Deployment Strategies

Introduction

As Elasticsearch deployments grow in complexity, so do the strategies needed to ensure that they remain efficient, scalable, and resilient. While the basic deployment of Elasticsearch can serve small-to-medium workloads, enterprise-level use cases often require advanced techniques for deployment, scaling, and optimization. This chapter explores these advanced strategies, focusing on how to prepare, deploy, and manage Elasticsearch in environments ranging from on-premises infrastructures to complex hybrid cloud systems. By understanding and implementing these strategies, organizations can maximize the performance and flexibility of their Elasticsearch clusters, while minimizing downtime and operational overhead.

The first sections of this chapter delve into the importance of pre-deployment planning, including how to size and configure your Elasticsearch cluster, based on your workload. Following that, we will explore different cloud-based deployment options, including using managed services such as Elastic Cloud, and deploying Elasticsearch on popular cloud platforms like AWS, GCP, and Azure. Additionally, we will cover Docker and Kubernetes-based deployments, ideal for modern, containerized environments. Finally, this chapter examines scaling strategies, and offers techniques for performance tuning and optimization, helping to ensure that your Elasticsearch deployment can handle growth and peak workloads, without compromising speed or reliability.

Structure

In this chapter, we will discuss the following topics:

- Pre-Deployment Planning
- Cloud Deployments
- Docker and Kubernetes Deployments

- Hybrid Deployments
- Scaling Strategies
- Performance Tuning and Optimization

Pre-deployment Planning: Sizing, Capacity, and Topology

In the world of Elasticsearch and the broader Elastic Stack, deployment is a critical phase that can make or break the success of your stack. The efficiency and effectiveness of your Elastic Stack deployment depend heavily on pre-deployment planning. This planning involves understanding and determining the appropriate sizing, capacity, and topology for your deployment. Let us dive into these three fundamental aspects.

Sizing

Sizing is the process of determining the appropriate hardware and software resources needed for your Elastic Stack deployment. Proper sizing ensures that your system can handle the expected load, provide quick responses, and maintain high availability. Here are certain key factors to consider:

- **Data Volume:** Estimate the amount of data your cluster will need to index and store. Consider both the current and future data growth.
- **Query Load:** Analyze the expected query load on your cluster. Consider peak times, frequency, and complexity of the searches.
- **Indexing Rate:** Determine the rate at which the data will be ingested. High ingestion rates may require more powerful hardware.
- **Retention Period:** Decide how long you need to keep the data. Longer retention periods will increase storage requirements.
- **Replication Factor:** Decide on the number of replicas for high availability. More replicas mean more storage and processing power.

The following steps can help you size your Elastic Stack deployment effectively:

1. **Baseline Metrics:** Start with baseline metrics from a smaller test deployment or historical data from similar applications.
2. **Elastic Sizing Guides**: Use Elastic's official sizing guidelines and tools like the Elasticsearch Service Sizing Guide.
3. **Pilot Testing:** Conduct pilot tests to validate your sizing assumptions. Adjust based on real-world results.

Capacity Planning

Capacity Planning goes hand in hand with sizing, but focuses on ensuring that your deployment can scale to meet future demands. It involves anticipating growth and planning for additional resources, without compromising performance.

The following are the key considerations for capacity planning:

- **Scalability:** Plan for horizontal scaling (adding more nodes) and vertical scaling (upgrading hardware) as data and query load increase.
- **Performance:** Ensure your cluster can maintain performance standards as capacity grows. Consider the impact on indexing, querying, and storage.
- **Resource Utilization:** Monitor CPU, memory, disk I/O, and network usage to avoid bottlenecks.
- **Budget:** Factor in the costs of additional resources, including hardware, cloud services, and maintenance.

To ensure effective capacity planning, consider the following steps:

1. **Monitoring Tools:** Use monitoring tools such as Elastic Stack's own Kibana, as well as other tools like Prometheus and Grafana, to track resource usage.
2. **Scaling Strategies:** Develop strategies for both scaling out (adding nodes) and scaling up (increasing node capacity).
3. **Regular Reviews:** Periodically review the capacity plans to ensure that they align with the current and projected needs.

Topology Design

Topology Design refers to the logical arrangement of nodes and their roles within your Elasticsearch cluster. An efficient topology can enhance performance, fault tolerance, and manageability.

The following are common node roles in an Elasticsearch cluster:

- **Master Nodes:** Responsible for cluster management and state. Ensure that you have dedicated master nodes to avoid performance degradation.
- **Data Nodes:** Handle data storage, indexing, and querying. Plan for enough data nodes to manage your data volume and query load.
- **Ingest Nodes:** Preprocess documents before indexing. Use ingest nodes, if you have heavy data transformation needs.
- **Client Nodes:** Act as load balancers for search requests. Useful in large clusters to distribute the query load.

We recommend the following steps for effective topology design:

1. **Node Roles:** Assign specific roles to nodes, based on their hardware capabilities and workload requirements.
2. **High Availability:** Design for high availability with multiple master nodes (at least three) and sufficient replicas of your data.
3. **Network Configuration:** Optimize network settings for inter-node communication and data transfer efficiency.

Pre-deployment planning is a cornerstone of a successful Elastic Stack deployment. By carefully considering the sizing, capacity, and topology, you can create a robust, scalable, and high-performing Elasticsearch cluster. These efforts will pay off in the form of smoother operations, quicker response times, and a better overall user experience.

In the next section, we will explore various deployment architectures and strategies, including on-premises, cloud, and hybrid deployments. Understanding these options will further enhance your ability to deploy and manage the Elastic Stack effectively.

Cloud Deployments

Elasticsearch is widely adopted in cloud environments due to its scalability and flexibility. Cloud deployments provide the advantage of managed services, reducing operational overhead, and offering elasticity to adjust to the varying workloads. This section explores the most common cloud platforms for Elasticsearch: Elastic Cloud, AWS, GCP, and Azure, and provides insights into how to deploy Elasticsearch in each.

Deploying on Elastic Cloud

Elastic Cloud is the official managed Elasticsearch service provided by Elastic, the creators of Elasticsearch. It offers a seamless experience with automatic updates, security configurations, and performance tuning. Deploying on Elastic Cloud provides access to the latest features, including Elasticsearch, Kibana, and APM.

Key Features:

- **Managed Service:** Elastic handles all the infrastructure, including backups, updates, and monitoring.
- **Global Presence:** Available in multiple regions, allowing for localized deployments and compliance with the regional regulations.
- **Seamless Scaling:** Both vertical and horizontal scaling options are available, with no downtime.

- **Security:** Built-in security features such as encryption, Role-Based Access Control (RBAC), and compliance certifications (for example, SOC 2 and HIPAA).
- **Integrations:** Offers native integration with other Elastic Stack components such as Kibana and Logstash.

We will focus on Amazon OpenSearch Service which is the successor to Amazon Elasticsearch Service. Amazon OpenSearch Service provides a managed Elasticsearch service with additional features and enhancements.

Steps to Deploy on Elastic Cloud:

1. **Sign Up:** Start by creating an Elastic Cloud account at elastic.co.
2. **Create a Deployment:** Select a cloud provider (AWS, GCP, or Azure), choose a region, and set the deployment size, based on your expected workload.
3. **Configure Settings:** Customize deployment settings such as node size, availability zones, and security configurations.
4. **Access Kibana:** After deployment, access Kibana directly from the Elastic Cloud console to manage and monitor your cluster.
5. **Scaling and Monitoring:** Use the Elastic Cloud console for scaling the cluster, or monitoring performance metrics.

AWS: Using Amazon Elasticsearch Service

Amazon Elasticsearch Service (Amazon ES) is a fully managed service that makes it easy to deploy, operate, and scale Elasticsearch on AWS. Amazon ES provides built-in integrations with other AWS services, including AWS Lambda, S3, and CloudWatch, making it an excellent choice for organizations already using AWS.

Key Features:

- **Managed Service:** AWS manages Elasticsearch clusters, handling patching, backups, and scaling.
- **AWS Integration:** Tight integration with AWS services such as S3 (for data storage), CloudWatch (for monitoring), and VPC (for secure networking).
- **Security:** Offers security options such as VPC access, IAM roles, and AWS KMS for encryption at rest.
- **Scaling Options:** Both vertical and horizontal scaling with seamless data replication across availability zones.

To deploy Elasticsearch on AWS, we can use these approaches:

- Using Amazon OpenSearch Service (successor to Amazon Elasticsearch Service)
- Elasticsearch on Amazon EC2 instances
- Elasticsearch from AWS Marketplace (third-party services - by Elastic, AWS partners)

Steps to Deploy on Amazon Elasticsearch Service:

1. **Access the AWS Console:** Go to the Amazon OpenSearch Service console.
2. **Create a Domain:** Define the domain name, and choose a deployment region as well as an instance type.
3. **Configure Access Control:** Set up VPC access or public access with AWS IAM policies to control who can access the cluster.
4. **Select Instance Types**: Choose from a variety of instance types, including memory-optimized and storage-optimized instances.
5. **Monitoring and Scaling:** Use CloudWatch for performance monitoring, and scale the cluster as needed, using the AWS console.

If you want to get more features and control over your Elasticsearch deployment, you can opt for deploying Elasticsearch on Amazon EC2 instances, or using third-party services available on AWS Marketplace. You can see Elasticsearch on AWS Marketplace in *Figure 8.1*.

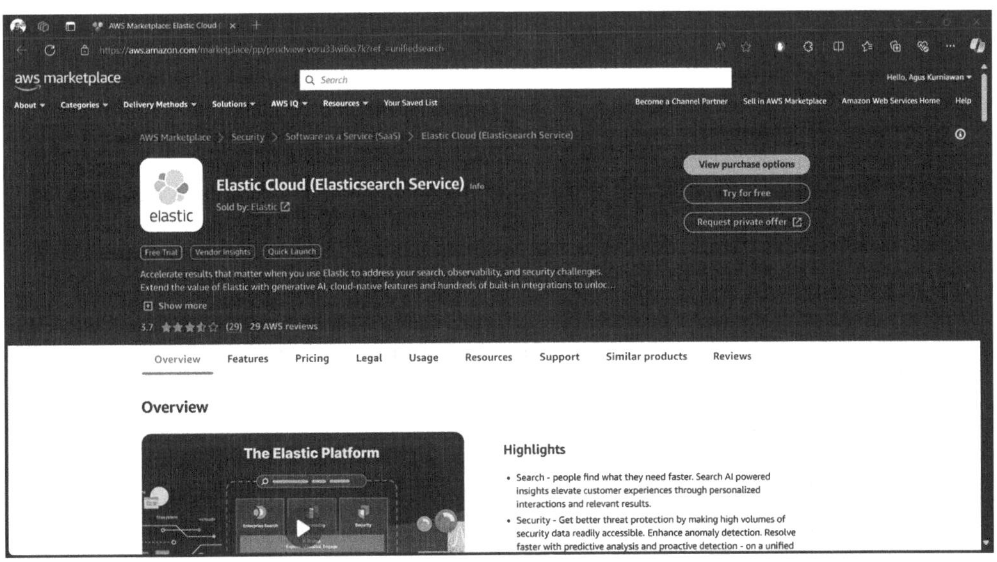

Figure 8.1: *Elasticsearch on AWS Marketplace*

GCP: Leveraging Google Cloud Platform's Services

Google Cloud Platform (GCP) provides several options for deploying Elasticsearch, including deploying your own managed cluster using Google Kubernetes Engine (GKE) or using third-party Elasticsearch services available on GCP Marketplace. GCP offers a highly scalable infrastructure, ideal for big data and AI/ML workloads.

Key Features:

- **Compute Flexibility:** Deploy Elasticsearch on GKE, Compute Engine, or GCP Marketplace-managed services.
- **Integration with Google Services:** Seamless integration with services like Google BigQuery, Google Cloud Storage, and Pub/Sub.
- **Performance Monitoring:** Use Google Cloud Monitoring and Logging for real-time insights into your Elasticsearch performance.
- **Scalability:** GCP's flexible compute resources allow for dynamic scaling to handle large data sets and high query loads.

Steps to Deploy Elasticsearch on GCP:

1. **GCP Console:** Log into the GCP console.
2. **GKE or Compute Engine:** Choose between deploying Elasticsearch on GKE for containerized environments or Compute Engine for virtual machines.
3. **Use Helm Charts (GKE):** If deploying on GKE, use Helm charts to manage the deployment of Elasticsearch nodes.
4. **Set Up Networking:** Configure VPC networks for secure communication between nodes, and set up firewall rules.
5. **Monitoring:** Use Stackdriver or Google Cloud Monitoring for alerting and performance monitoring.

Azure: Integrating with Azure's Elasticsearch Solutions

Microsoft Azure offers Elasticsearch through its partner solutions on the Azure Marketplace, or you can manually deploy Elasticsearch on Azure Virtual Machines. With its deep integration into Azure's ecosystem, you can build secure, scalable Elasticsearch clusters, using managed services like Azure Kubernetes Service (AKS) or Virtual Machines.

Key Features:

- **Azure Integration:** Leverage Azure services such as Azure Blob Storage, Azure Monitor, and Azure Active Directory for a tightly integrated experience.
- **High Availability:** Deploy Elasticsearch across Azure's availability zones for fault tolerance.
- **Security:** Integrates with Azure Active Directory (AAD) for authentication, and supports Azure Key Vault for managing encryption keys.
- **Scaling:** Elastic clusters can scale dynamically, either through manual configuration or automatic scaling with Azure Monitor metrics.

Steps to Deploy Elasticsearch on Azure:

1. **Azure Marketplace:** Search for Elasticsearch in the Azure Marketplace to deploy managed clusters.
2. **AKS or VMs:** Choose between deploying Elasticsearch on Azure Kubernetes Service (AKS) for containerized workloads or Virtual Machines for traditional deployment.
3. **Networking:** Set up VNet for secure communication, and control network access using Network Security Groups (NSGs).
4. **Integration with Azure Monitor:** Monitor cluster health, using Azure Monitor for real-time performance insights.
5. **Scaling:** Scale up or down using Azure's scaling features, either manually or based on resource usage.

Docker and Kubernetes Deployments

Deploying Elasticsearch with Docker and Kubernetes provides flexibility, scalability, and automation for containerized environments. Docker enables packaging Elasticsearch into containers, while Kubernetes offers orchestration for deploying and managing those containers at scale. This section explores how to containerize Elasticsearch and the Elastic Stack components, as well as how to leverage Helm charts and Kubernetes operators for managing large-scale Elastic deployments.

Dockerizing Elastic Stack Components

Dockerizing Elasticsearch and other Elastic Stack components (Kibana, Logstash, Beats) allows developers to easily package and deploy these services across various environments. Docker containers provide consistency, portability, and an isolated environment, which simplifies Elastic Stack deployments.

Benefits of Dockerizing Elastic Stack:

- **Portability:** Elasticsearch can be containerized and run on any platform that supports Docker, ensuring consistent behavior across environments.
- **Isolation:** Each component of the Elastic Stack (for example, Elasticsearch, Kibana, and Logstash) runs in its own container, allowing for modular scaling and updates.
- **Ease of Management:** Docker Compose can orchestrate multi-container deployments, simplifying the management of Elasticsearch clusters with Kibana and Logstash.
- **Consistency:** Containers eliminate differences between development and production environments, ensuring that Elastic Stack behaves the same regardless of where it is deployed.

Steps to Dockerize Elasticsearch:

1. **Pull Official Images:** Use the official Docker images for Elasticsearch, Kibana, Logstash, and Beats available on Docker Hub.

   ```
   docker pull elasticsearch:8.x
   docker pull kibana:8.x
   docker pull logstash:8.x
   ```

2. **Set Up Docker Compose:** Create a **`docker-compose.yml`** file to define your multi-container setup. For example, a basic setup might look like this:

```
version: '3'
   services:
     elasticsearch:
       image: elasticsearch:8.x
       environment:
         - node.name=es01
         - cluster.name=docker-cluster
         - discovery.type=single-node
       ports:
         - "9200:9200"
       volumes:
         - esdata:/usr/share/elasticsearch/data
     kibana:
       image: kibana:8.x
       ports:
         - "5601:5601"
       depends_on:
         - elasticsearch
   volumes:
     esdata:
```

This configuration spins up both Elasticsearch and Kibana containers.

3. **Run Containers:** Once the **`docker-compose.yml`** is set up, start the containers:

   ```
   docker-compose up
   ```

   Elasticsearch and Kibana will run as separate containers, with Kibana depending on Elasticsearch.

4. **Monitoring and Scaling:** Docker makes it easy to monitor logs and scale containers by adding more nodes to the Elasticsearch service. To scale Elasticsearch horizontally, you can simply add more nodes to your **`docker-compose.yml`** file.

Here are certain common use cases for Dockerized Elastic Stack components:

- **Local Development:** Developers can quickly spin up Elastic Stack components locally for development and testing.
- **CI/CD Pipelines:** Dockerized Elasticsearch is used in Continuous Integration (CI) pipelines to ensure consistent behavior in testing environments.
- **Microservices Architecture:** Deploy Elasticsearch alongside other services in a microservices environment, using Docker.

Helm Charts and Kubernetes Operators for Elastic Stack

Kubernetes is ideal for orchestrating Elasticsearch deployments at scale, particularly in production environments where availability, scaling, and rolling updates are critical. Helm charts and Kubernetes Operators provide powerful tools to automate the deployment and management of Elasticsearch clusters on Kubernetes.

Helm Charts for Elasticsearch

Helm is a Kubernetes package manager that simplifies the deployment of applications on Kubernetes by packaging them as charts. Elastic offers official Helm Charts for deploying Elasticsearch, Kibana, and other Elastic Stack components.

We have many benefits of using Helm charts for Elasticsearch deployments:

- **Simplified Deployment:** Helm charts provide pre-configured templates for deploying Elastic Stack components, reducing the complexity of managing YAML files.
- **Configuration Management:** Helm allows for easy customization of the deployment via a **`values.yaml`** file, where you can define cluster size, node roles, storage, and much more.

- **Version Control:** Helm enables version-controlled deployments, making it easier to upgrade or roll back Elastic Stack versions.

Helm is one of CLI tools to manage Kubernetes applications, and it is a package manager for Kubernetes. Helm CLI is available for Linux, Windows, and macOS. You can install Helm CLI by following the instructions on the official Helm website, https://helm.sh/docs/intro/install.

After the Helm CLI is installed, you can deploy Elasticsearch using Helm Charts. Here are the steps to deploy Elasticsearch using Helm Charts:

1. **Add Elastic Helm Repo:**

   ```
   helm repo add elastic https://helm.elastic.co
   helm repo update
   ```

2. **Install Elasticsearch Helm Chart:**

   ```
   helm install elasticsearch elastic/elasticsearch -f values.
   yaml
   ```

   In the **`values.yaml`** file, you can configure resources such as CPU, memory, number of nodes, storage classes, and network policies.

3. **Monitor and Scale**: Kubernetes handles the scaling of pods, and you can monitor the health of your Elasticsearch cluster via **`kubectl`** or integrated tools like Prometheus and Grafana.

   Sample **`values.yaml`** for Elasticsearch:

   ```
   replicas: 3
   resources:
     requests:
       cpu: "1"
       memory: "2Gi"
     limits:
       cpu: "2"
       memory: "4Gi"
   volumeClaimTemplate:
     accessModes: [ "ReadWriteOnce" ]
     storageClassName: "standard"
     resources:
       requests:
         storage: 10Gi
   ```

Helm charts allow for a straightforward and automated setup of Elasticsearch clusters, suitable for both small and large environments.

Kubernetes Operators for Elasticsearch

Kubernetes Operators extend Kubernetes functionality by automating the lifecycle management of stateful applications like Elasticsearch. The Elastic Cloud on Kubernetes (ECK) operator, provided by Elastic, simplifies the deployment, scaling, and management of Elasticsearch clusters in Kubernetes environments.

Benefits of Using ECK:

- **Automated Management:** ECK handles complex cluster operations such as scaling, upgrades, backups, and node replacements.
- **Custom Resource Definitions (CRDs):** ECK uses CRDs to manage Elasticsearch clusters declaratively, making it easy to scale clusters, and update configurations.
- **Resiliency:** Kubernetes operators ensure that Elasticsearch clusters remain available by automatically detecting and recovering from failures.
- **Security:** ECK supports security features such as TLS encryption, user authentication, and Role-Based Access Control (RBAC) within Kubernetes.

Steps to Deploy Elasticsearch Using ECK:

1. **Install the ECK Operator**:

```
kubectl create -f https://download.elastic.co/downloads/
eck/2.14.0/crds.yaml
```

Next, we shall install RBAC roles and the operator:

```
   kubectl apply -f https://download.elastic.co/downloads/
eck/2.14.0/operator.yaml
```

Verify that the operator is running:

```
   kubectl -n elastic-system logs -f statefulset.apps/elastic-
operator
```

2. **Create an Elasticsearch Cluster:** Define a Custom Resource (CR) that specifies the desired cluster configuration.

```
apiVersion: elasticsearch.k8s.elastic.co/v1
kind: Elasticsearch
metadata:
  name: quickstart
spec:
  version: 8.15.1
  nodeSets:
  - name: default
    count: 1
```

```
        config:
          node.store.allow_mmap: false
```

Apply the configuration:

```
kubectl apply -f elasticsearch.yaml
```

3. **Monitor and Scale:** ECK automatically manages scaling and failure recovery. You can monitor cluster health using kubectl or tools like Kibana and Prometheus.

We have several advantages of using ECK:

- **Seamless Upgrades:** ECK can manage rolling upgrades of Elasticsearch versions with minimal downtime.
- **Data Management:** ECK integrates with Persistent Volume Claims (PVCs) to manage data storage and backup across Kubernetes nodes.
- **Multi-Tenancy:** ECK enables the deployment of multiple Elasticsearch clusters in the same Kubernetes environment, making it ideal for multi-tenant environments.

Hybrid Deployments: Combining On-Premises with Cloud

Hybrid deployments allow organizations to leverage the flexibility and scalability of cloud infrastructure, while maintaining control over on-premises resources. Elasticsearch's architecture makes it a good fit for hybrid deployments, where part of the infrastructure runs in the cloud, and part on-premises. This strategy is particularly useful, when organizations want to maintain data sovereignty, meet regulatory requirements, or make a gradual transition to the cloud.

Benefits of Hybrid Deployments

- **Data Sovereignty:** Sensitive data can remain on-premises, while less critical workloads or backups can be handled in the cloud.
- **Cost Optimization:** Compute-heavy workloads can be handled by scalable cloud resources, while less demanding operations are managed on-premises.
- **Disaster Recovery:** Cloud resources can act as a backup for critical data, ensuring business continuity in the event of an on-premises failure.
- **Elasticity:** Cloud infrastructure provides flexible scaling, allowing organizations to handle peak loads, without investing in on-premises hardware.

Strategies for Hybrid Elasticsearch Deployment

1. **Data Tiering:** Store the critical data on-premises, while leveraging cloud storage for less frequently accessed data. Elasticsearch's hot-warm architecture can be adapted, where "*hot*" data is stored on-prem and "*warm*" data in the cloud.
2. **Cross-Cluster Search (CCS):** Elasticsearch's CCS allows queries to span across both on-prem and cloud clusters. This can be useful for integrating data sources from both environments, without moving all the data into one place.
3. **Snapshot and Restore:** Regular snapshots of your on-prem Elasticsearch cluster can be stored in cloud storage (AWS S3, GCP Storage, and so on) for disaster recovery. Snapshots can be restored in a cloud cluster, when necessary.
4. **Hybrid Indexing:** Cloud services can handle write-heavy indexing, while the on-prem cluster focuses on read operations, thus distributing the load.

Example Scenario: An organization with strict data residency requirements could store customer data on-premises, while using a cloud-based Elasticsearch deployment to analyze application logs, which have less stringent residency requirements. By using cross-cluster search, the organization can gain insights from both data sources, without compromising compliance.

Scaling Strategies: Horizontal vs. Vertical Scaling

Elasticsearch's distributed nature allows for flexible scaling strategies, depending on the workload and infrastructure. Scaling Elasticsearch can be accomplished in two primary ways: Horizontal scaling (scaling out) and vertical scaling (scaling up).

Horizontal Scaling

Horizontal scaling involves adding more nodes to the Elasticsearch cluster, distributing the data and workload across multiple instances. This method is most effective, when dealing with large data volumes or high query throughput.

Benefits:

- **Fault Tolerance:** By adding more nodes, data can be replicated across multiple machines, ensuring that if one node fails, another can take over.
- **Improved Performance:** Each node in the cluster contributes to data processing and indexing, so adding more nodes can distribute the load more evenly, and improve performance.

- **Flexibility:** Horizontal scaling allows for seamless expansion of storage and compute resources, without downtime.

Considerations:

- **Network Latency:** As the number of nodes increases, inter-node communication may add latency, particularly in multi-zone or multi-region clusters.
- **Cluster Management:** A larger cluster requires more overhead for managing node configurations, monitoring, and shard allocation.

Best Practices:

- Use shard allocation settings to ensure that data is evenly distributed across nodes.
- Regularly monitor cluster health to prevent node failures from disrupting the entire cluster.
- Utilize dedicated master nodes to avoid performance bottlenecks as the cluster grows.

Vertical Scaling

Vertical scaling involves increasing the resources (CPU, memory, and disk) of individual nodes in the Elasticsearch cluster. This approach is ideal for scenarios where adding more nodes is impractical, or the cluster primarily handles low-volume data with high computational requirements.

Benefits:

- **Simplicity:** Vertical scaling does not require adding or managing more nodes, simplifying the architecture.
- **Lower Latency:** Since there is no need to replicate data across multiple nodes, latency from inter-node communication is minimized.
- **Memory-Intensive Workloads:** Elasticsearch benefits from large amounts of memory, particularly when dealing with large aggregations or complex queries. Vertical scaling allows you to allocate more heap memory to individual nodes.

Considerations:

- **Hardware Limitations:** Vertical scaling is limited by the physical constraints of your hardware such as maximum CPU and memory capacity.
- **Single Point of Failure:** Unlike horizontal scaling, vertical scaling places more reliance on individual nodes which could lead to single points of failure.

Best Practices:

- Regularly monitor resource utilization (CPU, memory, and disk) and tune node settings accordingly.
- Ensure that Elasticsearch nodes have adequate heap memory, and use the recommended 50% heap-to-memory ratio.
- Consider upgrading storage to SSDs to improve query performance, and reduce IO latency.

When to Choose Horizontal vs. Vertical Scaling:

- **Horizontal Scaling:** Ideal for growing data volumes and distributed workloads, where fault tolerance and scalability are important.
- **Vertical Scaling:** Suitable for small-to-medium deployments, or when workloads require more memory and CPU, but not necessarily more nodes.

Performance Tuning and Optimization

Optimizing Elasticsearch for performance ensures that queries run quickly and efficiently, minimizing the impact on resources, while maximizing throughput. Performance tuning requires attention to several key areas, including indexing, querying, and hardware configurations.

Key Areas for Performance Tuning

- **Indexing Performance:**
    - **Shard and Replica Configuration:** Over-allocating shards can lead to inefficiencies. Aim for shard sizes between 20-40GB, and allocate replicas based on the desired fault tolerance.
    - **Bulk Indexing:** For large datasets, use the bulk indexing API to reduce the overhead of indexing individual documents.
    - **Document Structure:** Keep document sizes manageable by storing only necessary fields, and using efficient data types (for example, using keyword for structured fields instead of text).
    - **Index Templates:** Pre-define index settings and mappings to optimize how Elasticsearch stores and queries data.
- **Query Performance:**
    - **Efficient Use of Aggregations:** Aggregations are resource-intensive, so limit the scope of queries with filters and must clauses.

- **Query Caching:** Elasticsearch automatically caches query results. Ensure that queries are structured to benefit from cache re-use, particularly in read-heavy workloads.
- **Pagination:** Use search-after or scroll APIs for deep pagination, instead of traditional pagination, which can lead to slower queries as Elasticsearch has to scan through results.
- **Field Data:** Avoid high cardinality fields in aggregations as they consume a large amount of heap memory.

- **Hardware and Cluster Tuning:**
  - **Heap Memory:** Elasticsearch heavily relies on heap memory for performance. Ensure that the nodes are allocated sufficient heap space (typically 50% of the available memory). Regularly monitor for garbage collection issues.
  - **Disk and Storage:** SSDs are recommended for Elasticsearch clusters, as they offer faster read/write speeds compared to HDDs, improving indexing and query performance.
  - **Network Configuration:** Optimize network settings by reducing latency between nodes, ensuring fast communication within the cluster.
- **Thread Pools and Caching:**
  - **Thread Pools:** Tune thread pool settings for indexing and search workloads, ensuring enough threads are available to handle incoming tasks, without bottlenecks.
  - **Caching:** Elasticsearch uses various caches (node-level and query cache). Regularly clear caches, if they start consuming too much memory, or adjust cache settings to fit the workload.
- **Monitoring and Alerts:**
  - Use monitoring tools such as **Elastic's Stack Monitoring**, **Prometheus**, and **Grafana** to track cluster performance in real time. Set up alerts to monitor resource usage (CPU, memory, disk) and cluster health.
  - Regularly check cluster logs for slow queries, indexing bottlenecks, and shard-related issues.

Performance tuning in Elasticsearch is an ongoing process that involves monitoring workloads, adjusting configurations, and fine-tuning query patterns. By carefully managing resource allocation, and optimizing shard allocation, bulk indexing, and query structures, you can significantly improve Elasticsearch's performance, while maintaining system stability.

Conclusion

In this chapter, we explored the advanced deployment strategies necessary for managing Elasticsearch in a variety of environments, from cloud-based solutions to hybrid deployments. Understanding how to plan, deploy, and scale Elasticsearch using modern tools such as Docker, Kubernetes, and cloud services allows organizations to create highly flexible and resilient infrastructures. By carefully balancing horizontal and vertical scaling strategies, optimizing performance through fine-tuning, and leveraging cloud-native features, Elasticsearch clusters can meet the demands of growing data and complex search workloads.

As deployments evolve, so also must the strategies for maintaining their efficiency and performance. The insights gained from this chapter provide a strong foundation for building robust Elasticsearch systems, but real-world challenges often present unique problems and opportunities. In the next chapter, we will dive into practical case studies, where these advanced strategies are applied in real-world scenarios. These examples will highlight how organizations have tackled specific challenges with Elasticsearch, offering valuable lessons for your own deployment journey.

Points to Remember

- **Pre-Deployment Planning:**
  - Plan cluster size, capacity, and topology based on data volume, query load, and future growth.
  - Consider redundancy, availability zones, and failover strategies for high availability.
- **Cloud Deployments:**
  - Elastic Cloud provides a fully managed Elasticsearch service with automatic scaling, updates, and security.
  - AWS, GCP, and Azure offer managed Elasticsearch services integrated into their ecosystems, simplifying deployment and scaling.
  - Hybrid cloud setups can balance on-prem control with cloud scalability, using cross-cluster search for unified queries.
- **Dockerizing Elasticsearch:**
  - Docker allows for isolated, consistent deployments of Elasticsearch, and Elastic Stack components.
  - Use Docker Compose to orchestrate multi-container setups for Elasticsearch, Kibana, and Logstash.
  - Dockerized deployments are portable, and make it easy to move between development, testing, and production environments.

- **Kubernetes and Helm:**
  - Helm charts provide pre-configured templates to simplify deploying Elasticsearch on Kubernetes.
  - The Elastic Cloud on Kubernetes (ECK) operator automates Elasticsearch cluster management, including scaling, upgrades, and backups.
  - Kubernetes enables dynamic scaling and resilience, with ECK handling cluster recovery, and resource optimization.
- **Hybrid Deployments:**
  - Hybrid deployments use a mix of on-premises and cloud infrastructure for cost optimization, data sovereignty, and disaster recovery.
  - Cross-Cluster Search (CCS) enables querying across both environments, without moving data.
  - Use cloud storage for snapshot backups of on-premises clusters to improve resilience.
- **Scaling Strategies:**
  - Horizontal scaling adds nodes to the Elasticsearch cluster to distribute data and workload.
  - Vertical scaling increases individual node resources (CPU, memory, and so on), ideal for smaller clusters or high-memory workloads.
  - Choose horizontal scaling for distributed workloads and vertical scaling for memory- and CPU-intensive tasks.
- **Performance Tuning:**
  - Optimize indexing by managing shard size, using bulk indexing, and setting proper shard and replica configurations.
  - Improve query performance by using caching, structuring queries efficiently, and managing high cardinality fields.
  - Monitor resource usage (CPU, memory, and disk) as well as adjust settings like heap memory and thread pools accordingly.
- **Monitoring and Optimization:**
  - Use monitoring tools such as Elastic Stack Monitoring, Prometheus, and Grafana to track cluster health and performance.
  - Regularly review logs and cluster health metrics to detect slow queries, indexing bottlenecks, or shard imbalances.
  - Set up alerts for resource utilization issues, and respond proactively to performance bottlenecks.

Multiple Choice Questions

1. What is the main advantage of using Elastic Cloud for Elasticsearch deployments?
   a. Full control over all cluster configurations.
   b. Automatic updates, scaling, and security management.
   c. Requires manual patching and upgrades.
   d. Limited to small-scale deployments.
2. Which feature in Elasticsearch allows querying across multiple clusters, including both on-premises and cloud deployments?
   a. Replica Shards
   b. Snapshot and Restore
   c. Cross-Cluster Search (CCS)
   d. Vertical Scaling
3. What is the primary difference between horizontal and vertical scaling in Elasticsearch?
   a. Horizontal scaling increases node resources, while vertical scaling adds more nodes.
   b. Horizontal scaling adds more nodes, while vertical scaling increases node resources.
   c. Horizontal scaling reduces the number of shards, while vertical scaling increases the number of shards.
   d. Horizontal scaling is limited to cloud deployments, while vertical scaling is for on-premises.
4. What is the purpose of using Helm charts in Kubernetes deployments of Elasticsearch?
   a. Helm charts automate the querying process in Elasticsearch.
   b. Helm charts provide pre-configured templates for easy deployment of Elasticsearch clusters.
   c. Helm charts handle backups and snapshots in Elasticsearch clusters.
   d. Helm charts are used to create custom queries for Elasticsearch data.

5. Which method is best for improving Elasticsearch indexing performance, when dealing with large data sets?
    a. Use high cardinality fields in every index.
    b. Optimize bulk indexing to reduce individual document indexing overhead.
    c. Decrease the number of replicas to improve indexing speed.
    d. Disable query caching to speed up indexing.

Answers

1. b.
2. c.
3. b.
4. b.
5. b.

Questions

1. What are the critical factors to consider during pre-deployment planning for an Elasticsearch cluster?
2. Discuss how aspects like data volume, query load, redundancy, and growth expectations influence cluster sizing and topology.
3. What advantages do managed Elasticsearch services such as Elastic Cloud offer over self-hosted deployments?
4. Compare the benefits of managed services (for example, automatic updates, scaling, and security) with the control and flexibility of self-hosted setups.
5. How does a hybrid deployment strategy for Elasticsearch balance on-premises infrastructure and cloud resources?
6. Explore the benefits of hybrid deployments, including cost optimization, data residency, disaster recovery, and workload distribution.
7. When should you choose horizontal scaling over vertical scaling in an Elasticsearch cluster, and what are the key differences between the two?
8. Compare horizontal and vertical scaling, focusing on how they address different workload types, performance needs, and resource limitations.

9. How does Dockerization improve the portability and consistency of Elastic Stack deployments, and what are the key steps in Dockerizing Elasticsearch?
10. Explain how Docker helps create consistent, portable environments for Elasticsearch, Kibana, and Logstash, and describe the setup process with Docker Compose.

Key Terms

- **Elastic Cloud:** A fully managed service by Elastic for deploying and managing Elasticsearch, Kibana, and other Elastic Stack components in the cloud.
- **AWS Elasticsearch Service:** Amazon's managed Elasticsearch service integrated with AWS ecosystem tools such as S3, CloudWatch, and IAM.
- **GCP Elasticsearch:** Elasticsearch services available on Google Cloud Platform, offering options to deploy on GKE (Google Kubernetes Engine) or through managed services.
- **Azure Elasticsearch:** Elasticsearch deployments on Microsoft Azure, either through self-hosted virtual machines or partner-managed services.
- **Docker:** A containerization platform that enables Elasticsearch and other Elastic Stack components to run in isolated, consistent environments across different infrastructures.
- **Docker Compose:** A tool for orchestrating multi-container Docker applications, simplifying the management of Elasticsearch, Kibana, and Logstash deployments.
- **Kubernetes:** A container orchestration platform that automates the deployment, scaling, and management of containerized applications, including Elasticsearch.
- **Helm:** A Kubernetes package manager that uses pre-configured charts (templates) for easy deployment and management of applications like Elasticsearch clusters.
- **Elastic Cloud on Kubernetes (ECK):** A Kubernetes operator provided by Elastic that automates Elasticsearch cluster management tasks such as scaling, upgrades, and fault recovery.
- **Hybrid Deployment:** A strategy that combines on-premises infrastructure with cloud resources, allowing flexibility in scaling, data sovereignty, and cost optimization.
- **Cross-Cluster Search (CCS):** An Elasticsearch feature that allows queries to span across multiple Elasticsearch clusters, including on-premises and cloud clusters.

- **Horizontal Scaling:** Adding more nodes to an Elasticsearch cluster to distribute data and processing load, improving fault tolerance and query throughput.
- **Vertical Scaling:** Increasing the resources (CPU, memory, and storage) of individual nodes in an Elasticsearch cluster to handle more intensive workloads without adding nodes.
- **Shard:** A portion of an Elasticsearch index used to distribute data across nodes in a cluster, allowing for parallel processing and efficient data retrieval.
- **Replica:** A copy of a shard in Elasticsearch, used to provide redundancy, fault tolerance, and load balancing in the cluster.
- **Bulk Indexing:** An Elasticsearch feature that allows indexing multiple documents in a single operation, improving efficiency and reducing overhead.
- **Query Caching:** A performance feature that stores the results of frequent queries in memory, improving response time for similar queries.
- **Persistent Volume (PV):** A Kubernetes storage resource that persists data even if the container is restarted or replaced, commonly used for Elasticsearch data storage.
- **Thread Pool:** A set of worker threads in Elasticsearch responsible for processing indexing and search operations. Proper tuning of thread pools can improve performance under load.
- **Heap Memory:** Memory allocated to Elasticsearch's Java Virtual Machine (JVM) for caching and data processing. Optimal heap memory settings are critical for cluster performance.
- **Hot-Warm Architecture:** An Elasticsearch strategy where "`hot`" data (frequently accessed) is stored on high-performance nodes and "`warm`" data (less frequently accessed) on lower-cost nodes.
- **Snapshot:** A backup of Elasticsearch indices that can be stored locally or in the cloud, used for disaster recovery and restoration of data.

CHAPTER 9
Case Studies

Introduction

In today's digital landscape, organizations generate vast amounts of data from various sources, including application logs, performance metrics, security events, and endpoint activities. Managing and analyzing this data efficiently is crucial for maintaining system reliability, optimizing performance, and strengthening security. The Elastic Stack (ELK) provides a powerful solution for ingesting, processing, and visualizing data in real time, enabling organizations to gain actionable insights. This chapter presents a series of case studies demonstrating how different industries have successfully implemented the Elastic Stack to solve real-world challenges.

Each case study explores a specific domain, such as real-time log analysis, system performance monitoring, application performance management, uptime assurance, Security Information and Event Management (SIEM), and endpoint protection. By examining these use cases, we will uncover the challenges organizations faced, the architectural solutions they implemented using the Elastic Stack, and the tangible benefits, they achieved. These examples illustrate how organizations across various sectors–including e-commerce, SaaS, banking, healthcare, and enterprise security–have leveraged Elastic's capabilities to drive operational efficiency, enhance user experiences, and mitigate risks.

By the end of this chapter, readers will gain a deeper understanding of how the Elastic Stack has been applied in various real-world scenarios through a series of case studies. Rather than focusing on the technical deployment or implementation details, this chapter reviews the key challenges organizations have faced, and how they leveraged Elastic Stack to address them. Whether the objective is to optimize application performance, enhance security monitoring, or ensure high availability, these case studies provide valuable insights into the practical benefits and strategic impact of Elastic Stack solutions across different industries.

Structure

In this chapter, we will discuss the following topics:

- **Logs:** Real-time Log Analysis for E-commerce
- **Metrics:** Monitoring System Performance for a Global SaaS Platform
- **APM (Application Performance Monitoring):** Enhancing User Experience for an Online Banking Application
- **Uptime:** Ensuring 99.999% Availability for a Healthcare Portal
- **SIEM (Security Information and Event Management):** Proactive Threat Detection for a Large Enterprise Network
- **Endpoint:** Enhancing Endpoint Security for a Distributed Workforce

Logs: Real-time Log Analysis for E-commerce

In the fast-paced world of e-commerce, the ability to analyze logs in real-time can be the difference between delivering a seamless customer experience, and losing revenue due to system downtime or user frustration. E-commerce platforms generate a massive volume of logs from various sources, including web servers, payment gateways, and user interactions. This case study explores the challenges faced by an e-commerce platform, the solution implemented using the ELK stack, and the benefits achieved.

Challenge Overview

The e-commerce platform struggled with fragmented logging systems, making it challenging to identify and resolve issues efficiently. During promotional events, the platform experienced significant traffic spikes, leading to delayed responses and occasional downtime. Errors in payment processing, cart abandonment, and sluggish server performance often went undetected until after customer complaints were received. Furthermore, the lack of a centralized system for log analysis hindered compliance with data retention policies which are critical for auditing and regulatory requirements. The company needed a robust, scalable, and real-time log analysis solution to address these challenges effectively.

Solution Architecture

To overcome these challenges, the platform implemented a comprehensive solution using the ELK stack. **Logstash** was configured to aggregate logs from diverse sources, including application servers, payment gateways, and web traffic logs. The data was normalized and enriched to provide consistent and meaningful insights.

The logs were then indexed and stored in an **Elasticsearch cluster**, optimized for fast searches and queries. Elasticsearch's distributed nature ensured high availability and the ability to scale horizontally, making it suitable for handling traffic surges during peak periods.

To provide real-time visibility, **Kibana dashboards** were set up to monitor Key Performance Indicators (KPIs) such as transaction success rates, server health, and error trends. The platform also integrated an **alerting mechanism** with tools like PagerDuty and Slack, ensuring that anomalies were detected and addressed instantly.

The entire solution was deployed in a scalable architecture, leveraging containerization and orchestration tools for ease of management and reliability. This architecture not only improved log analysis, but also set a foundation for future enhancements such as machine learning-based anomaly detection.

Benefits and Outcomes

The implementation of the ELK stack brought numerous benefits to the e-commerce platform. **Enhanced troubleshooting capabilities allowed the DevOps team to reduce error resolution time by 70%, as centralized logging made it easy to trace and address issues**. Real-time alerts enabled swift action, minimizing the impact on customers, and improving platform reliability.

Customer experience improved significantly as performance bottlenecks were identified and mitigated during peak traffic hours, leading to a reduction in cart abandonment rates. Operational efficiency increased as the DevOps and support teams were able to collaborate using shared dashboards and streamlined workflows.

The company also gained **data-driven insights into user behavior**, enabling them to offer targeted promotions and personalized recommendations. Compliance with regulatory standards was achieved through efficient log retention and audit trails, further solidifying the platform's reputation for reliability and trustworthiness.

Metrics: Monitoring System Performance for a Global SaaS Platform

Global SaaS platforms operate under strict performance expectations to ensure seamless user experiences. With users spanning multiple time zones and regions, performance issues in any part of the system can significantly affect customer satisfaction and retention. This case study highlights the challenges faced by a global

SaaS platform, the monitoring solution implemented using the ELK stack, and the resulting benefits.

Challenge Overview

The global SaaS platform faced significant challenges in monitoring its system performance across multiple regions. The distributed nature of its infrastructure, with data centers spread worldwide, made it difficult to gain a unified view of system health. Performance issues such as latency, high memory usage, and disk IO bottlenecks were often detected only after users reported problems.

The platform lacked a comprehensive system to track real-time performance metrics, making it challenging to predict and prevent potential outages. The inability to correlate performance metrics with logs added further complexity to troubleshooting. Additionally, the company needed to maintain stringent Service Level Agreements (SLAs) with enterprise customers which required proactive monitoring and reporting capabilities.

Solution Architecture

To address these challenges, the SaaS platform implemented an ELK stack-based solution, focusing on **metrics monitoring**. The solution started with **Metricbeat**, a lightweight shipper for collecting metrics from system components such as CPU usage, memory utilization, and network bandwidth. Metricbeat was deployed across all servers in the distributed infrastructure.

The collected metrics were ingested into **Elasticsearch, enabling centralized storage and real-time querying**. Elasticsearch's scalability ensured that the platform could handle the large volume of metrics generated by a global infrastructure. **The data was enriched with metadata such as region and service tags, to facilitate detailed analysis and correlation.**

Kibana dashboards were configured to visualize system performance metrics across regions. Custom visualizations and heatmaps provided insights into server health, regional performance variations, and trends over time. Alerts were configured to notify teams about threshold breaches, such as high CPU usage or slow response times, through integration with tools such as Slack and Microsoft Teams.

The solution also enabled correlation between logs and metrics, combining the power of Elastic Observability. This integration allowed teams to trace issues from high-level metrics down to specific logs, drastically reducing the time required for root cause analysis.

Benefits and Outcomes

The implementation of the ELK stacks for metrics monitoring provided the SaaS platform with several key benefits. First, the platform achieved **proactive performance monitoring**, allowing teams to detect and address issues, before they affected the end-users. Threshold-based alerts ensured rapid response to critical problems, improving system reliability.

The unified view of system performance across regions enabled the platform to identify patterns, and optimize resource allocation, reducing operational costs. For example, underutilized servers in specific regions were reconfigured to balance the load, improving overall efficiency.

The integration of logs and metrics streamlined troubleshooting and incident management, reducing Mean Time to Resolution (MTTR) by 60%. Teams could quickly correlate performance degradations with specific events or code changes, ensuring faster fixes, and improved platform stability.

Additionally, the platform met its SLA requirements with enterprise customers by providing detailed performance reports and real-time dashboards. These capabilities enhanced customer trust and satisfaction, positioning the company as a reliable partner for mission-critical applications.

Application Performance Monitoring (APM): Enhancing User Experience for an Online Banking Application

Application Performance Monitoring (APM) is crucial for modern online banking applications, where users expect seamless transactions, low latency, and high reliability. Any performance degradation in such applications can lead to user frustration, reduced trust, and financial losses. This case study focuses on how an online banking application leveraged APM with the Elastic Stack to enhance the user experience, and maintain service reliability.

Challenge Overview

The online banking application faced significant challenges in ensuring a smooth and responsive user experience. With millions of daily transactions, the application had to handle complex workflows involving account management, fund transfers, and bill payments. However, intermittent performance issues such as slow response times and occasional transaction failures were reported by users, especially during peak usage hours.

The development and operations teams lacked visibility into the root causes of these issues. Traditional logging and metrics monitoring provided fragmented insights, making it difficult to pinpoint the source of performance bottlenecks. Moreover, the banking application was subject to stringent compliance requirements, necessitating detailed monitoring and reporting for audits. The organization required a robust APM solution to gain granular insights into application performance, and proactively address issues before they impacted the users.

Solution Architecture

To tackle these challenges, the online banking application integrated Elastic APM into its existing Elastic Stack setup. **Elastic APM agents** were deployed across the application's backend services, including APIs, microservices, and database layers. These agents were configured to capture the detailed performance data such as transaction durations, database query times, and HTTP request latencies.

The collected APM data was sent to **Elasticsearch**, where it was indexed and made available for real-time analysis. Elasticsearch's distributed architecture ensured scalability and fault tolerance, making it ideal for handling the large volume of performance data generated by the application.

Kibana APM dashboards were set up to visualize key performance metrics such as transaction throughput, error rates, and latency trends. These dashboards enabled the operations team to monitor performance in real-time and identify anomalies. The APM setup also included **distributed tracing**, allowing the team to trace transactions end-to-end, from user requests to backend responses, and identify bottlenecks in specific services or database queries.

To enhance the user experience further, the organization implemented **alerting mechanisms** for proactive issue detection. Alerts were triggered, when critical thresholds such as response times or error rates, were breached. These alerts were integrated with tools such as PagerDuty, enabling instant notifications for the support team. Additionally, periodic performance reports were generated to meet compliance requirements, and provide insights into long-term performance trends.

Benefits and Outcomes

The implementation of Elastic APM brought transformative benefits to the online banking application. With end-to-end transaction tracing and real-time monitoring, the operations team could quickly identify and resolve performance bottlenecks. This reduced the Mean Time to Resolution (MTTR) for critical issues by 65%, ensuring that the users experienced minimal disruptions.

The proactive alerting system allowed the team to address potential issues before they escalated, resulting in improved uptime and reliability. For instance, alerts on database query delays helped identify and optimize slow queries, leading to faster transaction processing during peak hours.

From a user perspective, the application's responsiveness improved significantly, leading to increased customer satisfaction and trust. The ability to trace and resolve performance issues at a granular level also ensured that critical financial transactions were processed without errors, bolstering the platform's reputation.

Furthermore, the organization achieved compliance with regulatory standards by maintaining detailed performance logs and reports. This not only simplified audits, but also provided valuable insights for capacity planning and infrastructure optimization. Overall, the Elastic APM solution enabled the online banking application to deliver a superior user experience, driving customer retention and business growth.

Uptime: Ensuring 99.999% Availability for a Healthcare Portal

High availability is a critical requirement for healthcare portals, as they provide vital services such as appointment scheduling, medical record access, and teleconsultation. Downtime in these systems can lead to delays in patient care and loss of trust. This case study explores how a healthcare organization leveraged the Elastic Stack to ensure 99.999% availability for its portal, overcoming significant operational challenges.

Challenge Overview

The healthcare portal faced several challenges in maintaining high availability and reliability. With thousands of patients and healthcare providers accessing the system daily, even minor downtimes could have severe repercussions. The system experienced occasional outages caused by server failures, application crashes, and high traffic surges during peak usage times.

The organization also struggled with the lack of visibility into uptime metrics across its infrastructure. Traditional monitoring tools provided basic server status checks, but failed to detect issues at the application level or during specific workflows such as prescription management. Furthermore, compliance with healthcare regulations required robust uptime monitoring and reporting to ensure service continuity.

The organization needed a solution that could proactively monitor system uptime at both the infrastructure and application levels, while providing detailed insights for incident response and compliance.

Solution Architecture

To ensure high availability, the healthcare portal implemented Elastic Heartbeat alongside the existing Elastic Stack setup. **Elastic Heartbeat, a lightweight monitoring agent, was deployed to continuously check the availability of critical system components, including web servers, APIs, and database services.** Heartbeat was configured to perform both HTTP and TCP checks, simulating user interactions to detect application-level issues.

The uptime data collected by Heartbeat was sent to **Elasticsearch**, where it was indexed and analyzed in real-time. This centralized storage allowed the organization to correlate uptime metrics with other observability data such as logs and system metrics for comprehensive monitoring.

Custom **Kibana dashboards** were designed to display uptime statuses, response times, and failure trends. These dashboards provided a clear view of the system's availability across various components and regions, enabling quick identification of problem areas. **Alerting mechanisms** were integrated to notify the support team via email and messaging tools like Slack whenever downtime or latency exceeded predefined thresholds.

To achieve fault tolerance, the Elastic Stack deployment itself was configured in a high-availability architecture. Multiple Elasticsearch nodes were deployed across different availability zones, ensuring resilience against hardware failures. Load balancers and auto-scaling mechanisms were also implemented to handle traffic surges, and maintain service reliability.

Benefits and Outcomes

The adoption of Elastic Heartbeat and the Elastic Stack significantly improved the healthcare portal's uptime and reliability. Proactive monitoring allowed the team to detect and resolve issues before they affected users, ensuring consistent service delivery. Downtime incidents were reduced by over 90%, and the portal achieved the targeted 99.999% availability.

The integration of uptime monitoring with other observability data provided deeper insights into the root causes of issues. For instance, correlations between downtime and server resource usage helped the team identify and optimize resource bottlenecks. This improved the efficiency of incident management, and reduced the Mean Time to Recovery (MTTR).

From a compliance perspective, the system's detailed uptime logs and reports simplified audit processes, and demonstrated adherence to healthcare regulations. The organization's ability to ensure uninterrupted access to critical healthcare services strengthened patient trust and satisfaction.

In addition, the high-availability architecture supported by the Elastic Stack provided resilience against unforeseen failures such as hardware malfunctions and traffic spikes. The scalability of the solution allowed the healthcare portal to seamlessly handle increasing user demand, ensuring long-term reliability and performance.

SIEM (Security Information and Event Management): Proactive Threat Detection for a Large Enterprise Network

In today's cyber threat landscape, large enterprises face persistent security challenges. Proactively detecting and mitigating threats requires a robust and scalable Security Information and Event Management (SIEM) solution. This case study examines how a large enterprise network leveraged the Elastic Stack to implement a SIEM system for enhanced security monitoring and threat detection.

Challenge Overview

The enterprise operated a large and distributed network with thousands of endpoints, including servers, workstations, and IoT devices. It faced challenges in identifying and responding to security threats such as unauthorized access, malware infections, and insider threats. The existing security tools were disjointed, creating blind spots, and making it difficult to correlate events across the network.

Real-time threat detection was another significant challenge. Logs from firewalls, intrusion detection systems (IDS), and endpoint devices were siloed, delaying incident detection and response. Furthermore, compliance with industry standards, such as GDPR and ISO 27001, required detailed reporting and audit trails, which the organization struggled to maintain with its legacy tools.

The organization needed a centralized, real-time SIEM solution that could ingest and analyze security events at scale, detect anomalies, and provide actionable insights for threat mitigation.

Solution Architecture

The enterprise implemented Elastic Security, built on the Elastic Stack, to address its SIEM needs. **Filebeat** and **Auditbeat** were deployed across the network to collect security event data from endpoints, servers, and network devices. These lightweight agents were configured to capture logs, user activity, process data, and network traffic.

The collected data was ingested into a centralized **Elasticsearch cluster** which provided powerful search and analytics capabilities. Elasticsearch's scalability allowed the system to handle millions of events per second, ensuring real-time data ingestion and analysis.

Kibana Security Dashboards were configured to visualize security metrics such as failed login attempts, unusual user activity, and network anomalies. The organization also leveraged Elastic's machine learning capabilities to detect anomalies, and identify potential threats based on behavioral patterns.

Detection rules and alerting mechanisms were set up for key security events such as privilege escalations, malware activity, and suspicious network traffic. Alerts were integrated with the Security Operations Center (SOC) workflow, enabling immediate response through tools such as ServiceNow and Slack.

The solution also included compliance-focused features such as role-based access control and detailed audit logs, ensuring that the system met regulatory requirements. Data retention policies were implemented using Elasticsearch's lifecycle management features, optimizing storage, while adhering to compliance standards.

Benefits and Outcomes

The Elastic SIEM solution transformed the enterprise's security operations, enabling proactive threat detection and response. By centralizing security event data, the organization eliminated blind spots, and gained complete visibility into its network. Real-time alerts allowed the SOC team to respond to the threats within minutes, significantly reducing the risk of data breaches.

The integration of machine learning enhanced the organization's ability to detect sophisticated threats such as zero-day exploits and insider attacks. Anomaly detection based on user behavior and network activity provided early warnings for potential incidents, enabling the team to act before damage occurred.

Operational efficiency improved as the SOC team could correlate events across different sources such as firewalls and endpoint devices, using the unified Elastic Security interface. The streamlined workflows reduced the Mean Time to Detect (MTTD) and Mean Time to Respond (MTTR) to incidents by over 50%.

Compliance requirements were also met with ease, thanks to detailed reporting, audit trails, and role-based access controls. The organization's ability to demonstrate adherence to regulatory standards during audits enhanced its reputation, and minimized compliance risks.

Overall, the Elastic SIEM solution provided the enterprise with a scalable, cost-effective, and proactive approach to threat detection and security monitoring. This implementation not only strengthened the organization's security posture, but also reduced operational overhead and improved stakeholder confidence.

Endpoint: Enhancing Endpoint Security for a Distributed Workforce

The shift to a distributed workforce has made endpoint security more critical than ever. With employees accessing corporate resources from a wide range of devices and networks, enterprises face new challenges in protecting sensitive data and systems. This case study explores how an organization leveraged the Elastic Stack to enhance endpoint security, and mitigate risks associated with a distributed workforce.

Challenge Overview

The organization's workforce became increasingly distributed due to remote work policies. Employees accessed corporate systems, using a mix of company-issued and personal devices, often over unsecured home or public networks. This shift introduced a range of security challenges, including vulnerability to malware, unauthorized access, and data exfiltration.

Traditional endpoint security tools struggled to scale with the growing number of endpoints, and lacked the centralized visibility needed to detect and respond to threats effectively. Moreover, the organization faced difficulty monitoring compliance with security policies across diverse devices and operating systems. These challenges were compounded by the need to ensure compliance with regulations such as GDPR and HIPAA which require robust endpoint monitoring and reporting.

Solution Architecture

To address these challenges, the organization deployed Elastic Endpoint Security, a component of Elastic Security, across all devices used by its workforce. The solution began with the installation of **Elastic Agent** on endpoints which provided comprehensive monitoring and protection against threats such as ransomware, malware, and phishing attacks.

The Elastic Agent collected the endpoint data, including file integrity changes, process activity, and network connections, and sent it to a **centralized Elasticsearch cluster**. The cluster was configured for high availability to handle data from thousands of endpoints in real-time.

Using **Kibana**, the organization built custom dashboards to monitor endpoint activity, detect suspicious behavior, and visualize security incidents. **Predefined detection rules and behavioral analytics helped identify threats such as unauthorized software installations, unusual data transfers, and privilege escalations.**

To enhance response capabilities, **automated remediation actions** were configured for specific threats. For example, devices identified as compromised could be quarantined automatically, while administrators received real-time alerts for further investigation. Integration with third-party tools such as ticketing systems and communication platforms, streamlined incident management workflows.

The Elastic solution also supported endpoint encryption and device compliance monitoring. By leveraging Elasticsearch's indexing and query capabilities, the organization implemented detailed compliance audits, ensuring that all endpoints adhered to security policies and regulatory requirements.

Benefits and Outcomes

The deployment of Elastic Endpoint Security significantly improved the organization's ability to protect its distributed workforce. By providing real-time visibility into endpoint activity, the solution allowed the security team to detect and respond to threats within minutes, reducing the risk of data breaches and other incidents.

Automated threat detection and remediation enhanced operational efficiency, enabling the security team to focus on more complex challenges, instead of the routine tasks. For instance, the automatic quarantine of infected devices reduced the time and effort required to contain malware outbreaks.

The unified dashboards and centralized monitoring provided by Elastic Security enabled the organization to maintain consistent security policies across a diverse range of devices and operating systems. This improved compliance with internal policies and regulatory standards, simplifying audit processes, and reducing the risk of penalties.

From a user perspective, the solution operated seamlessly in the background, ensuring robust protection without impacting device performance or employee productivity. The organization also achieved cost savings by consolidating its endpoint security and monitoring tools into a single, scalable Elastic Stack implementation.

By addressing endpoint security challenges comprehensively, the organization was able to support its distributed workforce confidently, ensuring data security, regulatory compliance, and a resilient IT environment.

Conclusion

The case studies in this chapter have demonstrated how organizations across various industries have leveraged the Elastic Stack to solve real-world challenges. From real-time log analysis in e-commerce to proactive threat detection in enterprise security, each case study highlights the impact of centralized data collection, visualization, and analytics in improving operational efficiency, security, and system reliability. By reviewing these examples, we gain insights into how businesses use Elastic

Stack to enhance decision-making, streamline troubleshooting, and maintain high-performance infrastructures.

While this chapter focused on reviewing practical use cases, it is important to recognize that the Elastic ecosystem extends beyond the traditional ELK stack. **In the next chapter, Beyond ELK: Integrating Other Elastic Products, we will explore the additional tools and capabilities within the Elastic ecosystem** such as Elastic Security, Elastic APM, and Elastic Observability. These solutions offer even more advanced analytics, machine learning, and security features that further enhance the power of Elastic in modern IT environments.

Points to Remember

- **Real-World Applications of Elastic Stack:** The Elastic Stack has been successfully applied across industries such as e-commerce, SaaS, banking, healthcare, and enterprise security to enhance observability, performance monitoring, and security.
- **Real-Time Log Analysis:** Centralized log collection and real-time analysis using Elasticsearch and Kibana help organizations detect issues faster, reduce troubleshooting time, and optimize system performance.
- **System Performance Monitoring:** Metricbeat enables SaaS platforms to track the key performance metrics such as CPU, memory, and network usage, improving resource allocation, and maintaining uptime.
- **Application Performance Monitoring (APM):** Elastic APM allows businesses to trace transactions across distributed systems, identifying performance bottlenecks, and ensuring a seamless user experience.
- **Ensuring High Availability:** Elastic Heartbeat is used to monitor uptime and availability, helping organizations achieve their availability goals, and comply with SLAs.
- **Security Information and Event Management (SIEM):** Elastic Security centralizes security event monitoring, helping enterprises detect threats proactively, investigate anomalies, and comply with security regulations.
- **Endpoint Protection:** Deploying Elastic Agent on endpoints provides real-time monitoring, and automated threat response, ensuring security for a distributed workforce.
- **Observability Beyond Logs:** Combining logs, metrics, APM, and security data within Elastic Stack provides a holistic approach to system monitoring and optimization.
- **Business Impact:** Organizations using Elastic Stack experience reduced downtime, improved system efficiency, faster threat detection, and better compliance with regulatory standards.

- **Next Steps:** Beyond the traditional ELK stack, Elastic offers additional products such as Elastic Security, Elastic Observability, and Machine Learning-based analytics which we will explore in the next chapter.

Multiple Choice Questions

1. What was the primary challenge faced by the e-commerce platform in the real-time log analysis case study?
    a. Lack of a centralized logging system for identifying and resolving issues.
    b. High costs associated with Elastic Stack deployment.
    c. Slow database performance due to excessive indexing.
    d. Inability to store logs for more than 24 hours.
2. How did the SaaS platform improve system performance monitoring using Elastic Stack?
    a. By using Logstash to collect and store logs from all servers
    b. By deploying Metricbeat to collect real-time system metrics
    c. By replacing its existing cloud infrastructure with on-premise servers
    d. By disabling non-essential logging to reduce storage costs
3. What key feature of Elastic APM helped improve the performance of the online banking application?
    a. Distributed tracing to analyze transaction flow
    b. Removing the need for performance monitoring
    c. Replacing Elasticsearch with a relational database
    d. Disabling security monitoring for faster transactions
4. In the healthcare portal case study, which Elastic tool was used to monitor system uptime and availability?
    a. Filebeat
    b. Metricbeat
    c. Heartbeat
    d. Auditbeat

5. How did Elastic Security help the enterprise network improve its SIEM capabilities?
    a. By providing centralized security event logging and real-time threat detection
    b. By reducing network bandwidth usage across the infrastructure
    c. By replacing traditional antivirus software with a firewall
    d. By preventing all external access to the corporate network

Answers

1. a.
2. b.
3. a.
4. c.
5. a.

Questions

1. How does real-time log analysis benefit e-commerce platforms, and what challenges does it help to resolve?
2. What role does Elastic APM play in improving application performance, and why is it particularly important for online banking applications?
3. How does Elastic Security enhance SIEM capabilities for large enterprises, and what advantages does it offer over traditional security monitoring tools?
4. Why is uptime monitoring critical for healthcare portals, and how does Elastic Heartbeat help organizations achieve high availability?
5. In the context of endpoint security for a distributed workforce, what are the key challenges organizations face, and how does Elastic Stack provide a solution?

Key Terms

- **Elastic Stack (ELK):** A suite of tools including Elasticsearch, Logstash, Kibana, and Beats, used for searching, analyzing, and visualizing data in real-time.
- **Log Analysis:** The process of collecting, indexing, and analyzing logs to monitor system health, troubleshoot errors, and optimize application performance.

- **Observability:** A comprehensive approach to monitoring systems by collecting logs, metrics, and traces to gain insights into performance and security.
- **Metricbeat:** A lightweight shipper for collecting system metrics such as CPU, memory, disk usage, and network traffic.
- **Application Performance Monitoring (APM):** A technique used to track application transactions, measure latency, and identify performance bottlenecks.
- **Distributed Tracing:** A method of tracking requests across multiple services to identify slow-performing components in an application.
- **Elastic Heartbeat:** A tool used to monitor system uptime by performing periodic checks on endpoints, APIs, and services.
- **Service Level Agreement (SLA):** A contractual agreement that defines the expected service uptime, performance standards, and response times.
- **Security Information and Event Management (SIEM):** A centralized system for collecting, analyzing, and responding to security events across an organization.
- **Elastic Security:** A security solution within the Elastic Stack that provides SIEM, endpoint protection, and threat detection capabilities.
- **Filebeat:** A lightweight log shipper that collects and forwards log data from servers, applications, and cloud environments.
- **Auditbeat:** A tool for monitoring security-related data such as user activity, system calls, and file integrity changes.
- **Anomaly Detection:** The use of machine learning models in Elastic to identify unusual patterns in the log data that could indicate security threats or system failures.
- **Endpoint Security:** Protection mechanisms designed to secure individual devices (laptops, servers, workstations) from malware, unauthorized access, and data breaches.
- **Threat Intelligence:** The process of gathering and analyzing security data to detect and prevent cyber threats in real-time.

CHAPTER 10
Beyond ELK: Integrating Other Elastic Products

Introduction

The Elastic Stack, commonly known as ELK (Elasticsearch, Logstash, and Kibana), has become the go-to solution for log management, analytics, and observability. However, Elastic provides a broader ecosystem of tools beyond the traditional ELK stack. In this chapter, we explore how other products such as Beats, Elastic APM, and Elastic Enterprise Search can enhance data ingestion, application monitoring, and search capabilities, making your observability and search solutions even more powerful.

Structure

In this chapter, we will discuss the following topics:

- Introduction to Beats
- Beats vs. Logstash: Understanding the Differences
- Using APM for Application Performance Monitoring
- Best Practices for Using APM for Application Performance Monitoring
- Exploring Elastic Enterprise Search
- Endpoint: Enhancing Endpoint Security for a Distributed Workforce

Introduction to Beats

Beats are lightweight data shippers designed to collect, process, and send data to Elasticsearch or Logstash. Unlike Logstash, which is a robust but resource-intensive data processing pipeline, Beats are designed to be efficient and purpose-built for specific data collection needs.

There are multiple types of Beats, each serving a distinct purpose:

- **Filebeat**: Used for collecting and forwarding log files.
- **Metricbeat**: Captures system and application metrics.
- **Packetbeat**: Monitors network traffic.
- **Winlogbeat**: Gathers Windows event logs.
- **Auditbeat**: Collects security audit data.
- **Heartbeat**: Checks service uptime and availability.

By deploying Beats on servers, cloud instances, or containers, organizations can collect various forms of telemetry data, without burdening their infrastructure. Beats integrate seamlessly with Elasticsearch, offering built-in dashboards in Kibana for instant visualization. This lightweight approach makes Beats an ideal choice for real-time monitoring and logging at scale.

Beats vs. Logstash: Understanding the Differences

When it comes to data ingestion within the Elastic Stack, two primary components are used: **Beats** and **Logstash**. While both tools are integral to the Elastic ecosystem and serve the purpose of collecting and forwarding data to Elasticsearch, they are designed for different use cases and environments. Understanding the differences between Beats and Logstash helps in choosing the right tool for your specific needs.

Lightweight vs. Heavyweight Data Ingestion

Beats are lightweight, single-purpose data shippers. They are optimized for simplicity and efficiency, running as small agents on your servers or containers. Each Beat is tailored for a specific type of data:

- **Filebeat** for log files
- **Metricbeat** for system and application metrics
- **Packetbeat** for network traffic
- **Winlogbeat** for Windows event logs
- **Auditbeat** for security audit data
- **Heartbeat** for uptime monitoring

Beats are designed to consume minimal system resources, making them ideal for large-scale deployments where multiple servers need to ship data simultaneously.

Logstash, on the other hand, is a robust, feature-rich data processing pipeline. It is designed to handle complex data transformations, parsing, and enrichment. Logstash supports numerous input sources and output destinations, allowing it to act as a central hub for diverse data streams. **It can process and transform data using filters**, **perform conditional logic**, and **enrich data with external sources**.

Data Transformation and Enrichment

Beats primarily focus on data collection with minimal transformation. They offer basic functionalities like filtering log lines or adding metadata but do not perform advanced data manipulation. If you need straightforward log forwarding without complex processing, Beats are the perfect choice.

Logstash excels in data transformation and enrichment. It can parse unstructured data, split logs, remove fields, and perform conditional logic. For example, Logstash can:

- Convert CSV files into structured JSON.
- Parse logs using Grok patterns.
- Enrich data with GeoIP information.
- Handle complex data pipelines.

This makes Logstash a better fit for scenarios where data needs to be heavily processed, before indexing in Elasticsearch.

Scalability and Resource Usage

Beats are more scalable due to their lightweight nature. They can be deployed across a large number of servers without consuming significant resources. This makes them suitable for high-throughput environments, where data needs to be shipped quickly and reliably.

Logstash is resource-intensive, and typically requires dedicated infrastructure, especially when handling large volumes of data. It is not as scalable as Beats for simple log forwarding tasks, but is powerful for complex data pipelines.

Deployment and Configuration

Beats are easy to deploy and configure. They come with pre-built modules for popular data sources, offering quick setup and predefined dashboards in Kibana. Their configuration is straightforward, making them accessible even for non-experts.

Logstash has a more complex configuration syntax, with separate pipelines for input, filter, and output stages. This allows for fine-grained control over data processing, but requires more expertise to manage.

Choosing between Beats and Logstash

The choice between Beats and Logstash depends on your specific requirements:

Use Beats when:

- You need lightweight, efficient data shippers.
- Minimal data transformation is required.
- You have a large number of servers or containers.

Use Logstash when:

- Complex data parsing and transformation are needed.
- You require enrichment from external sources.
- You have diverse data inputs and outputs.

Combining Beats and Logstash

In many cases, Beats and Logstash can be used together for a comprehensive data ingestion pipeline. Beats can be deployed on the edge to collect data and send it to Logstash, which then processes and enriches the data before forwarding it to Elasticsearch. This combination leverages the strengths of both tools, providing efficient data collection and powerful processing capabilities.

By understanding the key differences and use cases of Beats and Logstash, you can design an effective data ingestion strategy that meets the needs of your observability and analytics workflows.

Using APM for Application Performance Monitoring

Elastic APM (Application Performance Monitoring) is a specialized component of the Elastic Stack designed to track application performance, monitor distributed traces, and detect bottlenecks in real-time. It helps developers and operations teams gain deep visibility into how applications behave in production environments.

Elastic APM works by using APM agents which are installed in applications to capture traces and performance metrics. These agents support multiple programming languages, including Java, .NET, Python, Node.js, Go, and Ruby. The collected data is then sent to an APM Server which forwards it to Elasticsearch for indexing and analysis.

Some key features of Elastic APM include:

- **Tracing distributed applications:** Visualizing how requests propagate across different services.
- **Error and exception tracking:** Identifying slow requests, exceptions, and error-prone code paths.
- **Performance metrics:** Monitoring response times, memory usage, CPU load, and many more.

With Kibana's APM UI, teams can easily analyze application bottlenecks, detect anomalies, and optimize performance. Elastic APM is especially useful for microservices-based architectures, where tracing interactions between multiple services is critical.

Best Practices for Using APM for Application Performance Monitoring

Application Performance Monitoring (APM) is essential for maintaining high-performing applications, detecting bottlenecks, and ensuring an optimal user experience. Elastic APM provides a robust solution for monitoring distributed applications, tracking request traces, and identifying slow-performing services. However, to maximize its effectiveness, it is crucial to follow the best practices in deployment, configuration, and analysis.

Deploy APM Agents Strategically

APM agents collect performance metrics and traces from applications, but deploying them improperly can introduce overhead. Follow these best practices:

- **Identify critical services:** Deploy APM agents on key microservices, API endpoints, and backend applications that directly impact performance.
- **Use supported agents:** Ensure that you are using the latest version of Elastic APM agents for languages like Java, .NET, Python, Node.js, Go, or Ruby.
- **Limit unnecessary tracing:** Only monitor relevant transactions to reduce resource usage and storage consumption.

Define Key Performance Indicators (KPIs)

Setting clear KPIs helps measure application performance effectively. Some critical metrics to track include:

- **Response time:** Measure how long API requests take to complete.
- **Throughput:** Analyze the number of requests per second to identify spikes in demand.
- **Error rates:** Detect failed requests and exceptions that impact user experience.
- **Database query performance:** Monitor slow SQL queries that cause delays in application response times.
- **Service dependencies:** Understand how external services impact application performance.

Optimize Sampling for Performance Efficiency

APM can generate a large volume of trace data which can overwhelm Elasticsearch storage if not managed properly. To optimize performance:

- **Use adaptive sampling:** Configure APM agents to collect only a percentage of requests, instead of capturing all the traffic.
- **Prioritize slow transactions:** Ensure that traces for slow-performing requests are captured with high detail.
- **Exclude unnecessary endpoints:** Avoid monitoring low-priority or background jobs that do not affect performance.

Leverage Distributed Tracing

Modern applications rely on microservices, making distributed tracing critical for understanding request flows across multiple services. The best practices include:

- **Enable distributed tracing across all services:** Ensure that APM agents are installed across all interconnected microservices.
- **Use trace correlation:** Link logs, metrics, and traces to get a holistic view of how requests flow through the system.
- **Visualize service dependencies:** Use Kibana's **APM Service Map** to understand dependencies and detect performance bottlenecks.

Monitor Errors and Exceptions

Detecting errors early helps prevent system failures, and improves application stability. Consider these practices:

- **Enable automatic error tracking:** Elastic APM automatically captures exceptions and error logs.
- **Set up alerts for critical failures:** Configure notifications in Kibana or integrate with Slack, PagerDuty, or email to get real-time alerts.
- **Analyze stack traces:** Use stack traces to diagnose and fix recurring issues in the code.

Analyze and Optimize Slow Transactions

Identifying slow transactions is key to improving performance. Follow these strategies:

- **Set response time thresholds:** Define what is considered a slow request, and prioritize fixing those exceeding the limit.
- **Break down transactions into spans:** Analyze which parts of the code, queries, or external calls contribute to delays.
- **Optimize database queries:** Identify inefficient SQL queries or missing indexes, using APM's query performance monitoring.

Integrate APM with Logging and Metrics

To get a complete observability solution, Elastic APM should be used alongside logging and infrastructure monitoring:

- **Link APM traces with logs:** Use Elastic Stack's centralized logging to correlate performance issues with logs.
- **Monitor system metrics with Metricbeat:** Track CPU, memory, and network usage to detect infrastructure-related performance issues.
- **Combine APM with alerting:** Set up alerts in Kibana to get notified about anomalies in real-time.

Regularly Review and Tune APM Settings

APM monitoring is not a one-time setup; it requires continuous improvement:

- **Periodically review the collected data:** Remove unnecessary spans or traces to optimize storage and performance.

- **Upgrade APM agents:** Ensure you use the latest agent versions to benefit from performance improvements and bug fixes.
- **Fine-tune configurations:** Adjust sampling rates, span collection, and error tracking, based on observed system behavior.

Secure APM Data and Access

Since APM collects sensitive performance data, it is essential to secure access:

- **Use role-based access control (RBAC):** Restrict who can view, and manage APM data in Kibana.
- **Encrypt data transmission:** Ensure that APM agents and Elasticsearch communicate securely over TLS.
- **Control data retention**: Implement data lifecycle policies to archive or delete old traces and logs.

Use Kibana Dashboards for Visualization

A well-structured dashboard in Kibana provides instant insights into application performance:

- **Create custom dashboards:** Design visualizations for KPIs, error rates, and slow transactions.
- **Use real-time analytics:** Leverage Kibana's real-time monitoring capabilities to detect issues as they happen.
- **Drill down into root causes**: Investigate performance issues by correlating traces, logs, and system metrics.

Exploring Elastic Enterprise Search

Elastic Enterprise Search provides a powerful way to implement full-text search across different data sources, making it ideal for organizations looking to improve information retrieval in websites, applications, and internal knowledge bases.

The key products under Elastic Enterprise Search include:

- **App Search:** A streamlined solution for building powerful search experiences in web and mobile applications. It comes with relevance tuning, analytics, and customizable search UI components.
- **Workplace Search:** Designed to centralize content search across multiple business applications such as Google Drive, Microsoft 365, Slack, and Confluence.

Elastic Enterprise Search builds on the core capabilities of Elasticsearch, while offering **pre-built connectors**, **search analytics**, and **AI-driven relevance tuning**. With support for RESTful APIs and UI tools, developers can quickly integrate advanced search capabilities, without needing extensive expertise in search algorithms.

Thus, by leveraging Elastic Enterprise Search, organizations can ensure that employees and customers find relevant information faster, improving productivity and user experience.

Conclusion

Throughout this book, we have explored the powerful capabilities of the **Elastic Stack (ELK)**–a widely adopted solution for log management, search, and observability. While Elasticsearch, Logstash, and Kibana form the foundation of this ecosystem, Elastic offers a broader suite of tools that can take your data analytics, monitoring, and search capabilities to the next level.

In this final chapter, we examined **how Beats, Elastic APM, and Elastic Enterprise Search** integrate seamlessly with the traditional ELK stack, expanding its capabilities beyond basic log ingestion and visualization.

- **Beats vs. Logstash:** We learned that **Beats** provide lightweight, and efficient data collection from distributed systems, while **Logstash** offers powerful transformation and enrichment capabilities. Choosing the right tool depends on whether you prioritize scalability and simplicity (Beats) or require complex data processing pipelines (Logstash). In many cases, a **hybrid approach**–using Beats for collection and Logstash for transformation–delivers the best results.
- **Application Performance Monitoring (APM):** Observability extends beyond logs and metrics, and **Elastic APM** provides deep insights into application behavior, distributed traces, and bottlenecks. By following best practices, such as **strategic** agent deployment, error tracking, distributed tracing, and KPI monitoring, organizations can ensure optimal application performance and quick issue resolution.
- **Enterprise Search:** While Elasticsearch is a powerful search engine, **Elastic Enterprise Search** offers specialized solutions such as **App Search** and **Workplace Search** to provide an enhanced search experience across web applications and business tools. This expansion allows organizations to **deliver fast, relevant, and AI-driven search experiences** tailored to end-user needs.

As the volume and complexity of data continue to grow, **a unified approach to observability, search, and analytics** is becoming essential. The modern enterprise demands solutions that can handle **logs, metrics, traces, security events, and structured/unstructured data** all in one ecosystem.

The **Elastic Stack has evolved** beyond its origins, offering **machine learning-driven anomaly detection, security analytics, real-time monitoring, and full-text search capabilities**—all within a single, scalable platform. With **continued advancements in AI, cloud-native deployments, and edge computing**, Elastic is well-positioned to remain a leading choice for organizations looking to extract value from their data.

Therefore, by understanding **how to choose the right components, optimize performance, and integrate additional Elastic solutions**, you can **build scalable, efficient, and intelligent observability** as well as **search architectures** that support business growth and innovation.

Points to Remember

- **Beats** are lightweight, single-purpose data shippers designed for efficient data collection with minimal processing.
- **Logstash** is a more powerful but resource-intensive data pipeline that supports complex transformation, filtering, and enrichment.
- **Use Beats**, when you need scalable, low-latency data forwarding.
- **Use Logstash**, when you need to parse, transform, and enrich data, before sending it to Elasticsearch.
- **A hybrid approach** (Beats for collection + Logstash for transformation) often provides the best balance between efficiency and flexibility.
- **Elastic APM** provides deep visibility into application performance, distributed traces, and error tracking.
- **Deploy APM agents strategically** to monitor critical services, while minimizing resource overhead.
- **Monitor key performance indicators (KPIs)** like response time, throughput, error rates, and database query performance.
- **Use distributed tracing** to track requests across microservices, and detect bottlenecks.
- **Optimize sampling rates** to balance detailed tracing with storage efficiency.
- **Integrate APM with logs and metrics** for a comprehensive observability strategy.
- **Set up alerts and dashboards** in Kibana to proactively detect and resolve issues.
- **Elastic Enterprise Search** expands search capabilities beyond Elasticsearch for specialized use cases.
- **App Search** enables developers to implement powerful, relevance-tuned search in web and mobile applications.

- **Workplace Search** centralizes content search across multiple business applications (Google Drive, Microsoft 365, Slack, and so on.).
- **Leverage AI-driven relevance tuning** to improve search accuracy, and user experience.
- **Enterprise Search simplifies integration** with pre-built connectors and analytics for tracking search performance.
- The **Elastic Stack has evolved** beyond ELK, offering **APM, Beats, and Enterprise Search** to enhance observability and search solutions.
- **Choosing the right tools**–whether Beats vs. Logstash, APM for monitoring, or Enterprise Search for information retrieval–is critical for an effective deployment.
- **Elastic is a unified data platform** capable of handling logs, metrics, traces, security, and search needs in a scalable, efficient way.
- **Future observability trends** will continue to integrate **AI, cloud-native solutions, and real-time analytics**, making Elastic Stack a key player in modern IT ecosystems.

Multiple Choice Questions

1. What is the primary difference between Beats and Logstash?

    a. Beats perform complex data transformation, while Logstash is only for data collection.

    b. Beats are lightweight data shippers, whereas Logstash is a more powerful data processing pipeline.

    c. Beats store data directly in Elasticsearch, while Logstash only works with Kibana.

    d. Beats and Logstash are used interchangeably with no major differences.

2. Which of the following is NOT a type of Beat?

    a. Filebeat

    b. Metricbeat

    c. Packetbeat

    d. Querybeat

3. When should you prefer Logstash over Beats?
    a. When minimal resource usage is required.
    b. When complex data transformation and enrichment are needed.
    c. When collecting system metrics from multiple servers.
    d. When monitoring uptime of web services.
4. What is the main function of Elastic APM?
    a. Securely store logs in Elasticsearch.
    b. Monitor application performance, traces, and error tracking.
    c. Manage Kibana visualizations and dashboards.
    d. Perform full-text search across enterprise applications.
5. Which best practice is recommended for using Elastic APM efficiently?
    a. Enable APM agents on every single application component, regardless of its importance.
    b. Use adaptive sampling to optimize performance, and reduce storage consumption.
    c. Disable distributed tracing to reduce unnecessary monitoring.
    d. Use Elastic APM only for frontend applications.

Answers

1. b.
2. d.
3. b.
4. b.
5. b.

Questions

1. In what scenarios would you choose Beats over Logstash? Are there cases where combining both tools would be beneficial? Explain your reasoning.
2. What are some of the key challenges in Application Performance Monitoring (APM), and how does Elastic APM help overcome them? What best practices would you follow to optimize APM for a microservices-based system?

3. How does distributed tracing improve application observability in Elastic APM? Can you describe a real-world example where tracing requests across services could help identify and resolve performance bottlenecks?

4. How does Elastic Enterprise Search extend the capabilities of Elasticsearch? In what situations would you use App Search or Workplace Search, instead of setting up a custom Elasticsearch index?

5. The Elastic Stack has evolved beyond ELK (Elasticsearch, Logstash, and Kibana) with tools like APM, Beats, and Enterprise Search. In your opinion, what are some future trends in observability, search, or AI-driven analytics that could further enhance the Elastic ecosystem?

Key Terms

- **Beats:** Lightweight data shippers that collect and forward logs, metrics, and other data to Elasticsearch or Logstash.
- **Logstash:** A data processing pipeline that collects, transforms, and enriches data before sending it to Elasticsearch.
- **Elastic APM (Application Performance Monitoring):** A solution for tracking application performance, analyzing transactions, and identifying bottlenecks.
- **APM Agent:** A small software component that collects application performance data, and sends it to the APM server.
- **Distributed Tracing:** A technique used in APM to track requests across multiple microservices to diagnose performance issues.
- **Transaction:** A unit of work in an application such as an API request or database query monitored in Elastic APM.
- **Sampling Rate:** A method used in APM to control the percentage of transactions recorded, reducing storage costs and performance overhead.
- **Service Map:** A visualization in Kibana's APM UI that shows dependencies and interactions between different application components.
- **Error Tracking:** The ability of Elastic APM to capture and report application exceptions and failures.
- **Elastic Enterprise Search:** A suite of search solutions built on Elasticsearch, including App Search and Workplace Search.
- **App Search:** A pre-built search solution that provides relevance tuning, search analytics, and a search-ready UI for applications.
- **Workplace Search:** A tool that centralizes enterprise content search across multiple platforms such as Google Drive, Microsoft 365, and Slack.

- **AI-driven Relevance Tuning:** A feature in Enterprise Search that optimizes search results, based on user interactions and content relevance.
- **Full-text Search:** A search technique used by Elasticsearch and Enterprise Search to retrieve documents, based on textual content.
- **Observability**: A holistic approach to monitoring system performance by collecting logs, metrics, and traces.
- **Metricbeat**: A Beat that collects system and application performance metrics.
- **Filebeat**: A Beat that collects and forwards log data.
- **Packetbeat**: A Beat that monitors network traffic and protocol usage.
- **APM Dashboards**: Kibana visualizations that display application performance metrics, error rates, and response times.
- **Hybrid Data Pipeline**: A strategy that combines Beats for lightweight data collection and Logstash for heavy data processing.

Index

E

G

H

I

J

K

L

M

N

P

R

S

T

V

W